The Technique of Choral Writing

The Technique of Choral Writing

A Comprehensive Guide to Composing and Arranging for Vocal Ensembles

Matthew D. Nielsen, DMA

The Technique of Choral Writing:
A Comprehensive Guide to Composing and Arranging for Vocal Ensembles

First Edition.

Proofreaders:	Cynthia Nielsen, Carolyn Nielsen, Alex Benestelli
Beta Readers:	Jay Carter, DMA
	Elizabeth Johnson Knight, DMA
	Hannah Johnson McLaughlin, PhD
	Jules Pegram, DMA
	Joseph Sowa, PhD
	Gregório Taniguchi, MM
Copy Editor:	Diane Cady
Cover Design:	Cory Klose

© 2024 by Matthew D. Nielsen. Santa Monica, California.
All rights reserved.

No part of this book may be used or reproduced in any manner whatsoever without written permission from the author.

Printed in the United States.
1st Printing

ISBN 979-8-218-43594-3
Library of Congress Control Number: 2024911364

The publisher has no responsibility for the persistence or accuracy of URLs for external or third-party internet websites referred to in this publication, and does not guarantee that any content on such websites is, or will remain, accurate or appropriate.

For my mother,
the best proofreader I was blessed to have.

Table of Contents

Acknowledgements   x

Part I

Chapter 1
Introduction   2
   My Experience and Perspective 4
   Who this book is for. 4
   How to use this resource 5
   Composing and Arranging. 5
   Misconceptions About Choral Music 6
   Disclaimers 7

Chapter 2
Setting Words   11
   Languages 12
   Syllabification 13
   Melodic Stress and Metric Stress 14
   Further Syllabification Considerations 17
   Syllabic and Melismatic Word Setting 19
   Vocalises 22
   Blending Text Settings and Textures 26
   Text Painting. 31
   Underlay 36
   Continuing Study 37

Chapter 3
Considering the Vocal Instrument   39
   Breathing. 41
   Range and Tessitura 46
   Register and Passaggio 47
   Key Signatures 50
   Vowels and Consonants 51
   Stamina 54
   Finding Pitches 56
   Variation Between Singers 57
   Soloists Versus Choristers 58
   Vibrato 60
   Performing From Memory. 61
   A Word About Referring to the "Masters" 62
   Other Needs of Singers 64
   Continuing Study 65

Chapter 4
Sopranos 67
- General Range 67
- Introduction 68
- General Description 68
- Role in the Ensemble 70
- Other Considerations 70
- Example passages 72

Chapter 5
Altos 73
- General Range 73
- Introduction 74
- General Description 75
- Role in the Ensemble 76
- Other Considerations 77
- Example passages 77

Chapter 6
Tenors 78
- General Range 78
- Introduction 79
- General Description 79
- Role in the Ensemble 81
- Other Considerations 82
- Example passages 82

Chapter 7
Basses 84
- General Range 84
- Introduction 85
- General Description 85
- Role in the Ensemble 87
- Other Considerations 88
- Example passages 88

Chapter 8
Other Voices 90
- Countertenors 90
- Children's voices 94
- Cambiata 98

Chapter 9
Various Choral Ensembles — 101
- Choirs Based on Size 103
- Choirs Based on Ability 110
- Choirs Based on Purpose or Function 115
- Continuing Study 132

Chapter 10
Divisions — 134
- Standard Divisions 136
- Three-Part Divisions 138
- Double Choir Divisions 140
- Extensive Divisions 143
- Extensive Parts 145
- Solos 147
- Continuing Study 151

Part II

Chapter 11
Principles of Voicing and Balance — 154
- Voice Strength and Balance 155
- Chord Voicing Examples 156
- Chord Spacing 164
- Vowel Balance 167
- Other Chord Voicing Considerations 167
- Voice Crossing 169
- Unison Doublings 171
- Octave Doublings 174
- Continuing Study 182

Chapter 12
Choral Textures — 184
- How Much Is Too Much? 185
- Texture Changes 189
- Melody-Focused Textures 190
- Harmony-Focused Textures 197
- Gesture-Focused Textures 199
- Variants 203
- Composites 204
- Continuing Study 210

Chapter 13
Instrumental Collaboration — 212
- Piano 214

Organ	219
Harp	225
Obbligato Instruments	228
Chamber Ensembles	231
Full Orchestra	243
Wind Band	258
Continuing Study	262

Chapter 14
Extended Techniques and Special Effects — 265

Notation	268
Vocal Hygiene	268
Pitched Vocalizations	269
Unpitched Vocalizations	284
Non-Vocal	294
Requiring multiple singers	298
Other techniques	303
Continuing Study	306

Chapter 15
Engraving Choral Parts — 307

Layout and Front Matter	308
Text	312
Syllabic Slurs and Phrasing	315
Expression, Dynamic, and Technique Markings	317
Keyboard Reductions	317
Printing and Other Considerations	318
Continuing Study	319

Chapter 16
Closing Thoughts — 321

Habits for Continual Practice	322
Conclusion	324

Appendix A — 328

Choirs Based on Size	328
Choirs Based on Ability	328
Choirs Based on Purpose or Function	330

Appendix B — 334

List of Examples	334

Bibliography — 340

Index — 344

Acknowledgements

First thanks are for the support and enthusiasm from my longtime friend and colleague, Joseph Sowa, who encouraged me to keep working on this book, assuring me of its merit, and affirming its value.

Many thanks to the help and support of Hannah Johnson McLaughlin and Sarah Bowe for their input and suggestions for Chapter 14 of this book. Their experience, research, and insight has been invaluable.

Thanks to the Doheny Memorial Library at the University of Southern California, the Marta and Austin Weeks Music Library at the University of Miami, and the music library at the University of California at Los Angeles.

My gratitude to Andrea Zomorodian for loaning me a laptop to finish this book after my own laptop decided to shuffle off this mortal coil.

Lastly, my deepest, most heart-felt gratitude to my family who have shown continuing support and encouragement along my musical journey. Especially my father and mother, Dale and Cynthia.

Part I

Chapter 1

Introduction

The human voice is the oldest musical instrument and through the ages it remains what it was, unchanged; the most primitive and at the same time the most modern, because it is the most intimate form of human expression.
— Ralph Vaughan Williams

Since the earliest evidence of written music the human voice has repeatedly found a venerated place on our pages. Through poverty, riches, violence, ritual, ruin, war, plague, devastation, rebirth, and love, its presence has endured. Vocal music has evolved dramatically, and yet it remains rooted firmly in our most fundamental practice of musical expression.

More music has been written for the human voice than any other instrument or group of instruments in Western music. Most of this is thanks to the mountains of music composed during the Renaissance and Early Baroque periods by some of the most prolific musical minds in history, and today the canon continues to rapidly expand.

Choral music makes up a significant part of the canon of Western art music and failing to understand how to effectively write for this group is a lost opportunity. To ignore writng for the human voice is to miss out on one of the largest and most enthusiastic music markets in North America and much of the rest of the world. Many choirs are eager to commission and perform new music in a way that many orchestras struggle with.

And yet, there appears to be precious little written about how to write for vocal ensembles. It seems that some must believe that these techniques and principles are learned through osmosis. However, based on the scores of substandard choral music I've encountered, it isn't working. This situation isn't necessarily because the music is poor but because the composer or arranger exhibited little working knowledge about the human voice or the choral idiom. I have even seen choral arranging classes taught by music theory professors who had little to no experience with choral ensembles—and confessed as much—but were nevertheless teaching students how to write for choirs. It was the blind leading the blind.

In *The Technique of Orchestration*, Kent Kennan and Donald Grantham dedicated two whole pages in Appendix D (right before the bibliography) on writing for choirs. While I otherwise love this book, and I'm glad they thought to write about choirs at all (not every orchestration book I've encountered thought to include or discuss singers), two pages hardly suffices in discussing how to compose and arrange for this singular collective of musicians—with or without an orchestra. This book is written in response to those two pages, and my hope is that it can help remedy that lack of working knowledge I saw during my music education.

In many cases, the most idiomatic choral music I've encountered has been written by composers and arrangers who either are singers themselves and have sung in choral ensembles for years or from those who took pains to learn without being singers themselves. Thankfully, being a singer isn't a prerequisite to learning how to write well for choirs—but it doesn't hurt—and those same lessons can be learned without being in a choral ensemble, just as one doesn't need to play every instrument to write effectively for the orchestra.

For one who may have little or no experience with the choral idiom, it can be a confusing and intimidating world from the outside looking in. It is a decidedly different world from our instrumental counterparts, culturally, aesthetically, methodically, or pedagogically. When it comes to understanding even the fundamentals of the voice, students can sometimes feel abandoned in the wilderness to search alone. I hope the new student to choral writing can take comfort in this: I have found the choral art-form to be one of the most diverse, inclusive and welcoming communities I have ever encountered, and newcomers are always welcome. There is choral music for everyone, but more importantly, choral music is for everyone. Keep an open heart and an open mind and you will find your place in it.

My Experience and Perspective

I have been involved with choral singing for as long as I can remember. My parents took our family to church where congregational singing was in our cultural DNA. As a child, I sang in our town's local children's choir: Valley Voices. While I sang in high school choir for only one year, I became heavily involved in choral singing in college. I sang for a total of nine years in multiple collegiate ensembles. Beginning in 2012, I began a career as a professional singer working in several different ensembles across the United States.

While I've been singing my whole life, my professional training in choral music has mostly revolved around conducting these ensembles, including two graduate degrees in choral music. Alongside my training in conducting, I began to seriously study composition and arranging, although not in a formal setting. My studies have mostly consisted of one-on-one lessons and decades of mentoring from several different professors of choral music, composition, and organ during their office hours. These mentors included Ronald Staheli, retired chair of choral studies at Brigham Young University, and Morten Lauridsen, distinguished professor emeritus at the University of Southern California. Additionally, I have poured over countless choral scores as a singer and conductor while also studying them as a budding composer and arranger.

My perspective of choral music comes from a North American experience, with most of my training taking place in the Mountain West and West Coast regions. Even though I come from one particular choral environment, I strive to keep an eye on as many different choral scenes around the globe as best as I can.

Who this book is for

This book is my attempt to help composers and arrangers write more idiomatic choral music. It is written for many different groups of individuals, but primarily it is written for music students studying composition, choral arranging, and orchestration. With that in mind, I presume the reader will have already learned music theory, part-writing, and have taken a survey of music history.

If you've sung in choirs for an extended period of time, some of these principles will probably be obvious. Indeed, this book has some sections that contain information that will be redundant for experienced choral musicians. With that said, I still believe that music education and choral conducting students will find great value in this book. Even with years of choral performance experience it still takes study, practice, and time to learn these principles. I learned very quickly in my composition lessons that I still had many things to learn about choral arranging even though I had sung in choirs for most of my life. Also, while conductors and educators may believe they will never compose music, arranging music for their choirs is almost an inevitability. Having basic knowledge of writing for their ensembles will go a long way in programming and ultimately offering engaging and meaningful performances.

Beyond the setting of higher education, this book can also be useful for musicians who have long since left their formal studies but feel that they still have gaps in their knowledge regarding choral arranging. This may be especially true if you feel that you had limited experience with choral forces during your school years. It's never too late to learn something new about writing for choirs.

How to use this resource

You should not feel obligated to read this book from cover to cover unless that's your desire. While the knowledge found in earlier chapters will be helpful when reading subsequent chapters, it may not necessarily be a prerequisite. Feel free to skip to the chapter or sections that you feel will be most helpful to you first and fill out the rest of the knowledge as need arises. Skim the parts you feel don't need your immediate attention and re-read them when you feel it's time for a deeper dive.

At the end of each chapter will be sections for additional listening, and in some cases, suggestions for practice. Where relevant I've divided those between shorter exercises that can be done in a few minutes and exercises meant for long term projects or practice that can be lengthened over days, weeks, or even months. These are optional resources available for further practice, and while I hope these will be helpful, feel free to modify them in any way or create your own assignments and listening lists.

Composing and Arranging

For those not familiar with the terms, a composition is an original piece of music with the vast majority or all of the music being original, with little to no previously composed materials. Very often in choral music we will also refer to a composition as a "setting," which comes from the idea that the composer is setting a text to new, original music. An arrangement is a piece of music based on previously composed material from any number of sources including their own previously composed materials.

Both of these forms are valuable categories in the canon of choral music. Original compositions and arrangements of previous materials are both well represented in concert programs from nearly all choral ensembles across the globe. Some composers (especially those in academia) may look down their noses at arrangements as lesser art than composing original music. While it is wonderful to create original compositions, arrangements are not inherently of less value or less worthy of our attention than original compositions. After all, composing involves the same skill set in arranging these motifs in various garments of musical gestures.

Writing effective and engaging arrangements takes a great amount of skill and creativity. I would argue that it takes just as much creativity as setting a text with original materials. Some very talented and successful arrangers have written in both of these categories; others have leaned into one or the other. Some musicians find that their skill set and creative mind works better in composing while others in arranging. Students should never be discouraged from working in one or the other.

A large amount of mass settings from the Renaissance—especially the Late Renaissance—were based on previously composed materials, sometimes by the composers themselves and sometimes by another composer who they admired. It doesn't make these mass settings any less valuable or impressive. A great deal of Johann Sebastian Bach's output were arrangements of—or at the very least heavily borrowed and quoted from—Lutheran chorale tunes. It doesn't take away one iota from his genius in how he arranged these melodies into works of art. Many of the composers we esteem as "masters" have written arrangements including Ralph Vaughan Williams, Arnold Schoenberg, Béla Bartók, Sergei Rachmaninoff, Benjamin Britten, and Arvo Pärt.

Misconceptions About Choral Music

I have sometimes heard from composition students and their teachers that writing for vocal ensembles is limiting in multiple ways, including their range, timbre, ability, and ambition for new music or a lack of adventure to tackle exceptionally challenging repertoire. That choirs are not eager to take on new music is one of the limits I hear about most often from my composer colleagues. Vocal ensembles are perceived as less likely than other musicians to reach out and commission a new work or to accept unsolicited scores being sent to them. From my perspective as a life-long choral musician, I don't think anything could be further from the truth.

Yes, you will find some conductors are not eager to accept or look through unsolicited scores sent their way nor are they eager to program something new or find the funding for a new commission. However, I believe that this is very much the minority of choral conductors. Many ensembles will have mission statements reflecting a desire to bring new music to the choral scene. Some ensembles' sole purpose is dedicated entirely to both commissioning and performing new music. Of course, not every ensemble has made it their mission to explore new music and that should be respected. For more information about the different kinds of choral ensembles, consult Chapter 9.

I sometimes hear from composers a complaint about conductors and singers whining about how their music is too hard and that's why they don't sing it. After glancing at their scores, I can say that it's not so much that it's too hard but that it's not idiomatic. There is a difference between challenging the conventions of the voice and writing in a way that isn't viable.

Another misconception is that the choir is monochromatic. It certainly can be, but this misconception is often rooted in the idea that singers only produce sound in a single, fixed way.[1] The voice is not a fixed instrument; it is actually incredibly flexible. Many vocal artists have made a living out of offering a range of different timbres by physically changing the shapes of their resonating chambers. There is much more to the voice than just *bel canto* technique and more information can be found in Chapter 14 of this text.

Disclaimers

Ranges

My greatest fear when writing this text is that some readers will skip to the ranges for each voice, take one glance and think that's all there is to know. The last thing you should do is look at the singer's ranges and think that everything is free game all the time without restraint. Limiting one's learning about the human voice to memorizing its ranges is only learning one very

---

[1] Deke Sharon and Dylan Bell, *A Cappella Arranging*. Lanham (MD: Rowman & Littlefield, 2012), 49.

small part of how to compose for choral ensembles. You've learned about the heights and depths but have yet to understand anything in between or even that the extremes of the ranges are not sustainable in a healthy way.

Meanwhile, it's practically impossible to pin down exact ranges for singers because every singer and every group of singers is different. As Nikolai Rimsky-Korsakov explained in his book on orchestration: "While the range of an instrument is exactly governed by its construction, the compass of the voice, on the other hand, depends on the individuality of the singer."[2]

In this text, I will give different ranges, one for untrained voices and another for trained voices. But keep in mind that these are not definitive, exact ranges, but instead guiding principles for general considerations. You will almost certainly find singers who will be the exceptions to the ranges marked here. You may find a soprano who can sing freakishly high and can float there for extended periods, but don't expect the rest of the section to be able to sing the same way. Be mindful to not let your awareness of these exceptions become what you expect from every other singer.

International Phonetic Alphabet

Throughout this book, I will be using symbols from the International Phonetic Alphabet (IPA) in square brackets [ ] to describe specific vowels sounds. For readers not familiar, IPA is a system of phonetic symbols used universally by collegiate, professional, and some volunteer singers to agree on what vowels and consonants they should sing. While the system has its limitations, it's a great point of departure when negotiating any language.

If you're not familiar with IPA, now is a great time to find a resource to help you become familiar.[3] This is a system that is learned by virtually every college voice and choral conducting student in the United States and used frequently in rehearsals. As virtually all choral music is based on phonetic sounds, learning it as a composer will be very beneficial and help communicate your exact intentions. This is especially helpful when working with less familiar languages in the choral canon, as well as neutral vowel sounds. More about languages in Chapter 2.

---

2   Nicolai Rimsky-Korsakov, *Principles of Orchestration* (New York: Dover Publications, 1964), 142.

3   A resource that I regularly return to is ipachart.com which allows you to click on a symbol and hear a recording produced by the phonetics lab at UCLA of what that symbol sounds like.

A few words about gender

Previous choral culture used to divide choral forces into the binary of "men" and "women," or "boys" and "girls." This has always been problematic for a number of reasons, most commonly by the presence of countertenors[4] in the alto section.

Singers who have trans and nonbinary gender identities are finding a more welcoming space in the choral landscape in light of further acceptance and inclusion. Consequently, using binary or unnecessarily gendered language may not be helpful for many of these people.[5] Thankfully, this practice is being phased out. Proper etiquette in a choral setting is to call each section by its designated name (soprano, alto, etc.). This practice includes talking about children's choirs; the preferred terms are "trebles" or simply "children."

In this book, I will follow these new practices of calling sections by their names rather than putting an emphasis on the gender of those singers. I will also refer to certain voice parts as people who were assigned a specific sex at birth, regardless of any chosen gender expression.[6] If you find yourself stuck referring to sopranos and altos as "women" or "girls" and tenors and basses as "men" or "boys," I invite you to make a conscious effort to change that habit.

Pluralizing Non-English Words

In any book about music, many non-English words will be used, including words from Italian, German, French, and Latin to name a few. Many of these non-English words are nouns and making them plural has been a point of contention at times. For example, is the plural of *ictus* supposed to be *icti* or *ictuses*? Celli or cellos? Both are correct but for different reasons because languages express pluralization differently. "Celli" uses the plural suffix from Italian while "cellos" uses the plural suffix from English. As I am a native English speaker, I have chosen to use the latter throughout this book.

Use of Examples

I have endeavored to find musical examples of high quality from works that will be accessible to virtually everyone with an internet connection.

---

4 Countertenors are male-assigned singers who sing in their falsetto register and most often sing the alto part in choral music. See Chapter 8 for more information.

5 Matthew L Garrett and Joshua Palkki, *Honoring Trans and Gender-Expansive Students in Music Education* (New York: Oxford University Press, 2021), 177-178;182.

6 Garrett and Palkki, *Honoring Trans and Gender-Expansive Students in Music Education*, 25.

I have also sought to use a variety of examples from a variety of composers from different periods and countries of origin. While some composers and their compositions may be great examples (or indeed the earliest example) of a specific principle, I have attempted to favor sharing examples from a wider variety of composers rather than examples from a smaller number of composers.

In some instances, certain engraving practices specific to certain composers or publishing houses are maintained in these examples. Some of these practices may be outdated or will be directly contradicted by me later in the text or by others. However, in the spirit of *sic erat scriptum*, they are maintained in these examples as printed except when lack of context or clarity may necessitate some adjustments.

Regarding examples from the Renaissance and Baroque periods, for simplicity and ease of reading, I have chosen to use performance edition practices for these examples rather than attempting to represent their sources as closely as possible. Doing so will involve adding bar lines and halving (and sometimes quartering) note values, as well as transposing and/or assigning different voice parts and clefs than those listed in the source. Again, the purpose of this is for ease of reading for most readers.

Chapter 2

Setting Words

Poetry is the true source of my music.
— Hugo Wolf

*The setting to music of a poem must be an act of love,
never a marriage of convenience.*
— Francis Poulenc

    The primary difference between singers and instrumentalists is the ability to include words directly and naturally in our music making. Even orchestral tone poems don't quite compare when words are seamlessly interwoven into a musician's sound production.
    The words themselves are often the catalyst for the composition and are very likely to drive the direction of the music. Words can determine the length of the work, the form, tone, tempos, dynamics, and any sort of word-painting or programmatic features that may be inspired by the chosen text. Even when the music is written in a manner that is contrary from the text, the words still dictate how the work is crafted.
    Too often I will see a composer setting music for choirs without (what appears to be) much consideration to the text. It is almost as if the text is a necessary but reluctant vehicle they are forced into or even an obstacle to their compositional ends. Composers and arrangers need to understand that they are not just writing music for vowels sounds and consonants that get in the way of

their ideas. They are creating a setting for words, phrases, sentences, stanzas, poems and other forms of the written word that convey meaning, subtext, and pathos. We can, and will, consider wordless choral and vocal music after understanding the basics of word settings.

Setting texts to music can seem rather straightforward, and for the most part the principles are conventional without many deviations. In this chapter, we will consider the different facets of settings words in choral music.

Languages

Singing is shared across virtually every culture, and consequently one can find vocal music in almost any language. In choral music every language is possible and indeed welcome. With that said, there are a number of languages that come up more often in Western art music. The most often-used languages in choral literature are—in no particular order—Latin, Italian, French, German, and English. Spanish, Russian, and Hebrew are used less often, but are languages that many singers are familiar with. Much less often used but still significant in choral music are Swedish, Norwegian, Korean, Finnish, Estonian, Latvian, and Portuguese.

Whatever language you chose to compose in, it's vital to be at least basically familiar with the language and its idiosyncrasies, as well as challenges that may be presented to the musician tasked with performing it. One doesn't need to restrict their composition to their mother-tongue alone, but if the plan is to set a text in a language not their own, one must be sensitive to that language and respect it. Understanding each word individually as well as how it fits into the larger context is a step that cannot be skipped.

While the responsibility for pronunciation ultimately belongs to the performing musicians, providing International Phonetic Alphabet (IPA) pronunciations for languages that are used less frequently[1] will go a long way in making your music accessible to and performed by more ensembles—not to mention making sure that words are pronounced accurately and building good will with the performers. Just make sure that the IPA guides you provide are accurate.

As almost any choral musician will tell you: never assume that a native speaker won't be present in the audience. I have been shocked by how often a native speaker of any given language will be present at a choral concert in North America despite the lowest of odds. One example: when I was in high

---

1   IPA guides are not necessary when writing with the most often-used lanugages like Latin or Italian for example.

school, our choir sang Christmas music for free-will donations at a BART station in San Francisco. Our repertoire included music from all over the world including a carol from Hawaii. After performing this Hawaiian Christmas song, a commuter came up to our conductor to thank us for singing in their native language.

Syllabification

In many languages, multi-syllabic words will have their own respective, inherent musical quality due to having stronger and weaker syllables in their pronunciations. The term generally used to describe this hierarchy is "syllabic stress." For example, the English word "choral" should be pronounced with the strongest emphasis, or greatest stress, on the first syllable and the weaker emphasis, or less stress, on the second syllable. The word "syllable"—a three syllable word—should have the greatest stress on the first syllable, a weaker emphasis on the second, and the weakest on the last. This difference between a strong emphasis and a less strong emphasis is sometimes termed "primary stress" and "secondary stress."

In English, certain words, including single syllable words will also have an inherent hierarchy of requisite emphasis within a sentence based on whether the word is a noun or verb, an adjective or adverb, or whether the word is a conjunction, prepositions, or article. In general, we give the most emphasis to nouns (and sometimes pronouns) and verbs, less emphasis to adjectives and adverbs, and the least emphasis to conjunctions, prepositions, and articles. For example, in the sentence "Hope is the thing with feathers/that perches in the soul," the greatest stress will be placed on the nouns and verbs such as "hope," "thing," feathers," "perches," and "soul." The words "the," "with," that," and "in" will receive much less emphasis in the sentence as they are prepositions and conjunctions. Furthermore, in multi-syllabic words like "feathers" and "perches" the first syllable has greater stress, and the second syllable is unstressed.

Different languages have different rules about syllabic stress. Some languages are similar to English regarding syllabic stress, while others have other stress structures specific to their languages, and still others have little to no syllabic stress in their languages. If this hierarchy is present in a respective language, a musical setting of those words should reflect and respect that hierarchy. This syllabic hierarchy is reflected in music by aligning it within conventional musical hierarchy; it's important to have these stronger and weaker syllables or words reflected in your rhythmic and melodic structure. This is usually accomplished through melodic stress as well as metric stress.

Melodic Stress and Metric Stress

To emphasize words and syllables in choral music, we conventionally add stress through melody, rhythm, or both. Melodic stress is achieved through pitch level with higher pitches being given to words and syllables of stronger emphasis, and lower pitches for words and syllables of weaker emphasis. This practice, however, isn't always desirable or necessary and can be compensated by metric stress.

Metric stress is arguably more important in choral music than melodic stress, and in many ways, this is a principle best left intact and unbroken. Metric stress is where the strongest words and syllables are placed in the strongest parts of a meter. Traditionally, in duple times (2/2, 2/4, 6/8, etc.)—whether simple or compound time—the first beat is the strongest and the second beat is the weakest. Consequently, the strongest words and syllables should be placed on the first beat of duple time, and the weaker syllables on the second beat or the subdivisions. In triple time (3/2, 3/4, 9/8, etc.), the first beat conventionally receives the strongest emphasis, with the second beat getting the weaker emphasis, and the third beat receiving the weakest emphasis. Typically, in quadruple time (4/2, 4/4, 12/8, etc.), the first beat gets the strongest emphasis, the third beat gets the next strongest emphasis, beat two is a weaker emphasis, and beat four is the weakest emphasis. Subdivisions in these meters will also be places for words or syllables with weaker emphasis.

Placing the strongest words and syllables onto the strongest beats is how we set words with proper metric stress. Even if melodic stress isn't strictly followed, metric stress can compensate especially well.

One glaring example of this hierarchy that comes to mind is in the third verse of the hymn "Ten Thousand Times Ten Thousand." The fault lies with the poet, Henry Alford, who deviates in one line of his text. Alford writes the text of this hymn in iambic meter meaning it follows a pattern of weak syllable followed by a strong syllable. This is all fine and well until the seventh line of the third verse when Alford suddenly reverses the pattern and writes a trochee of strong syllable followed by a weak syllable and then returns to iamb.

Verse 1:
   Ten thousand times ten thousand
   In sparkling raiment bright,
   The armies of the ransomed saints
   Throng up the steeps of light:
   'Tis finished, all is finished,
   Their fight with death and sin;
   Fling open wide the golden gates,
   And let the victors in.

Verse 3:
   O then what raptured greetings
   On Canaan's happy shore!
   What knitting severed friendships up,
   Where partings are no more!
   Then eyes with joy shall sparkle
   That brimmed with tears of late,
   Orphans no longer fatherless,
   Nor widows desolate.

This jarring change in meter is even more pronounced in the music setting. In this case, it's not the composer's fault, but it is the composer's problem. Suddenly, for the third verse a weak syllable is now found on the downbeat and because it's a hymn in strophic form, it unfortunately has to stay that way.

Example 2.1: John Dykes, "Ten Thousand Times Ten Thousand."

If composing in a strophic form, departing from this pattern would be the fault of the poet and not the composer. However, I have seen plenty of examples of composers and arrangers composing outside of the constraints of strophic form and hymn meter that have made this unforced error.

Notable Exceptions

There are cases where certain musical and rhythmic forms fall outside of the conventional metric stress. Certain dance meters will call for a stronger emphasis on beat two for example, and syncopations will compel us to emphasize the subdivision of a beat. In these cases, the natural word stress will still dictate the metric hierarchy in the rhythmic setting.

A notable exception to this principle is Poulenc's settings of Latin texts. His Latin motets and masses are notorious for their egregiously incorrect syllable emphasis. This works for Poulenc because he does this consistently throughout—not just in each composition, but everywhere in his catalog of sacred works. He knows what the proper syllabification is and is intentionally emphasizing the wrong one. It's not a bug, it's a feature. This odd syllabification comes off as charming as it matches his musical tics as well as his overall attitude towards his esteemed religion, reflecting his disposition perfectly.

Example 2.2: Francis Poulenc, *Messe en Sol Majeur*, "Gloria."

Published by Editions Salabert. International Copyright Secured. All Rights Reserved. Reprinted by permission of Hal Leonard Europe.

Where it falls apart for most student composers and arrangers is setting syllables inconsistently and turning to odd patterns by accident or because they've composed themselves into a corner. When words are incorrectly syllabified on occasion, it comes across less as charming and more as clumsiness with the language and words. This is a mistake when writing for choirs. Intimacy with the language and words is paramount to successful vocal writing, no matter the style.

Further Syllabification Considerations

Depending on the text, language can get complicated quickly. Composers have been tackling awkward and non-metered texts since the first mass settings and Latin sequences were composed. Most of these challenges are easier to manage with melismatic settings, but in syllabic settings, the struggle can become more taxing.

Poetry from periods where strict meter with consistent word stresses was paramount to the prevailing style can fit into a musical meter—and into a strophic form—quite easily. Very often hymn texts from Christian music traditions and their hymn tunes are so well regulated that provided the meter is identical, hymn texts and hymn tunes can be swapped and are interchangeable.

However, in later periods when strict meter is not the desired aesthetic for poetry—or if you would prefer to set prose rather than poetry—setting words into an inflexible musical meter can present a real challenge.

Speech-like Rhythms

Very often when working with a challenging text composers will set the text in a way that imitates, or closely follows, natural speech rhythms. For example, in *Walden Pond*, Dominick Argento has chosen to set passages of Henry David Thoreau's *Walden*. Setting prose can be a challenge in choral music, and Argento's solution is to attempt to imitate speech patterns found in the prose. Argento makes sure to keep the most important words and the most important syllables of each word in proper metric stress throughout, departing only for a syncopated attack for the word "high."

Example 2.3: Dominick Argento, *Walden Pond*, "The Pond."

© Boosey & Hawkes. Reproduced by permission of Boosey & Hawkes.

Mixed Meters

Using mixed meters is another solution that composers turn to when setting texts that don't follow a strict meter. The primary goal behind incorporating mixed meter is to ensure that correct word stress is maintained. This practice also allows a text setting to follow a more natural speech-like setting as discussed above.

Example 2.4: Gerald Finzi, *Seven Poems of Robert Bridges*, "My spirit sang all day."

© 1939 Oxford University Press.
© Renewal assigned 1969 to Boosey & Hawkes Music Publishers Ltd. Reproduced by permission of Boosey & Hawkes.

Syllabic and Melismatic Word Setting

Words can be set generally in two ways: syllabically and melismatically. In syllabic word setting each syllable is sung on a single note. In melismatic settings syllables are sung across multiple pitches.

Syllabic settings are especially effective when one desires a musical gesture that is speech-like and declamatory in nature. Here's an example from a madrigal by Claudio Monteverdi:

Example 2.5: Claudio Monteverdi, *Il quarto libro de madrigali a cinque voci*, "Si, ch'io vorrei morire."

Syllabic word settings can also be found in other textures. Here's another passage from the same composition by Monteverdi with imitative entrances:

Example 2.6: Claudio Monteverdi, *Il quarto libro de madrigali a cinque voci*, "Si, ch'io vorrei morire."

Examples of syllabic word settings are also abundant in Romantic choral music, especially the partsongs of Mendelssohn, Brahms, and Elgar, among many others. These Romantic settings aren't necessarily meant to be declamatory or even speech-like as was the case with many baroque settings.

Example 2.7: Felix Mendelssohn, *Sechs Lieder*, op. 59, "O Täler weit."

Example 2.8: Johannes Brahms, *Liebeslieder Waltzer*, op. 52, "Nein es ist nicht auszukommen."

Melismatic settings were very popular in the Renaissance and Baroque periods. The following two examples are from the later years of these two epochs.

Example 2.9: Robert White, *Lamentations of Jeremiah*.

Example 2.10: George Frederic Handel, *Messiah*, "And He shall Purify."

Extensive melismatic passages have fallen in and out of favor with audiences throughout the centuries, but one can still find the occasional example of melismatic word settings in modern music.

Example 2.11: Gabriel Jackson, "In the beginning was the Word."

© Oxford University Press 2010. All rights reserved.

Vocalises

With the slightest whiff of irony, any discussion of setting words to music must include choral music with no words. A vocalise is a sub-genre of vocal music that does not use a text. The word "vocalise" can also be used to describe a short vocal warmup exercise used in voice lessons. Incidentally, this sub-genre can also include wordless vocal exercises and phrases, much like an étude for voices. Vocalises can use a single vowel, multiple vowels, or meaningless syllables. One of the most well-known examples of this sub-genre for solo voice is in fact "Vocalise" by Sergei Rachmaninoff for soprano and orchestra.

Choral-orchestral repertoire has some wonderful examples of wordless choirs, for example *Daphnis et Chloé* by Maurice Ravel or *Flos Campi* by Ralph Vaughan Williams. Additionally, many film and television soundtracks have included the use of a wordless choir for a specific effect or aesthetic. Most choral-orchestral vocalises stay on the darker side of the vowel chart,[2] for example [a], [o], and [u].

Example 2.12: Maurice Ravel, *Daphnis et Chloé*.

Example 2.13: Ralph Vaughan Williams, *Flos Campi*.

---

2   More information about the vowel chart can be found in Chapter 3.

Although not as common, one can find a few examples of vocalises in a cappella music. A few such examples include some works by Jaakko Mäntyjärvi and Wolfram Buchenberg. Both of these composers employ meaningless syllables for their compositions, however, while meaningless, these syllables are chosen to craft a desired aesthetic. In the case of Mäntyjärvi, they are meant to have a certain sort of folksy, Nordic yokel quality and meant to imitate the sounds made by the Swedish chef from the Muppet show. By contrast, the Buchenberg is meant to sound like oscillations and space fields, and have a kaleidoscopic, almost psychedelic quality.

Example 2.14: Jaakko Mäntyjärvi, "El Hambo."

© 2005 SULASOL. All rights reserved. Walton Music Corp. admin. USA and Canada

Example 2.15: Wolfram Buchenberg, "Klangfelder Raumschwingungen Oszillationen."

© 2003 Wolfram Buchenberg. Used by permission.

Occasionally, a composer will not indicate any specific vowel or syllable to sing (as seen in the previous example from Ravel), or they may direct the musicians to sing with indeterminate syllables independently of each other. This is a perfectly acceptable practice, especially if you as a composer or arranger clarify this in a performance note. But be advised that by omitting any specificity in vowel choice you may not be pleased with the performer's choice of vowel. Granting indeterminacy requires accepting a loss of control. An example of a composer calling for indeterminate use[3] of meaningless syllables can be found in Dominick Argento's setting, "Everyone Sang."

Example 2.16: Dominick Argento, "Everyone Sang."

* In the textless passages each attacked pitch is to be sung to syllables of the chorister's own choosing--very spirited, jubilant and varied. The effect should be spontaneous and exuberant, not uniform.

© 1991 Boosey & Hawkes. Reproduced by permission of Boosey & Hawkes.

One word of caution: as we will discuss in Chapter 3, the vowel makes a huge contribution to the intonation of the choral ensemble. Intonation is determined by a unified fundamental pitch as well as unified vowels, which unifies the overtones of an ensemble's sound. Allowing singers to choose their own vowels at random (as Argento has indicated) means that fundamentally the music will never be truly in tune because the vowels are never unified.

Composing for a wordless choir is not only perfectly acceptable, but also it has given us a charming collection of literature that has a *je ne sais quoi* mystique to it. Some composers find it very freeing to compose without being bound to a text.

---

3   More information about indeterminate music can be found in Chapter 14.

Blending Text Settings and Textures

Most compositions have a combination of syllabic and melismatic settings. The ratio between syllabic or melismatic passages has shifted from epoch to epoch and at times becomes one of the defining characteristics of choral music from each period. Today, many composers will find a balance between syllabic and melismatic writing, although many will choose to compose syllabically by default with melismatic moments.

When considering text settings and how to pace a work accordingly, one good example to examine is Palestrina's most famous mass, *Missa Papae Marcelli*. The work includes the five movements from the Ordinary of the mass: "Kyrie," "Gloria," "Credo," "Sanctus," and "Agnus Dei." Three of these movements, "Kyrie," "Sanctus," and "Agnus Dei," involve relatively short texts, while two of them, the "Gloria" and "Credo," are rather lengthy, as shown in the chart below.

1. Kyrie eleison.
Christe eleison.
Kyrie eleison.

4. Sanctus, Sanctus, Sanctus,
Dominus Deus Sabaoth.
Pleni sunt coeli et terra gloria tua.
Osanna in excelsis.

Benedictus qui venit
in nomine Domini.
Osanna in excelsis.

5. Agnus Dei, qui tollis peccata mundi, miserere nobis.
Agnus Dei, qui tollis peccata mundi, miserere nobis.
Agnus Dei, qui tollis peccata mundi, dona nobis pacem.

2. Gloria in excelsis Deo.
Et in terra pax hominibus bonae voluntatis.
Laudamus te. Benedicimus te.
Adoramus te. Glorificamus te.
Gratias agimus tibi propter magnam gloriam tuam.
Domine Deus, Rex caelestis,
Deus Pater omnipotens.
Domine Fili unigenite, Iesu Christe.
Domine Deus, Agnus Dei,
Filius Patris.
Qui tollis peccata mundi, miserere nobis.
Qui tollis peccata mundi, suscipe deprecationem nostram.
Qui sedes ad dexteram Patris, miserere nobis.
Quoniam tu solus Sanctus.
Tu solus Dominus.
Tu solus Altissimus, Iesu Christe.
Cum Sancto Spiritu, in gloria Dei Patris.
Amen.

3. Credo in unum Deum.
Patrem omnipotentem,
factorem caeli et terrae,
visibilium omnium et invisibilium.
Et in unum Dominum
Jesum Christum,
Filium Dei unigenitum,
Et ex Patre natum ante omnia saecula.
Deum de Deo, lumen de lumine,
Deum verum de Deo vero.
Genitum, non factum,
consubstantialem Patri:
per quem omnia facta sunt.
Qui propter nos homines
et propter nostram salutem
descendit de caelis.

Et incarnatus est de Spiritu Sancto
ex Maria Virgine:
Et homo factus est.

Crucifixus etiam pro nobis sub Pontio Pilato:
passus, et sepultus est.

Et resurrexit tertia die,
secundum scripturas.
Et ascendit in caelum:
sedet ad dexteram Patris.
Et iterum venturus est
cum gloria judicare vivos et mortuos:
Cujus regni non erit finis.

Et in Spiritum sanctum Dominum,
et vivificantem:
Qui ex Patre, Filioque procedit.
Qui cum Patre, et Filio simul adoratur,
et conglorificatur:
Qui locutus est per Prophetas.

Et unam, sanctam, catholicam et apostolicam Ecclesiam.
Confiteor unum baptisma
in remissionem peccatorum.
Et expecto resurrectionem mortuorum
Et vitam venturi saeculi.
Amen.

Setting Words

Fresh from the Council of Trent (1546-1563) and its heated discussion surrounding polyphony and textual clarity, Palestrina's mass setting contains expansive, luxuriant polyphonic settings for the "Kyrie," "Sanctus," and "Agnus Dei" movements, and more practical, efficient, homophonic settings for the "Gloria" and "Credo" movements. Approaching the mass movements in this manner fleshes out the shorter movements, helps to trim up the longer movements, and more or less helps equalize the duration of all the movements. This improves the pace of the entire mass, and provides textual clarity to the wordiest mass movements.

Example 2.17: Giovanni Pierluigi da Palestrina, *Missa Papae Marcelli*, "Gloria."

Example 2.18: Giovanni Pierluigi da Palestrina, *Missa Papae Marcelli*, "Agnus Dei II."

The same consideration can be taken with our own text settings. Shorter texts can have the luxury of more time, more repetition and a more melismatic setting, while lengthier, more wordy texts can be set in a quicker and more efficient manner.

Mixing Syllabic and Melismatic Word Settings

While a composition will often have a mix of syllabic and melismatic word settings from section to section, one can also mix multiple word settings by having different parts singing simultaneously. This technique is quite common, with one or more parts singing a word or two in melismatic fashion while one or more parts sing a line more syllabically.

Example 2.19: Johann Sebastian Bach, *Mass in B minor*, BVW 232, "Sanctus."

Mixing Syllabic Settings and Vocalises

One can also assign one or more parts to sing a line more syllabically while having one or more parts sing their pitches on one vowel or multiple vowel sounds. This combination is very common in choral music and is one of the easiest and quickest ways to either add a variety of timbral colors to a choral work or to fix balance issues in a composition or arrangement.

Example 2.20: Maurice Ravel, *Trois Chansons*, "Trois beaux oiseaux du paradis."

Telescoping

Telescoping is layering different lines of the text to be sung by different parts simultaneously. This is a technique that we see emerge in the eighteenth century and was used most often in the mass settings of Haydn and Mozart. It was most likely employed to truncate the settings of the particularly wordy Gloria and Credo movements of the mass while needing to say all the words for the Mass to be considered licit or in conformity with the law.

Example 2.21: Josef Haydn, *Kleine Orgelmesse*, "Gloria."

The result is a rather messy, albeit efficient, way to get many words sung in a short period of time. As can be expected, intelligibility is lost as it's a real challenge for the average audience attendee to follow four lines of dense Latin text and comprehend it all—although the contemporary listeners would have been well familiar with this text already.

This technique is still employed in modern music, although not as often, nor as obviously as did Haydn or Mozart. This effect can be useful if one desires a messy cacophony of multiple words and sentences. If your goal is to overwhelm the listener, telescoping is an effective, workable option.

An example of this in modern music can be found in the first movement of *Path of Miracles* by Joby Talbot. In the first movement, the story of St. James's martyrdom is repeated in different languages representing the babel of different languages spoken by travelers on Camino de Santiago. Some of these retellings are consecutive, while others overlap or are sung simultaneously in various languages.

Example 2.22: Joby Talbot, *Path of Miracles*, "Reconcevalles."

Copyright © 2005 Chester Music Limited International. Copyright Secured. All Rights Reserved.

Keep in mind that while mixing text settings and telescoping can create specific desired textures unique to the genre of choral music, it can make intonation a challenge for the choir. As discussed in a previous section, for choral ensembles to be in tune both their fundamental pitches and the overtones created by their vowels need to be unified. Consequently, writing music with two different vowel sounds simultaneously will affect the choir's ability to tune as the overtones wont line up. This will be especially conspicuous at any cadences. If used in shorter instances this may not be a major concern, but can be during extended passages.

Text Painting

Text painting is another way that choral musicians refer to programmatic aspects or representative descriptions in their music. We can trace the origins of text painting in choral music back to secular works from the Renaissance period and examples can be found in French chansons as well as Italian and English madrigals.

The French were the first to formalize the forms of their secular music, as the chanson predates the other secular forms that would follow in Europe. Part of the evolution of their secular music was to pioneer the idea of using the music to imitate the sounds of other things. Clément Janequin was one of those who mastered this in works such as "Le chant des oiseaux," and "La Guerre." In "Le chant des oiseaux," Janequin attempts to imitate the sounds of various birds.

Example 2.23: Clément Janequin, "Le Chant des Oiseaux."

One particularly charming example in the French chanson canon comes from Passereau with his chanson "Il est bel et bon." The text describes women gossiping while feeding their chickens, and in the opening line, the repeating word "bon" sounds like the clucking of the chickens themselves.

Example 2.24: Pierre Passereau, "Il est bel et bon."

The secular music from the English Renaissance has no shortage of word painting examples. One example is "As Vesta was from Latmos Hill descending" by Thomas Weelkes. One of the numerous examples of word painting in this madrigal is the line "First two by two, then three by three together/Leaving their goddess all alone." Naturally, two parts sing "two by two," then a trio of parts chimes in for "three by three," and finally all six voices join in for "together." The lower five voices then drop out and abandon the first soprano to sing "all alone" as a solo.

Example 2.25: John Weelkes, "As Vesta was from Latmos Hill descending."

Looking now to twentieth-century French secular music, we can see that Ravel took inspiration from the programmatic chanson of the French Renaissance in one of his *Trois Chansons*. In the first movement, "Nicolette," the protagonist travels through the forest and encounters a wolf, a page, and an old lord. When Nicolette meets the wolf, the tenors and altos sing an [u]

vowel imitating a wolf howl. In the next section, the altos and tenors sing nonsense syllables ("ta ka ta ka") in sixteenth notes to represent Nicolette's quick footsteps while she runs away.

Example 2.26: Maurice Ravel, *Trois Chansons*, "Nicolette."

Another example from "Nicolette" involves meeting the page. When the page meets Nicolette, he asks if she's willing to be his "doux ami" (soft friend). To portray the page as a prepubescent boy, Ravel has all voices singing in very high registers and even has the tenors singing in falsetto.[4]

Example 2.27: Maurice Ravel, *Trois Chansons*, "Nicolette."

One of the most beautiful examples of text painting in twentieth-century Italian choral music has to be "Il giardino di Afrodite" from *Due Composizioni Corali* by Ildebrando Pizzetti. A setting of the Greek poet Sappho, the work is dense with examples of word painting. One particular example can be found on the words "Stormiscono le fronde, e ne discende

---

4   More information about falsetto can be found in Chapter 14.

molle sopore" (The leaves rustle and soft sleep descends from them.) where the tenors and basses sing in quickly moving sixteenth notes to represent the word "stormiscono" (they rustle). A few measures later, the sopranos, altos, first tenors, and second basses will sing a descending line for the phrase "e ne discende" (and it descends from there).

Example 2.28: Ildebrando Pizzetti, *Due Composizioni Corali*, "Il giardino di Afrodite."

© 1961 Casa Ricordi Srl. International Copyright Secured. All Rights Reserved. Reprinted by permission of Hal Leonard Europe.

During the turn of the twentieth century, text painting showed a certain resurgence in English choral music. One of the most successful English composers to implement this characteristic in his music was Benjamin Britten. Two notable examples come from his composition *Hymn to St. Cecelia*. The first example involves the words "And around the wicked in Hell's abysses/ The huge flame flicker'd and eas'd their pain." On the word "flame," the tenors and basses are instructed to sing a sforzando-piano to demonstrate this sudden dimming. Before the word "flicker'd," the sopranos and altos are instructed to diminuendo and then oscillate in different inversions of an E major triad, giving a wavering quality. Additionally, between the first and second syllable of the word "flicker'd," there is a very quick stop between the [I] vowel and the explosive [k] consonant, which imitates that ever-so-brief relief from hellfire.

Example 2.29: Benjamin Britten, *Hymn to St. Cecilia*, op. 23.

© 1942 Boosey & Co. Ltd. Reproduced by permission of Boosey & Hawkes.

A second example from *Hymn to St. Cecilia* is found in the words "I cannot grow;/I have no shadow/To run away from,/I only play." The running, scurrying lines from the sopranos and tenors paint an innocent, child-like imitative game, like a playground of unimpeachable amusement.

Example 2.30: Benjamin Britten, *Hymn to St. Cecilia*, op. 23.

© 1942 Boosey & Co. Ltd. Reproduced by permission of Boosey & Hawkes.

One particularly demonstrative example of text painting is "Dance, Clarion Air" by Michael Tippett, which has to be among the most delightfully flamboyant openings in choral music. The joyful skipping dotted eight notes give way to a very tall, open chord on the word "air," conveying a certain spaciousness and even weightlessness. This is followed by an echo, as if the air were answering back.

Example 2.31: Michael Tippett, "Dance Clarion Air."

Copyright © 1953 Schott Music Ltd., London. Copyright renewed. Used by permission of European American Music Distributors Company, sole U.S. and Canadian agent for Schott Music Ltd., London.

There are numerous more examples and endless possibilities when it comes to word painting ideas no matter the language. With that in mind it's important to remember that choral works do not need text painting to be effective or successful. Nor does the text painting need to be so explicit or demonstrative. Critics may consider it too demonstrative or too obvious, but if you want to do it, proceed tastefully.

Underlay

Another part of syllabification to consider is underlay. Underlay is the placement of syllables on specific notes and note changes. This technique originates from the Renaissance when composers would compose the music, dictating the pitches and rhythms, but simply would write the word under the first few pitches and expect the singers to know or decide for themselves where the syllables went on those pitches and rhythms. Composers and printers eventually began to be more specific with text placement, but underlay remains an issue when creating editions of early music.

In modern choral music, the composer is fully expected to dictate the underlay of each word and syllable. Clarity is provided in the underlay by adding slurs to pitches that share syllables.[5] This can be done easily in modern notation software and more details will be covered in Chapter 15.

The lower voices (very often the basses) sometimes get forgotten when setting text. Lower voices are sometimes asked to sing weird phrases that don't make any sense. While it is common in choral music to have a bass, or one of the inner voices, droning, it can have unintended consequences. Excessive use of droning can cause singers to lose interest. It also makes it tough sometimes for those singers to make to make a connection with the text.

Continuing Study

Suggested Exercises

Short
» Learn the symbols for vowel sounds in the International Phonetic Alphabet (IPA) and study the vowel chart. Learn the basic vowels and consonants of your vernacular language and practice writing words, then phrases, and eventually sentences in IPA.
» Practice translating words and phrases from IPA to American English, such as the following:
['tɑkoʊ]
[lɑs 'veɪgəs]
[kɹə'sant]
[gə'ɹɑʒ]
[gwɑkə'moli]

Long
» Practice setting the following texts metrically without pitch.
- Because I could not stop for Death/He kindly stopped for me
- "Hope" is the thing with feathers/That perches in the soul
- Glória in excélsis Deo
- Et in terra pax homínibus bonæ voluntátis
» Practice setting different movements from the mass metrically without pitch. Start with the "Agnus Dei" and the "Sanctus," then move onto the "Gloria" and the "Credo."

---

5   This practice is fully accepted in modern notation, but for scholarly and even performance editions of works from the Renaissance and Baroque periods, editors will purposefully avoid using slurs that clarify underlay.

Suggested Listening

Mass in B minor, BVW 232 - Johann Sebastian Bach
Liebeslieder Waltzes, op. 52 - Johannes Brahms
Hymn to St. Cecelia, op. 23 - Benjamin Britten
Trois Chansons - Claude Debussy
"Evening" - Ēriks Ešenvalds
"Salutation" - Ēriks Ešenvalds
Seven Poems of Robert Bridges - Gerald Finzi
Lagrime di San Pietro - Orlande de Lassus
Missa Papae Marcelli - Giovanni Pierluigi da Palestrina
"Which Was the Son of…" - Arvo Pärt
"The Beatitudes" - Arvo Pärt
Due Composizioni Corali - Ildebrando Pizzetti
Gloria - Francis Poulenc
Trois Chansons - Maurice Ravel
Daphnis et Chloé - Maurice Ravel
Flos Campi - Ralph Vaughan Williams

Chapter 3

Considering the Vocal Instrument

Your scientists were so preoccupied with whether or not they could that they didn't stop to think if they should.
— Dr. Ian Malcolm, *Jurassic Park*

Just as writing for the clarinet requires different considerations compared to writing for a viola, writing for the human voice also requires some basic considerations. Before we dive into the specifics for each voice type in later chapters, there are some general principles that apply to all voice parts that we shall consider in this chapter.

In my musical journey, I've seen a great deal of emphasis put on other instruments imitating the human voice. This can be summarized in the direction of *cantabile* or "with a singing quality." When this direction is given in a studio lesson, from the podium, or from composers themselves, instrumentalists know what that direction means and how they should respond. Upon this backdrop, I wish to say to my composing and arranging colleagues with all the love that I possess:

Writing for singers should start with singable lines.

The reader may ask, "what does 'singable' mean?" Many different teachers will tell you something different, and every composer will have a different idea. All I would do is point back to the writing of Palestrina: stepwise motion, carefully prepared leaps, avoiding extensive use of challenging intervals (such as descending 6ths and 7ths), staying within reasonable ranges and tessitura[1], and allowing space to breathe. This doesn't necessarily mean only writing legato lines. Once you understand how the voice operates in best practices then you can grow into other various textures and rhetorical gestures as well as special effects and extended techniques. I would only advise you to not attempt calculus before mastering arithmetic.

Let's just make one thing absolutely crystal clear: voices are not instruments. I will make some comparisons to instruments to try to convey a principle of vocal writing, but in truth, voices have no instrumental equivalent and can't do everything an instrumentalist can do, nor should they. There are times when a voice and instrument will align well enough in range to tempt us to treat them the same way, but this is a mistake as the registers and timbres will not line up the same way nor will their traditional roles with other instruments or sections. I have heard it said that "if a violin can play it, a soprano can sing it," and nothing could be further from the truth.

I once heard an account of a well-established composer who wrote a tenor part all the way down to a low E2. After you read subsequent chapters, you will understand that this is far beyond the range of tenors, and low even for many basses. Once, during a residency at a university, a student asked this composer why they wrote for the tenors to sing so low. The response from the composer was that they had been taught that tenors are the "cellos of the choir," and cellos can play a low E, so it made sense to them.

And even though no one asked, the same is true in reverse: instruments are not voices and can't do everything voices can do. Often, I will hear composers complain about the "limitations" of human voices, while seeming to completely miss what the human voice has to offer. It can't be stressed enough that there are plenty of things the human voice can do that other instruments aren't capable of, and composers shouldn't miss out on those incredible offerings just because they can't always keep up with the breakneck virtuosity or extreme ranges of other instruments.

If you've never sung in a choir before, never considered the vocal instrument or its idioms, or for some reason can't stomach the thought of reading this entire book, this chapter should hopefully give you a crash course on basic considerations for the human voice. This chapter will also help introduce you to a handful of the quirks of the vocal world and choral music-making that

---

1   Tessitura will be defined later in this chapter.

one might overlook. The goal of this chapter isn't to give the impression that one must walk on eggshells whenever composing for singers. It's an invitation to consider more than just the lowest and highest pitches of our ranges.

Breathing

Breath flow is fundamental to a singer's phonation, a common trait we share with aerophones like woodwind and brass instruments. Good vocal production is built on balanced phonation, or the way in which our vocal folds create sound through vibration. Balanced phonation involves making sure the sound is not too forced nor too breathy and is dependent on consistent airflow. As music becomes more extreme in either range or dynamics, faster breath flow is required to execute in a healthy and efficient way and faster airflow can lead to a quickly dwindling air supply. Singers must be given time and space to breathe, in the same way one would give time to a woodwind or brass player.

The question then arises about how often choral groups need to breathe and the short answer is that it depends on several factors. If the music is in the middle of the voice and at a moderate dynamic, voices are capable of singing for a decent amount of time before needing to breathe. If the music is more extreme in ranges or dynamics, the amount of time is shorter before breath needs to be renewed. Another factor is the level of training for the number of singers; amateur singers will need to breathe more often and trained singers very likely will be able to go longer. But individual singers must breathe, and each individual singer will have a different limit compared to the singer next to them.

There are times when it's appropriate to direct singers not to breathe in a specific spot where they may breathe otherwise. This may be at a structural pivot or in a place where it may make more sense textually to connect clauses or phrases together and are notated with a dashed slur. When this is done, it's very helpful to provide another opportunity for singers to breathe. You don't necessarily need to dictate every single breath, but you will need to allow them space and opportunities to renew their air supply. If you don't give singers space and time to breathe, they'll either take it anyway or allow their sound to die on the vine.

You may have seen a live performance or a video of a singer holding a note for an extended period of time, but don't be fooled. This is impressive, but it's a party trick. Most singers are not able to hold out notes for extended periods of time, at least not as a point of departure. Even if you have a soloist who can do this, reserve it for once per composition.

Moving further up in the hierarchy of needs, breathing can also be an expressive rhetorical tool of the ensemble. Very often in choral music, particularly in historical or older examples from the canon, breaths are not made explicit, and the music director will need to make a choice about where to have the ensemble breathe. Sometimes this choice is based purely on needs, but more often it is also based on the desired rhetorical phrasing. A music director can choose to take a breath or not when the opportunity presents itself. As an example, let's consider the first six measures of Mozart's "Ave verum corpus."

Example 3.1: Wolfgang Amadeus Mozart, "Ave verum corpus" K618.

Mozart didn't put in any breath marks, so the decision of where to breathe or not is left to us. Some will decide to perform this in two measure phrases—very often when performed on the very slow side of adagio—and have the ensemble breathe like so:

Example 3.2: Wolfgang Amadeus Mozart, "Ave verum corpus" K618 in two bar phrases.

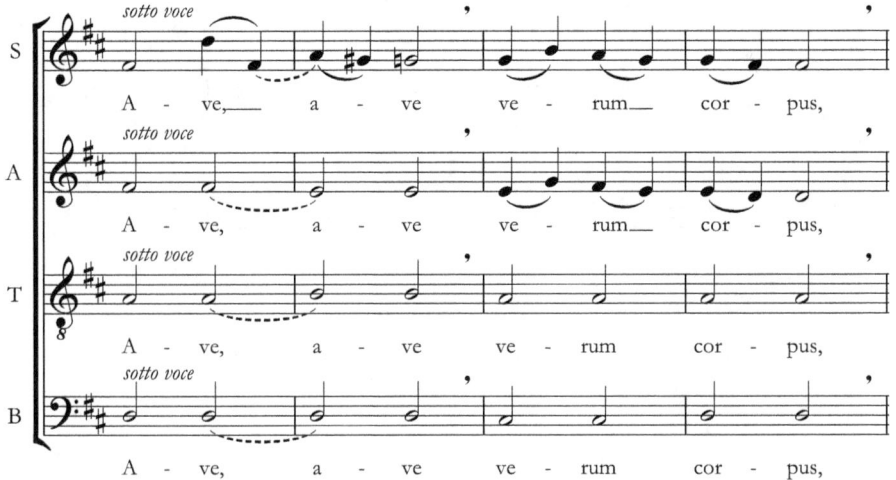

Other times, a music director will choose to perform this section in four measure phrases thusly:

Example 3.3: Wolfgang Amadeus Mozart, "Ave verum corpus" K618 in four bar phrases.

Still others will choose to perform this section by taking breaths at the commas in the text:

Example 3.4: Wolfgang Amadeus Mozart, "Ave verum corpus" K618 with breathing at commas.

I have heard all three of these choices in performance from ensembles of all levels with music directors of various prestige. Each of them has their merits, especially with certain ensembles and at certain tempos. As stated previously, you are not required to dictate every breath to the musicians. However, be mindful that the singers will need opportunities to breathe and places where they can make those choices.

Stagger Breathing

Some readers will be aware of a method to give the illusion of breathless singing called "stagger breathing." In this practice singers alternate between sustaining their singing to maintain the pitch while other singers take quick, silents breaths for themselves, and then vice versa. This practice is immensely helpful to maintain sounds for long periods of time, almost imitating an organ that can produce sounds for as long as the bellows pump air.

While stagger breathing is possible in many applications, it's not a panacea. It has a few limitations and choirs can't stagger forever on any given pitch. First, stagger breathing is a big challenge for smaller ensembles to pull off successfully, and impossible for groups that have one singer per part.[2] It

---

2 See Chapter 9.

is much easier with larger ensembles versus small. Stagger breathing is also a challenge when the music has lots of divided parts. This is especially a struggle if there's an uneven voicing in the sections. For example, if one singer is carrying much of the sound of a three or four voice section and they stop to breathe, it's like you've lost almost half the sound of that section, and the empty space becomes conspicuous.

Second, stagger breathing is also more challenging when singers are singing in higher parts of their voices, as well as at softer dynamics. These are parts where individual voices can be somewhat more exposed in the texture. Additionally, these are also times when voices are using faster airflow and subtly taking a quick breath can be difficult to do quietly.

Third, stagger breathing can be tough to do convincingly with amateur singers. To pull off stagger breathing well requires practice to leave the texture, breathe, and re-phonate without being noticed. Many amateur level singers just abruptly stop, gasp, and start singing again on a glottal onset.[3] It takes time to practice getting right. If I'm being honest, I've been surprised how many professional singers struggle with effective and discreet stagger breathing.

Fourth—but most subjectively—having choirs sing forever without breathing can be unsettling subconsciously for audiences. We understand that singers need to breathe, and whether we notice it or not, find it bizarre when we don't hear that. I remember listening to a lecture from an audio engineer about an experience he had while recording a singer. He had recorded several takes and edited together a performance from different takes, but later, he and others in the studio noticed that something was off. All the breaths the singer took had been edited out of the final performance and it gave the impression that the singer never breathed. The engineer ended up adding breaths back into the performance to try to restore that feeling of natural music making. Even though the vocal track became something of a Frankenstein's monster with different takes and random breaths added in, everyone in the room agreed that the final product came across as more natural and "real." Don't underestimate the humanity that comes with the sound of an audible breath. It reminds me of a quote by Igor Stravinsky who called the organ "the monster that never breathes."[4]

---

3   More on glottal onsets and glottal stops in Chapter 14.

4   Andrew Thomas, "The Organ in Some Striking Orchestral, Operatic and Choral Contexts." *The Musical Times* 151, no. 1912 (2010), 6060.

Range and Tessitura

The term "range" can be applied to both a musicians' voice as well as a written part in a composition or arrangement. In regards to a written piece, range defines the highest and lowest pitches—for any given part; tessitura is defined as where a majority of the pitches lie for that given part. For example, while a tenor part may span a reasonable range of D3 to G4, when most of the part lies between B3 and G4, that is the tessitura. Depending on where most of the pitches lie in the voice, the tessitura could be considered high or low, and in some cases problematically so.

It's important to consider both range and tessitura when composing and arranging for vocalists. One should, of course, make sure that pitches do not exceed reasonable ranges, and the same care should be taken to where the tessitura sits for any voice part. Avoid writing parts where the tessitura is too high, too low, or in awkward parts of the voice (which we will discuss in the next section). Refrain from parking singers in just one register of their voice for extend periods of time or even worse, through the entire piece. It's possible for a composition or arrangement to have an unreasonable range and a reasonable tessitura; simultaneously, it's possible for a composition or arrangement to have a reasonable range and an unreasonable tessitura.

There are many famous choral works where the tessitura is unrelentingly high, and while these are beautiful works of art, performing them in a live concert can be problematic and sometimes less than successful.[5] Choral conductors will sometimes resort to creative but unorthodox methods just to try to pull it off. These methods can sometimes include rotating portions of the choir to sing while others rest, then alternating so that other voices get an opportunity to rest while others sing.

When discussing the ranges of singers, whether specific to a certain voice part or not, there's much more to be considered besides the very highest and very lowest pitches available. The last thing you should do is look at the ranges in this book and think that everything between them is free game in all circumstances. The temptation is to see the range of a voice, look at the high note and think, "this is possible at all times and at all dynamics." Singers do not share that ability with our instrumental colleagues. This idea very often leads to unidiomatic and unreasonable writing.

Extreme ranges can be very fun to sing and exciting to listen to, but they aren't always necessary for a successful or effective composition. Remember,

---

[5] Indeed, I would say that there are some works that I've heard on recordings, but never heard live for this very reason.

just because you can doesn't mean you should. The soprano range in Fauré's *Requiem* is generally fairly conservative; the highest pitch is a G5, which they only sing once in the entire work. Additionally, consider that in the same work the sopranos aren't parked up in that high register the whole time either.[6]

Writing in extreme ranges or with extreme tessituras persistently and extensively may be a desired aesthetic, and perhaps what your art demands, but understand that you are making a tradeoff. The number of groups that are able or willing to perform your work will be smaller. It may not only be for ability concerns, but also for vocal hygiene or health concerns, especially if it's a middle school, high school, or university ensemble where students are still learning how to be stewards of their voices. If that's the kind of music you wish to compose, you are free to do so, but understand that the circle of possible performers will quickly dwindle. If that's the case, don't blame the singers or conductors who don't want to take it on. Just as it's your prerogative to write in that manner, it's the conductors' and singers' prerogative to pass on it.

Register and Passaggio

When most people hear the word "register" as it relates to the human voice, they often think of terms such as "head voice" or "chest voice." The concept of vocal registers is a contested idea among voice teachers and scientists, but for our purposes we will be working from a definition given by Manuel García:

> By the word register we mean a series of consecutive and homogenous tones going from low to high, produced by the development of the same mechanical principle, and whose nature differs essentially from another series of tones, equally consecutive and homogenous, produced by another mechanical principle.[7]

In other words, a register is a group of pitches that sound a similar way because they are produced by the vocal mechanism in a similar way. A singer moving outside these groups of notes, either to higher or lower pitches, will sound different because they are produced differently by the singer's instrument.

---

6   I will fully concede that the soprano solo in Movement IV of Fauré's *Requiem* has a tessitura in an awkward part of many sopranos' voices.

7   Scott McCoy, *Your Voice: An Inside View.* (Princeton: Inside View Press, 2004), 64.

The easiest—but far from perfect—instrumental analogy to the idea of registers is the different strings of a violin, viola, cello, or double bass. While it's possible to play a number of pitches on a lower string ("sul G" on violin for example), it will sound different than playing that same pitch on a higher string. Registers in the human voice work in a similar way. As a vocalist sings ascending pitches, they will need to switch to higher registers, or higher "strings," in order to keep moving up in their ranges.

Voice scientists generally agree there are at least two major registers based on laryngeal function: Thyroarytenoid-Dominant Production (TDP) and Cricothyroid-Dominant Production (CDP),[8] with one major break, or transition, between these two. Many teachers will have various names for these two general registers, most commonly these will be referred to as "chest tone" and "head tone." Within these larger registers, pedagogues will describe other breaks (or transition areas) when the production of the voice seems to change within these major laryngal productions.

Of course, there is some overlap of pitches among these neighboring registers that can be produced in both registers. This transition area is what Italians call passaggio, or passage. In English, however, we refer to these as "breaks" in the voice. This is probably because as we move through this transition area (if we don't transition to the next register) we reach a limit of the previous register, and it sounds as though our voice will break. While these registers, or the breaks between them, aren't entirely fixed, singers will usually encounter them in the same parts of their range, no matter what literature or style they sing.

Different voice pedagogues have trouble agreeing on the subject of register and passaggio. Some vocal pedagogues insist that there are different breaks in the voice, while some even argue that there aren't any at all. Pedagogues who argue that there are breaks in the voice also can't agree on how many there are. The only consensus they have is that many singers seem to have these breaks, and they can be difficult to navigate.

For the purpose of this book, we'll acknowledge that there are passaggios within TDP and CDP, along with the understanding that some breaks are easier to navigate than others. In general terms, many of these voice parts[9] will find significant breaks in the following places:

---

[8] McCoy, *Your Voice*, 65-66.

[9] My experience has shown me that there are voices that are exceptions to these guidelines, so don't be surprised when you find someone who doesn't fit neatly into any of these boxes.

Considering the Vocal Instrument 49

Sopranos generally have a break around E5 and F5.
Altos generally have a break around B4 and C5.
Tenors generally have a break around E4 and F4.
Basses generally have a break around B3 and C4.

As a composer or arranger, knowing this information should inform how to care for each voice part around these breaks between registers. The idea isn't to avoid these spots entirely, but rather to avoid parking voices in these places for extended periods of time or asking singers to sustain pitches in the break at extreme dynamics. Doing so would hinder ease of singing, create uncertainty around a singer's ability to execute during a performance, and possibly affect vocal hygiene in the long term.

An example of what to avoid can be found in Barber's setting of "Anthony O'Daly" from his choral cycle *Reincarnations*.[10] He calls for sopranos to sing on an E5 for twenty-three merciless measures. To make matters worse, he has the tenors and sopranos singing half-steps between E and F leading up to the climax of the movement at a very loud dynamic. Even though it's relatively short, it's tremendously taxing to sing.

Example 3.5: Samuel Barber, *Reincarnations*, "Anthony O'Daly."

Copyright © 1942 (Renewed) by G. Schirmer, Inc. International Copyright Secured. All Rights Reserved. Used by permission.

Lower breaks in the voice can be difficult to navigate at extreme dynamics but are generally easier the rest of the time. Higher breaks in the

---

10   It pains me to use this as a poor example because *Reincarnations* is a masterpiece of twentiety-century American choral music, even if much of it isn't written idiomatically for the voice.

voice can be difficult to navigate in general. Navigating these breaks requires the singer to shift mechanisms a little earlier than they need and to sing with a faster air flow than they normally would.

As a composer or arranger, it isn't necessary to fully understand what the voice is doing physiologically during these register shifts or navigating these breaks. What is necessary is understanding that registers and passaggios can be stumbling blocks in a singer's voice and to minimize putting singers into their breaks for extended periods of time, especially in extreme dynamics. Ultimately, the responsibility for navigating these breaks is down to the musicians themselves, but as a composer or arranger, you can help make their lives easier by avoiding these snares.

Key Signatures

In the world of equal temperament, and where A4 is at 440 Hz, key signatures can play an important role in the success of a performance—particularly for an a cappella work.

Vocal ensembles will sometimes sing in a neighboring key signature in a cappella music and take music up or down a half step (semitone). While it is not an uncommon practice for a choral conductor to experiment with singing a cappella works in adjacent keys, doing so can confuse our fellow musicians outside of the choral world. They often ask why we don't just stay with the key chosen by the composer or arranger.

Choral musicians do this for one of two reasons: First, if a piece is just generally too high, bringing it down a half step can provide a great deal of relief. Sometimes, making the shift downward from an A5 and an A♭5 can be a big relief to sopranos (although it can vary depending on the context). This can be especially helpful for music that was written in a setting when A4 may have been closer to 415 Hz and seems slightly too high in modern performance (more on this later in this chapter).

Second, it's to avoid key signatures where half steps (ti-do and mi-fa) are found on or near certain breaks in the voice. Half steps can be tricky for a vocalist, even highly trained ones, especially when in proximity to register shifts. Keys where the half steps lie close to the passaggio are often more difficult for the singers to execute with adequate intonation and will be more challenging to maintain pitch. As one solution, choral musicians will try to find an adjacent key that's easier for the singers to navigate their breaks, sing with ease, and ultimately, to keep in tune.

For example, the key of C major/A minor is a notoriously problematic key for singers to keep in tune because the half steps between E5 and F5 for sopranos and E4 and F4 for tenors are right where a major passaggio occurs. Similarly, the half steps between B4 and C5 for altos and B3 and C4 for basses are where another major passaggio lies. Moving up a half step to D♭ major or down a half step to B major will be a surprisingly helpful change. Similarly, the key of F is problematic because of the half steps between E and F again. Moving to E or F♯ are generally more successful keys in a cappella music. Oddly, in my experience I have also found the key of B♭ major to be a difficult one to keep in tune as well. I suspect this is because there are enough singers who have a break somewhere between A♮ and B♭ or between D♮ and E♭.

If you're workshopping a composition and the conductor moves your composition up or down a half step, be open to this new key and consider solidifying this adjustment in your engraved music. It can be easy to take offense when a group changes something that appears so fundamental to your writing, but in truth, this is an aspect that should be considered as flexible as something like dynamics or small tempo adjustments. It could strengthen the work's viability with a larger number of ensembles.

It's important to note that this practice of shifting to neighboring keys applies primarily to a cappella works and is not a general practice with accompanied works. Doing so would require engraving and distributing newly transposed instrumental parts. Most obviously, it's much easier for vocal ensembles to maintain pitch if they have one or more instruments helping them maintain it.

Having said that, even when a work is accompanied, those vocal problems related to half steps in proximity to register shifts are still there, and the choir will still struggle with intonation. This could become an issue with softer instruments that choirs can sometimes have a difficult time hearing, such as a nylon string guitar. Additionally, should you have the instruments tacet for a period of time, the choir may struggle to maintain pitch in the a cappella passages, which will be very evident when the instruments begin playing again.

Vowels and Consonants

As stated previously in Chapter 2, what sets singers apart from instrumentalists is the ability to include words directly and naturally in our music making. This, however, is a double-edged sword as the vowels and consonants that make those words can have a major impact on vocal production and how a vocalist will sound. Each vowel has its singular characteristic, and each resonates differently in the voice. Some vowels are easier to produce in different parts of a singer's range, while others are more challenging. Some vowels will also cause issues in higher registers as well as at louder dynamics.

For context, let's review the basics of vowel sounds using the vowel diagram most used by the International Phonetic Association:

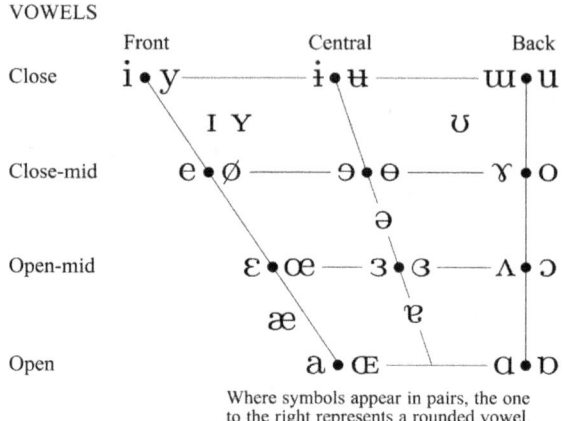

Where symbols appear in pairs, the one to the right represents a rounded vowel.

IPA Chart, http://www.internationalphoneticassociation.org/content/ipa-chart, available under a Creative Commons Attribution-Sharealike 3.0 Unported License. Copyright © 2018 International Phonetic Association.

Imagine this chart is a facsimile of the oropharynx in profile. On the left side of this chart is the front of the mouth and on the right is the back. The vowels placed on this chart indicate where the tongue is positioned in the mouth to create different overtones and produce their respective vowel sounds. To make the [i] sound, the tongue is high in the mouth and towards the front. To make the [u] sound, the tongue is also high in the mouth, but towards the back. You can notice this difference yourself if you alternate quickly between an [i] vowel and an [u] vowel, while keeping the lips the same shape. The [a] vowel requires the tongue to be at the bottom of the mouth and somewhat halfway between front and back. You can notice this as well if you alternate quickly between an [i] vowel and an [a] vowel while keeping the jaw from moving.

In general, singing the more open vowels from the lower half of the chart—like [a] or [ʌ]—will be easier to produce when singing in higher registers or louder dynamics compared to the vowels from the upper half of the chart—like [i] or [u].

When writing a vocalise (as discussed in Chapter 2), most composers will stick with vowels on the warmer side of the vowel chart: [a] to [u]. Very rarely does a composer venture much brighter or more forward than an [a] vowel unless they are looking for a particularly brassy, edgy, characterful, or obnoxious sound.

Vowel Modification

As pitches get higher or dynamics get louder, singers can't always maintain pureness of vowel and must modify their vowels. Vowel modification is the practice of migrating vowels from a more closed vowel to a more open vowel. For example, instead of singing with a true [i] sound, a singer (with at least a modest amount of training) will very often begin to modify this towards an [I] vowel, which is slightly more open. This will allow the musician to sing with a bit more open production to keep the voice working in a healthy and efficient manner, while trying to stay as close as possible to the original vowel sound. As music get higher or louder, however, another modification from [I] will be made to yet another slightly more open vowel, such as [e]. In cases of increasingly extreme dynamics and higher pitches, modification will move yet another vowel placement until ultimately modifying to either [a] or, for some singers, [ʌ].

As mentioned previously, vowel modification is done for two reasons: ease of phonation and quality of tone. In many cases, it's just not possible to sing pure closed vowels and maintain the dynamics required or in a manner that would be considered by most to be in good practice or healthy. Additionally, some will argue that it doesn't sound ideal when a singer is maintaining a pure closed vowel in extreme dynamics or higher pitches; others may argue that this is subjective. By modifying slightly, the goal is to maintain best practices and to try to maintain understanding of the text by the audience.

The reason why composers and arrangers should be aware of this practice is because the major drawback of vowel modification is that the more modifying a singer does, the more intelligibility becomes difficult to execute well, and audiences have a harder time understanding the text.[11] Pure vowels are important to intelligibility. Modifying the vowel by one step may not affect text intelligibility that much, but modifying more than that certainly will.

Writing music that is either in higher registers or requiring louder dynamics will result in the singers modifying many of their vowels, sometimes significantly. This is especially an issue when working with instrumental collaborators, and vocal ensembles will usually need to sing in higher registers and at louder dynamics to balance adequately, particularly when working with

---

11 One particularly memorable example in popular culture is how Justin Timberlake sings the words "it's gonna be me" has become a huge meme online.

larger ensembles such as an orchestra (more on this in Chapter 13). Should you have a large amount of text in these moments, the listener has very little chance of getting any meaningful text from the ensemble, which is already a challenge for choirs.

Asking singers to not modify in these scenarios—to try to maintain better text intelligibility—is not reasonable to ask. There's only so much that singers can do when the music is extremely high or extremely loud. A better strategy is leaving passages with lots of text for dynamics and textures that lend themselves to better understanding, and using fewer words for those louder, higher passages. This strategy is similar to Palestrina's text setting strategy for Missa Papae Marcelli as discussed in Chapter 2.

Consonants

As one can expect, consonants are vital to word intelligibility. In low to medium range pitches, along with low to middle dynamics, there is relatively little issue for the singer to put out a lot of consonants in their singing. As you may guess by the theme in this chapter, things get complicated with extreme dynamics and higher pitches.

As stated previously, as singers get higher and louder they will need to modify to more open sounds for vocal health and ease of singing. Many consonants require closing the mouth partially or entirely, the tongue to move around, or to morph through diphthongs to create various sounds. This is a challenge when one is already modifying and trying to maintain an open vocal tract. Singers will start to cheat on some consonants, both to maintain a legato line but also because it can be difficult to execute at extremes. That's why singers will sometimes sound like they've lost their dentures in high and loud passages.

Some singers truly see consonants as getting in the way of their vocal productions, and in many ways, this mindset is justified. As a composer or arranger, this is important to know for similar reasons as discussed in the previous section on vowel modification, and similar strategies can be employed here.

Stamina

Every type of musician has a length of time that they are comfortably able to rehearse or perform either certain passages, compositions, or in general. Some instrumentalists will have guidelines on how to avoid injury from repetitive motion, and some unions will enforce rules about breaks during rehearsals to avoid these injuries. Singers also have limits, but these limits are somewhat different from other musicians.

Rehearsal Related

The limits singers have for general phonation will be shorter than most instrumentalists. For example, while undergraduate piano students may practice for several hours every day, undergraduate voice majors may be limited by their teachers to one hour of individual, phonating practice to avoid fatigue and overuse injury, as the student will also probably have choral and opera rehearsals that same day. As singers mature, their stamina for extended rehearsals will increase. Most professional choirs will rehearse for no more than five or six total hours (including breaks) in a day, with a fifteen minute break after sixty minutes of rehearsal, and at least a sixty minute break after three hours.

This is one of the reasons why vocalists may have a reputation as wilting lilies: having a relatively shorter stamina and fatiguing quickly compared to instrumentalists. But remember, the vocal folds are only as long as the average human thumbnail[12] and can only handle so much work in one setting, especially in young singers whose voices are still maturing.[13]

Performance Related

Additionally, singers have a certain amount of stamina regarding range and dynamics. Singers have a limit regarding the extreme high and extreme low parts of their voices. Even while sopranos and tenors specialize in singing high, there is a limit to how long they can continuously and exclusively sing up in their vocal stratosphere and maintain good tone and pitch.

Likewise, singers have a limit regarding the extremes in dynamics. Singing very loud or extremely soft is of course a big part of choral music making, but there's a limit to how long musicians can sing in those dynamics and maintain good tone and healthy practices. It's not difficult to imagine the limits any voice has when asked to shout very loud or whisper for extended periods of time. Both of these practices are taxing on the human voice and will compromise vocal health if insisted on for too long a period of time.[14]

---

12   McCoy, *Your Voice*, 107.

13   This maturation process can continue through the age of 35.

14   Singers will sometimes refer to compositions that contain excessive amounts of high and loud singing as "a screamer" or "park and bark."

These concepts can be distilled down to the principle that voices should not stay stuck in one register of their voice (especially the extreme ends of range), or at one dynamic level for extended periods of time (as discussed in a previous section of this chapter). Voices should be able to move through their range and through different dynamics. All things in moderation of course. One doesn't necessarily have to have them move endlessly from register to register with no place to rest.

Allow times and places in your composition for singers to be able to rest and reset.[15] This doesn't necessarily mean having the entire ensemble be tacit simultaneously. If you notice you've been especially demanding of a certain voice or section, allow them the chance to rest. The voice is not a machine that can be worked into the dust, nor is it an instrument made from wood, metal, or plastic. The flesh becomes weak even if the spirit is willing.

Finding Pitches

Because singers cannot see their instrument and can't spontaneously sound out pitches at will (unless they have perfect pitch), singers need to find their pitches from some previous reference. When choirs begin a performance of an a cappella work, that reference is a pre-determined pitch, either from an instrument, a pitch pipe, a tuning fork, or another singer giving the pitch.

When reading music there are three general approaches a singer will use to find their pitch after a brief break. First, they will determine the relationship between the pitch they just finished singing and the new pitch. As an example, if they finished singing on an E♮, and after a few moments of rest then need to sing a B♮, the singer will consider the relation of a perfect fifth ascending or a perfect fourth descending.

Second, if the rest is somewhat longer, the musician will see if they can find their new pitch in another part in the measure just prior to their entrance. That can be a part sung by a singer or by an instrument. If they are entering on a G♮, they will look for a G♮ in the other parts in the previous measure. If they can't find that, they will find another pitch, such as one that's a step away, and work out an interval relation to their own.

Third, if there seems to be no clear relation from the previous material to what they are singing next, singers will have to take time to practice the transition, either in their own practice or together in rehearsal. It's not impossible

---

15   For more information about letting voices rest for musical purposes, see Chapter 12.

for us to learn and memorize odd key changes or unrelated pitches, but just like many other aspects of choral music, each of these things comes with a price to pay. In this case, that price is rehearsal time.

Once the pitch has been established in the memory through practice and rehearsal, finding pitches in performances is mostly a nonissue (unless it hasn't been practiced enough).

Voice Leading

The Common-practice period part-writing rules that are learned in music theory classes are especially important when writing for singers. Most trained vocalists spend an extensive amount of time learning how to sight read using conventional tonality and it's best to lean into this skill set as best as one can. In a post-tonal world, doing so can be frustrating for a singer when they encounter augmented seconds or diminished thirds or fourths, for example. And of course, in a post-tonal world, it may make complete sense to spell chords a certain way, especially for something like a keyboard reduction.

Singers respond much better to a line that is written with clearer, simpler intervals for ease of reading, even if that means spelling pitches enharmonically that don't make sense vertically, or in the broader context. For example, it's much easier for singers to read and sing a minor third than an augmented second.

There may come times when you'll need to make a choice regarding enharmonic pitches and how to spell accidentals. Lean toward what is best for the singer to read. This may even mean that you use one enharmonic spelling for the vocal part and another for the keyboard reduction. While imperfect, this is a preferable solution to make the music friendlier to read for both musicians.

Variation Between Singers

It's a challenge to explain to non-vocalists just how much variety of timbre there is from singer to singer. The difference between a cheap violin and an expensive violin is fairly pronounced. Likewise, the difference between an amateur singer and a professional singer is extremely apparent. But even among trained singers, the contrast from singer to singer can be vast.

Working with different singers in a single section isn't the same as comparing it to a section of violins, where each violin has variations of sound. It's closer to having a section staffed by violins, flutes, and trumpets. The variation of the singers' tone, even in the same section, can be that dramatic.

For examples of how professional soprano soloists, working in the same general genre of opera, can sound different from each other, consider the recorded performances of Natalie Dessay, Kiri Te Kanawa, and Jessye Norman. Opera singers have codified these differences in vocal timbre in the Fach system.[16]

What makes ensemble singing so incredible is the ability to amalgamate these different tones into a single unified sound. Even still, because of the variation of singers, a section of sopranos from one choir can sound very different from a section of sopranos in another choir. Even in the same choir, the sound of each section will almost inevitably evolve from season to season (sometimes in scholastic choirs from semester to semester). It's important to understand that these differences aren't necessarily good or bad; most often it is a difference between good and another kind of good.

And yet, even with large variations of timbres between singers in the same section, it all comes together in a wonder. This is the secret of the beauty of choral music: the amalgamation of all these variations into a sound that is more valuable than the sum of its parts.

Soloists Versus Choristers

One concept about vocal music that many music teachers and professors seem intent on conveying to compositions students is the difference between a soloist and a chorister. Even Kennan and Grantham took pains to emphasize this separation.[17] The prevailing idea used to be that choral singers or choristers have a pleasant but overall forgettable voice that was easy to blend with other singers, while the soloist was a singer with a stunning, distinctive, and significantly voice that is only capable of standing out.

This is not only a drastic oversimplification but now a somewhat dated paradigm of what actually happens in the vocal world today. In many ways, the difference between a soloist and a chorister that many people identify is really just the difference between a trained singer and an untrained (or undertrained) singer.

There are a few reasons why this mindset has endured for so long (and in many places continues to this day). For many years, the primary way to make a living as a classical vocalist was in opera—either as a soloist or paid chorus member—or as a soloist for an oratorio. Therefore, if you wanted to make a living in classical music as a vocalist, your training led you to be a soloist. Choral

---

16 This classification system is much less important in choral music overall. It should be noted that the Fach system is not subscribed to by every singer or teacher of singing.

17 Kennan and Grantham, *The Technique of Orchestration*, 394.

music was considered a waste of time because in the past it didn't lead to much paid work or meaningful career moves, and it was believed that blending into a choir harmed one's ability to sing out as a soloist. Making a living as a choral musician was less viable and less common, even if one tried to cobble together numerous jobs. This idea has of course been perpetuated by many classical voice teachers who made careers in that environment.

While ensemble singing still doesn't pay as well as solo singing, the landscape of classical singing has changed significantly in the last few decades and there are many more viable and sustainable paths in classical singing outside of solo opera or oratorio work. Audience tastes and performance practices have changed, and there are now career opportunities for ensemble singing, including early music ensembles and professional choral groups. Today, many professional choral ensembles are made up of singers who are also accomplished and beautiful soloists. Many of the colleagues that I sing next to in various professional choral ensembles also do a significant amount of solo work, and some have even been part of Grammy-winning recordings as soloists. While a small group of professional singers do specialize in one specific career path, many professionals do both successfully.

It's true that the vast majority of choral musicians in the United States are amateurs with little or no training. Choral music in the United States has mostly been an amateur sport for hundreds of years; only recently has the professional side of the choral music scene made any serious strides. However, as mentioned previously, the classical voice landscape has changed dramatically, and in some ways the mindset of the past is being erased every day.

Understanding the Distinctions

With all that said, there are a few differences that you should be aware of between traditional soloist and chorister practices that have stuck around in modern music making. Solo voices will classify themselves differently from ensemble singers, either in their voice part or their Fach (as mentioned briefly in the previous section). Most solo singers will categorize themselves into one of seven voice parts: soprano, mezzo-soprano, contralto, countertenor, tenor, baritone, and bass. In general, you will probably find that each of these may be asked to sing slightly higher ranges than have been indicated in Chapters 4-8.

The distinction between firsts and seconds is not used for nearly all soloists, so it's not a good idea to ask a soprano or tenor soloist if they are "a first or a second." Instead, many soloists will adhere to the Fach system[18] to

---

18 For more information about the Fach system, please consult *What the Fach?!* by Philip Shepard.

help further classify their voice type and repertoire specialization. The different Fachs can include (but are not limited to) other descriptive adjectives such as lyric, spinto, dramatic, etc. Part of the reason why they do this is to perform repertoire that works best in their vocal timbre, and to help them corner their place in the singing market and the roles they can get cast in.

Vibrato

Vibrato is a very controversial topic among singers, voice teachers, and music directors, and is very likely the reason for any heated conversation among any of the three. Very few subjects are as touchy to discuss in the field of vocal music. And yet, discuss it we must.

Let's begin with these principles in mind:

» Some singers have a natural inclination to produce a sound with a pronounced vibrato, while others do not. Neither of these makes a voice inherently superior.
» Some singers find it much easier and more sustainable to sing with full vibrato, while others find singing without vibrato to be easier and more sustainable.
» Some singers have found a way to comfortably move back and forth between singing with and without vibrato, while others find it to be extremely difficult or nearly impossible.
» Vibrato is more appropriate in some vocal literature and less appropriate in other vocal literature.

With these ideas in mind, vibrato is usually at the discretion of the musicians, without any comment from the composer. In previous generations, very accomplished ensembles in North America staffed with trained singers, would use vibrato as a point of departure, no matter the literature. Today, the idea in North America is to use vibrato for certain applications, but also to use straighter tone as a point of departure. Some of those applications may include monophony, dyadic and triadic harmonies, or climatic moments, but application can be uneven.

Composers will sometimes give directions for adding or removing vibrato from choral compositions and arrangements, but this is not conventional for most compositions. Also, keep in mind that giving directions about vibrato in the score does not guarantee that the musicians will comply.

Example 3.6: Eric Whitacre, "Go, Lovely Rose."

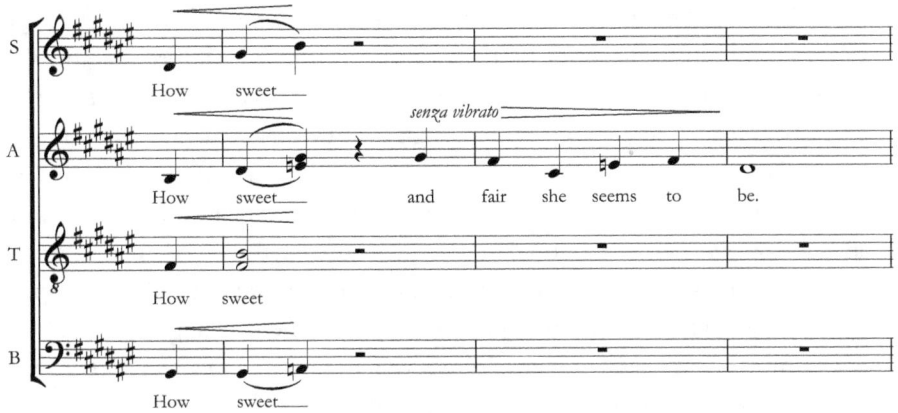

Copyright © 2001 Santa Barbara Music Press. Used by permission.

As a composer, you should be aware of the culture and, in a limited way, the mechanism around vibrato in singing, but in general, you should stay out of the fray yourself. The more you can keep yourself above board on this subject, the happier you'll be.

Performing From Memory

Many choral ensembles have a tradition of performing from memory. The purpose for this practice can include: allowing the singers to more fully commit to a performance; allowing them the freedom to more fully follow the conductor's gestures; permitting them to find a more personal, intimate connection with the music they may not be able to find otherwise; or more practically, freeing their hands and arms for clapping or other choralography.[19] This practice is one that we borrow from opera and music theater rather than from instrumental performance.

Some scores are easier to commit to memory and others quite difficult. Most choral conductors will choose to memorize shorter octavos—even entire concerts of octavos—but perform longer works from scores. The decision to perform from memory is one made by the ensemble and ultimately not your decision as a composer or arranger. However, there are some strategies you can employ to make your score easier to memorize instead of a burden.

A significant amount of choral music includes some sort of repetition, whether that repeated material is minimal or extensive. For example, many arrangements of strophic materials—such as a folk songs or hymns—have

---

19 Clapping and choralography will be discussed in greater detail in Chapter 14.

repeating verses and sometimes refrains. When repeating either these verses or refrains, it will be much easier to memorize them if the music is exactly the same or significantly different. Perhaps each verse is set differently and the refrains are repeated exactly the same except for the final refrain. Or the refrain is repeated but the last phrase or line is significantly different to the others.

What makes memorizing difficult is when a verse or refrain is repeated, but only one or two notes, rhythms, or words have been changed. These small changes are a huge burden on the memory, can easily be forgotten or overlooked, will require more repetitions to memorize, and take precious time away from general rehearsal. The same is true when memorizing words: having the sentence repeat exactly or change entirely is easier to memorize than two sentences where only one or two words are different.

This is not only difficult to memorize but it's not that compelling to an audience. Be honest with yourself as a composer or arranger: is the one small note or rhythm difference vital to the success of your work? Even without the burden of memorization, these small, easy to miss differences can trip up choral ensembles of all abilities and take up precious time. This might sound obvious to some readers, but this comes up fairly regularly in choral music.

As mentioned previously, you are not responsible as the composer or arranger for the choice to perform from memory but making it an easier choice for the performers is immensely helpful. This strategy is more suited for shorter forms, but it doesn't hurt to incorporate it with longer forms. Even when performing from a score, your music will be easier to learn and easier to perform if the singer isn't worried about any very small, minute alterations.

A Word About Referring to the "Masters"

When discussing writing for the choral ensemble, we should look back and consider the composers and arrangers who came before us and learn what lessons we can from their works and experiences. However, we must put some of their works into their context before looking to them as sacrosanct examples to be lifted up beyond reproach.

Considering that A4 was not standardized worldwide as 440 hertz until 1953,[20] we should consider pitch to be very relative and understand that it may not equate to our modern-day concert pitch. During the 1600s, cities up and down the Italian peninsula would vary in pitch by as much as a major third.[21]

---

20 Bruce Haynes, *History of Performing Pitch: The Story of "A"* (Lanham, MD: Scarecrow Press, 2002), 361.

21 Haynes, *History of Performing Pitch*, 70.

Additionally, different opera houses in the same city would tune to different pitches, and some opera houses and orchestras would tune to different pitches from season to season.[22] If a composer has written a choral work prior the middle of the twentieth century and it seems to be very high, it's very likely that it was pitched lower than it would appear in modern performance. When studying these scores, do not assume that what is written was always composed to be performed around 440 Hz.

How does this affect the way we should study masterpieces from far removed epochs? Let's consider Handel's *Dixit Dominus*—composed in 1707 while he was in Rome—where every voice part seems to be written excessively high for extended periods of time. When one considers that it was common for Roman instruments to be tuned to 392 Hz,[23] it's clear that it was meant to sound lower. Despite still being one of the most challenging works in the choral canon, it is somewhat more manageable for the vocalists at this lower pitch.

Additionally, we should also consider that if a composer was deaf from the middle of their career onward, they would not have heard how painfully high their music was to actually sing. Beethoven's *Missa solemnis* and *Symphony No. 9* are unparalleled works from the early Romantic period, but brutal to actually sing. Both are mercilessly high in the voice for extended periods of time, and much too loud for too long.[24] Below is an example of some of the unreasonable things Beethoven writes in the extremes of the voice. On its own, this is fairly difficult to execute, but one should keep in mind that this is simply one small excerpt from a work seems to be made almost entirely of passages just like this.[25] It's an extraordinarily challenging work to perform, even at 415 Hz. Consider as well, that the size of Beethoven's orchestra was considerably smaller than ones used today, and the instruments used in this period would have been somewhat quieter than modern ones.

---

22 Haynes, *History of Performing Pitch*, 360.

23 Haynes, *History of Performing Pitch*, 360.

24 The joke among singers is that it's easier to sing the solo parts than the choral parts for these two works because you get more time to rest.

25 Even though this is one example from *Missa Solemnis*, I had many, many passages to consider when lifting an excerpt for this chapter.

Example 3.7: Ludwig van Beethoven, *Missa solemnis*, op. 123 "Gloria in excelsis."

We should also consider that some of the great masters just didn't bother to learn—or perhaps in some cases accept—what was idiomatic for the human voice. One could argue that choral ensembles have since learned how to pull off performances of these otherwise less-than-successful attempts at writing for choirs, and that it's the composer's job to push the envelope and for the performers to catch up and figure out how to execute on their vision. I will concede there needs to be a certain amount of that, but the attitude of the composer or arranger must be one of empathy, deference, and humility rather than arrogance or condescension.

Singers can be just as enthusiastic to try new things, challenge themselves, and push their abilities by attempting difficult music as any of our instrumental colleagues. However, asking any musician to push the limits comes with an understanding that they are entitled to push back if they don't think they can make it work.

Ultimately, what we need composers and arrangers to understand is that your efforts will be more successful if you work with the voice and not against it. That may sound like a worthless platitude and yet it seems to elude many composers who are unfamiliar with the vocal idiom.

Other Needs of Singers

One of the needs of the singer that we sometimes find too embarrassing to mention is that when a musician is singing, saliva is being produced in their mouths and after a period of time, they will need to assimilate that buildup of saliva. Now, considering that the average human clears saliva from their mouths every one to two minutes,[26] this is going to come up during performances. You might be giving your singers enough time to breathe, but also make sure that they have enough time to clear their saliva.

This might seem odd to discuss or mention, but it has come up in my own choral rehearsals and performances, especially when singing strophic, homophonic pieces. One experience comes to mind: I was singing in a quartet and the bass part frankly had no breaks or places to rest. It barely even allowed time to breathe. There were several times in rehearsal when we would sing through the arrangement, and by the time we got near to the end, I had to make a choice to either stop making sounds and clear the saliva, to start drooling, or to start choking. If you don't give singers the opportunity to assimilate their saliva buildup, they will just take it.

Continuing Study

Suggested Exercises

Short
- » Describe the difference between range and tessitura.
- » Identify where traditional vocal breaks are in sopranos, altos, tenors, and basses.
- » Discuss why certain key signatures are friendlier to voices singing a cappella music and others are not.

Long
- » Practice singing your part in Mozart's "Ave verum corpus" and see how long you can sing comfortably before you need to take a breath.
- » Find a motet by Palestrina and count the number of intervals, both ascending and descending, that are found in the work. For example, count the number of ascending minor seconds, major seconds, minor thirds, etc. Analyze how many ascending and descending intervals Palestrina uses in that motet.
- » Find an acquaintance who has studied voice and politely ask them what they wish composers knew about their voice part.

---

26 Norfolk and Norwich University Hospitals. "The Normal Swallow," accessed April 24, 2004, https://www.nnuh.nhs.uk/departments/speech-andlanguage-therapy/swallowing/the-normal-swallow/.

Suggested Listening

Reincarnations - Samuel Barber
Missa solemnis, op. 123 - Ludwig van Beethoven
"Locus iste" - Anton Bruckner
"Evening" - Ēriks Ešenvalds
Dixit Dominus - George Frideric Handel
Ave Maria - Paweł Łukaszewski
"Màiri" - James MacMillan
"Ave Verum Corpus" - Wolfgang Amadeus Mozart
"The Beatitudes" - Arvo Pärt
Mass No. 2 in G Major - Franz Schubert
Symphony of Psalms - Igor Stravinsky
Missa Corona spinea - John Taverner
Gloria - Antoni Vivaldi

Chapter 4

Sopranos

She was a singer who had to take any note above A with her eyebrows.
— Montague Glass

General Range

1st Sopranos

General range: D4 thru A♭5
Trained range: C4 thru C6 (and sometimes higher)

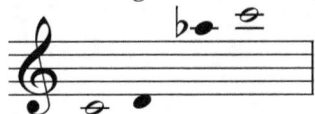

2nd Sopranos

General range: C4 thru F5
Trained range: B3 thru A5

Introduction

The soprano section is almost certainly the most praised and most criticized section of any choral ensemble. It's the first thing a listener notices about a choir's sound and it's likely among the most memorable aspects of a performance. Sopranos are almost constantly under the microscope; it's a wonder they can phonate at all.

In my experience, there are more sopranos interested in and participating in choral music than any other voice part.[1] Consequently, this group is usually the most competitive in an audition process and is most likely to be staffed by some of the most talented and accomplished artists of the ensemble. Beginning composers will often see this pool of talent with such capable voices and think the sky is the limit and end up writing parts that are abusive and not idiomatic. It's important to remember that this section needs to be treated reasonably.

The word soprano originates from the Latin *superius*, which sang above all the other voice parts, including the part previously know to be the highest, alto. In previous epochs, the *superius* part in religious music would have been sung by adolescent boys. Only during the development of secular music did women's voices begin to be part of ensemble music making in Europe. In this chapter, we will only consider female-assigned voices. More on children's voices can be found in Chapter 8.

Sopranos will exclusively use the treble clef. Previous generations of engravers would have used the "soprano clef" with the middle C on the bottom line of the staff. This transposition up a major 3rd can still be found in older editions of choral-orchestral repertoire. However, such practices have long been discontinued.

General Description

The lowest portion of most sopranos is the least generous part of their voices. In subjective terms, it can have a gentle velvetiness to it, but at other times it can be perceived as weak and sometimes aspirate. The lower part remains usable but in general, anything below F4 should only have lighter accompaniment to it or at the least be doubled with the altos. The chest voice can be accessed to bring out lower pitches, but using the chest voice in the lower

---

1 In collegiate settings, there are often so many sopranos that larger voices in this part—particularly with a few extra low notes—are often assigned to sing alto. Many will argue that this is detrimental, or at least less than ideal, to both the singer and the conductor.

register can have a somewhat juvenile character. It really can't be overstated how the lower voice of most sopranos is very often not their strength. Some high soprano voices truly don't even blossom until C5.

The middle voice has more power and more character to the tone. For some high sopranos, this part of the voice may still not add much more in terms of power or character. The high voice is where the voice becomes much stronger and begins to have a more silvery quality to it. It some cases, this part of the voice can be overwhelmingly powerful and overbalance the rest of the ensemble.

The very high part of the voice above A5 tends to change depending on the soprano. For some voices it stays quite fluty, while for others it becomes more piercing, and still for some it begins to sound strained. However, some voices sound strained in this range due to singing in straight tone and can sound more free and open when allowing some vibrato into the sound. Sometimes in this range the voices can begin to lose their descriptive characteristics and become almost "white" and featureless. This part of the voice can also vary in power from strong to quickly tapering off. These are some of the aspects that divide the first sopranos from the second sopranos in the minds of many conductors.

The most useful parts of the soprano voice are the middle and high parts, as they are the strongest and have the most character. However, as discussed previously in Chapter 3, it's important to not keep a voice stuck in one register for extended periods. Doing so may cause the voice to fatigue. Most sopranos will have a major register shift somewhere near E5 to F5. Parking the voice here for an extended period can also fatigue the voice even faster.

Agility

In general, sopranos are capable of extraordinary dexterity. Extensive runs and quick passages are possible and can sound thrilling. With training, some sopranos are capable of some truly astounding virtuosic vocal gymnastics. Most trained sopranos will be able to sing running sixteenth notes at a pretty good clip, though there's a limit to what is possible. Some sopranos who specialize in Bach, Handel, and Rossini will be able to handle many fast, agile lines.

For some singers, lithe and acrobatic singing is less of a possibility for them, and in general, untrained sopranos won't be able to execute as adeptly, but they will still have a fair amount of agility at their disposal. Some singers will also be better at upward runs, while others are more proficient at downward runs. Interestingly, in my experience, the division between singers who are more comfortable with one or the other is virtually tied.

Role in the Ensemble

As the highest voices in the choral ensemble, sopranos bring a great deal of brightness to the overall sound. Whether the overall timbre of the soprano sound is comparatively warm or brilliant, the section provides a clarity that is missing when just the lower voices are singing without them. Being the highest voice also naturally predisposes the section very often to sing the melody.

When not singing the melody, this section can offer a truly beguiling counter melody. This is, of course, in addition to other lovely upper harmonies either in a duet or in consort with the other upper voices. Sopranos are sometimes called to sing *ostinati*. This can be very effective, but if done too high or in the breaks for too long it can fatigue the voice quickly.

Duets with altos work especially well, particularly in parallel 3rds. Duets with tenors also work beautifully—in octave doublings or in parallel 6ths. Duets with the basses are more challenging but can be done in octave or two octave doublings under the right circumstances. Pairing with basses is usually quite successful in canon. More will be covered on this topic in Chapter 11.

Extra-musically, the soprano section can provide inspiration to the rest of the ensemble, being one of the most competitive and skilled sections in the ensemble. It can lend itself to some internal competition, but that is not your problem.

Other Considerations

I often hear sopranos anecdotally say that one of the things they despise being asked to do is to not sing for a period, only to suddenly sing very high in their range. This is particularly true when marked at softer dynamics. In fairness, most singers don't enjoy doing this, but for some reason sopranos are asked to do this regularly. It is reasonable, however, to have sopranos re-enter after being tacet at lower, middle, and even mid-high parts of their voice, especially if the dynamic is on the stronger side.

A particularly egregious example of what sopranos dread can be found in "Floret silva" from *Carmina Burana* by Carl Orff. The divided sopranos end a phrase on a F♯5 and A5 and, after being tacet for twelve measures, are directed to sing a high G5 and B5 at a pianissimo dynamic. The success rate of this passage in performance is usually mixed.

Example 4.1: Carl Orff, *Carmina Burana*, "Floret silva."

Copyright © 1937 Schott Music GmbH & Co. KG, Mainz, Germany. Copyright renewed. Used by permission of European American Music Distributors Company, sole U.S. and Canadian agent for Schott Music GmbH & Co. KG, Mainz, Germany.

Sopranos are the highest voices, and they can sing high in a very thrilling way; however, they are not machines and their higher register needs to be used rationally and reasonably. I once attended a rehearsal of a highly accomplished professional chamber choir in England that was rehearsing a very difficult composition where the sopranos were constantly singing high C, Ds, and Es. During break, I overheard one of the sopranos lament, "I just don't think [the composer] understands what they are asking us to do."

Example passages

Example 4.2: Johannes Brahms, *Zwei Motteten*, Op. 29, No 1 "Warum ist das Licht gegeben."

Example 4.3: Gabriel Fauré, *Requiem*, "Introit and Kyrie."

Example 4.4: James MacMillan, "O bone Jesu."

© Boosey & Hawkes Music Publishers Ltd. Reproduced by permission of Boosey & Hawkes.

Example 4.5: Ralph Vaughan Williams, "Silence and Music."

© Oxford University Press 1953. All rights reserved.

Chapter 5

Altos

The difference between a violin and a viola is that a viola burns longer.
— Victor Borge

General Range

1st Altos

General range: A3 to D5
Trained range: G3 to F5

2nd Altos

General range: G3 to C5
Trained range: E3 to E5

Introduction

The alto section is a tremendously important and consequential section, but sadly it's also a very underappreciated, undervalued, and underused section. It's also a section that seldom finds consensus among conductors voicing their ensembles. Experiences will vary, but some conductors will staff their alto sections with sopranos who happen to have darker, larger, or more dramatic voices.[1] Other conductors will staff their alto sections with voices who are less accomplished vocally but who have higher skill sets outside of vocal training such as sight-reading or aural memory. Part of the reason for doing this is because of the relative lack of true contralto voices compared to sopranos. Because of this, alto sections in some amateur and semi-professional groups can be staffed with a wide variety of timbres, in some of these cases, more so than the soprano section.

Most modern composers in the United States will primarily consider female-assigned voices when thinking of the alto section. Composers in the United Kingdom (or in very heavily Anglican-flavored ecclesiastical settings) will consider an alto section staffed by either countertenors, female-assigned singers, or both. In this section we are only considering the female-assigned voices. Countertenors will be covered in Chapter 8.

The word alto has its origins from the Latin *altus* meaning "high." This may be confusing at first, considering it's the middle part of the upper voices (soprano, alto, and tenor), and the low part for female-assigned singers. But historically, the tenor part was the first vocal part written and sung by the priesthood in a monastic setting, and the alto part would have been first sung by a countertenor (a male-assigned singer primarily using their falsetto register). Consequently, singing in falsetto above the tenor part would have been considered singing the high part. The term alto was used to describe the part above the tenor before female-assigned voices began singing it.

The alto part uses the treble clef almost exclusively. Some editions of early music, particularly from the Renaissance, will sometimes have alto parts written in an octave treble clef just as tenors do.[2] All professional singers and most semi-pro altos will be able to read the octave treble clef. However, with

---

1 Very often, the joke is that altos are simply sopranos who smoke. That may have been born out of kernel of truth in generations past, but it's definitely not true at the time of this publication.

2 This makes sense when you consider that these parts were written for countertenors.

female-assigned altos, the low register is not as usable as it is with countertenors and it makes less sense to use this clef in modern use.[3] Switching clefs is not an acceptable practice in modern choral music.

General Description

The lower part of the alto voice can have a rich, sultry, and sometimes smoky quality in contrast with the soprano's somewhat breathy quality with less character. However, do not mistake this richer quality to mean a great deal more power or projection. The lower register can still be easily covered; this is especially true if the tenors are singing in the same range as the altos. If the lowest part of the voice is pushed, it can sound pressed and without depth. This is not to say that the register can't be used in homophonic passages, but it carries a risk of being unbalanced.

The middle voice gains a bit more power, as well as more of the characteristic timbre of the voice. This part of the voice is capable of a great deal of flexibility and virtuosity, but it also contains a few breaks, which can be difficult for altos to navigate at quick tempos. It's a very useful register where altos will spend most of their singing time.

The higher voice has the most power and an intensely strong timbre. It's a much more generous part of the voice that lends itself well to a great amount of flexibility and versatility. This part of the voice can also provide a great amount of agility and dexterity. This register, as well as higher ones do require, however, a great deal of air and excessive singing in this register can be taxing.

The highest part of the voice, around E5 and F♯5, can have a tendency to sound strained and squeezed in a way that the soprano's voice in these same pitches would sound piercing or fluty (depending on the dynamics). Some composers will call for altos to sing in this range, which is meant more for sopranos than for altos. Writing in this range is sometimes done to achieve a strained and pushed effect or for dramatic purposes. However, it is not recommended for ensemble writing. Many trained mezzo-sopranos can sing these pitches happily and with great success, but most of the altos in a typical alto section will not.

Potential breaks in the voice may include a major break around D4 and E4, and another minor one around B4 and C5. The major break between altos'

---

3   Treble clef is not totally ideal as you may find yourself composing with more ledger lines; however, this is the current practice in choral writing as of publication.

Thyroarytenoid-Dominant Production (TDP) and Cricothyroid-Dominant Production (CDP) can be a major obstacle for the altos and a challenge to navigate.

Agility

Despite generally having richer, rounder voices then sopranos, trained altos very often have an almost equal amount of dexterity and agility to sopranos and tenors. This is especially apparent in the solo vocal writing found in Bach, Handel, and Rossini. And just like with trained soprano voices, this skill can translate very well into ensemble singing in a very exciting way.

As with other voices, less-trained voices will not be able to execute as well as trained voices and indeed, amateur voices should avoid anything more than moderate movement.

Role in the Ensemble

Whether they are aware of it or not, the alto section has a tremendous amount of influence on the overall tone of the choral ensemble, for good and for bad. Their sound can add a great deal of depth, warmth, and overall character to the ensemble's tone.

This section also bears a great deal of responsibility for the intonation of the overall ensemble and any poor intonation in the altos can have a contagious effect on the other singers. This is particularly important when considering your part-writing for this inner voice. Awkward voice-leading can add to the difficulty this section already faces to maintain pitch.

This voice adds a great deal of depth and richness to the sound of the ensemble. It duets very well as an inner voice. With the soprano section, it serves as a round, supporting sound to the brighter, lighter sound of the sopranos above. With the tenor section, the timbre hierarchy is inverted, with the rounder, warmer sound of the altos above and the brighter tenor sound serving in a supporting role. Altos can also pair very well with basses in octave doublings, which can be found in multiple instances in the choral canon. More on voicing in Chapter 11.

Other Considerations

Altos are very often given substandard writing. Some older hymn harmonizations have given altos two pitches for their entire part. Other times, altos (along with tenors) are simply given the leftover pitches in harmonization without much thought to singable or coherent part-writing. As a result, altos often get parts that are difficult to read, learn, and sing musically. These musicians are not second-class citizens in the choral community. They deserve better.

Example passages

Example 5.1: Anton Bruckner, "Os justi."

Example 5.2: Cyrillus Kreek, *Taaveti laulud (Psalms of David)*, "Taaveti laul Nr. 121 (Psalm 121)."

Example 5.3: Frank Martin, *Mass for Double Choir*, "Kyrie."

Example 5.4: Francis Poulenc, *Un Soir de Neige*, "La bonne neige."

Published by Editions Salabert. International Copyright Secured. All Rights Reserved. Reprinted by permission of Hal Leonard Europe.

Chapter 6

Tenors

Never look encouragingly at the brass...
— Richard Strauss

General Range

1st Tenors

General range: D3 to F#4
Trained range: C3 to B♭4 (and occasionally higher)

2nd Tenors

General range: C3 to F4
Trained range: B2 to A♭4

Introduction

Tenors, in many ways, are the heroes of choral ensembles, but you should never tell them that. In general, this section is most often asked to sing in their head tone—involving some sort of mix between TDP and CDP—and, except when at very loud dynamics, they don't often get to use their full voices. When they do sing in full voice, their voices can peel paint off the walls.

The word tenor comes from the Latin *tenere*, which translates as "to hold."[1] Tenors are among the first sections we have written music for. While it's true that the monophonic chants being notated and sung for millennia previously would have been sung by whichever members of the priesthood were there, that part in later antiphons was labeled as "tenor," which contained the original *cantus firmus*. Later, a high part would be added and referred to as *altus* or "high," and *bassus* or "low." After some time, the *cantus firmus* began to be sung by other parts and the tenor part could be free to sing other composed parts.

Tenor parts are written in a suboctave treble clef.

The "tenor clef"—which has middle C on the second line from the top of the staff—is antiquated for this application and is no longer acceptable to use in modern choral music. The bass clef should also not be used when tenors are given their own staff. The only time a bass clef should be employed is when writing on a grand staff, where tenors and basses share the lower staff.

General Description

An untrained or under-trained tenor's voice will mostly have an under-sung, almost anemic quality throughout. With training, even a moderate amount, a great deal more power and character can be found in different parts of their range. Do keep in mind that most tenor (and bass) voices are still experiencing cartilage ossification in the early to mid 20s and clear into their 30s

---

1   John Potter, *Tenor: History of a Voice* (New Haven: Yale UP, 2009), 5.

in some cases.[2] This ossification of the cartilage in the voice—well after vocal mutation—can explain why many high school and even college-age tenors may struggle with consistent tone and passaggio negotiations.

Like the soprano voice, the lowest part of the tenor voice can be somewhat weak and nondescript. The very lowest part of the voice can become uneven and sound a bit gravelly, with the power tapering off quickly.

The middle part of the voice adds much more of the characteristic timbre of the voice. The middle voice also adds power quite quickly that is maintained throughout the remainder of its range. This is an important lesson: tenors don't need to be in the highest part of their voice to find a relatively large amount of power and projection. However, there is no need for you to compensate by indicating a softer dynamic for the tenor part.

The middle high part of the voice adds even more power and brightness. This part of the voice is capable of a great deal of brilliance as well as flexibility. This is where the tenor voice is the strongest and can clearly pop out of the texture as needed.

The highest part of the voice maintains brightness but starts to lose some depth behind it. This is where there's a difference between the first and second tenors. First tenors will be able to sing in this range at different dynamic levels, including softer ones, which they can sing with a smooth, floaty quality. Second tenors will find less success singing softly or smoothly in this range.

Unlike the soprano and alto voices that taper off their power as they get to the highest parts of their voices, the tenor voice loses less of that strength as the voice tops out. The voice mostly hits a hard ceiling at its limits.

Potential breaks in the tenor voice include around E4 and F4. It's best not to leave tenors hanging around these pitches for too long or leave them exposed on their own in very soft dynamics. In many cases, it's better to get the voice up and over these breaks or have them singing in somewhat louder dynamics. Otherwise, the sound of this section can quickly atrophy.

Agility

Most tenors can possess a great deal of dexterity and, with training, are capable of some truly impressive virtuosic coloratura singing. This can be found in passages from Bach and Handel to Rossini and Donizetti. Running scales and leaps slightly larger than an octave are all possible with training. This also translates very well into an ensemble section.

---

2 Robert T Sataloff,. and Karen M. Kost, "The Effects of Age on the Voice, Part 1," *Journal of Singing* 77, no. 1 (Sept/Oct 2020), 63-64.

Like sopranos and altos, less-trained voices will not be able to execute as well as professionals. However, even less-trained tenors can sing with a healthy amount of movement, although not too extensively and not for extended periods of time.

Role in the Ensemble

The tenor section adds a significant amount of brightness and brilliance to the ensemble and helps especially as an inner voice. This section is a tremendous asset in the choral ensemble and provides composers with a great deal of flexibility and versatility by fulfilling multiple musical roles. As an inner voice, it helps provide a colorful addition to the choral fabric.

The relative brilliance and clarity provide a beautiful change of color and an easy alternative for a melodic voice to the sopranos. Traditionally, having the tenor sing the melody while the sopranos harmonize is called *fauxbourdon*[3] or *faburden* singing, and hymnals will sometimes offer alternative harmonizations in this style.

Example: 6.1 John Dowland harmonization of "Old Hundredth."

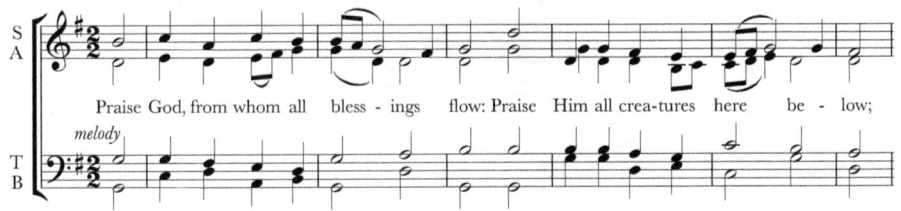

Even without the presence of sopranos and altos, the tenor is a great option for singing the melody either on its own or doubled with the basses (provided the range allows).

As an upper voice, it can serve as the "bass" voice of the three. In the higher register it sounds much loftier in character and gives the upper voices a floating, almost weightless sound. It can duet beautifully with its neighboring voices. In duet with the altos, it provides the same brighter timbre to serve in a supporting role to the rounder, richer alto color. In duet with the basses, it provides a brighter timbre, supported by the basses' warmer, rounder sound.

---

3   This term is most often referring to a style of writing in the late Middle Ages and early Renaissance. However, like many terms used over different epochs, it becomes used to describe this practice in hymnal harmonization as well.

82   The Technique of Choral Writing

The lower part of the voice—which doesn't serve a great amount of utility on its own or in four-part harmony—can be quite useful in one particular application: in close harmonies with the basses and baritones, the tenors can help create a rich, earthy sonority.

Other Considerations

For some tenor voices it can take quite a bit of time and patience to get the voice warmed up and in decent shape. Even still, there are times when the tenor voice refuses to cooperate regardless of training or time spent warming up. The more training a tenor has, the less likely this is to happen or the more likely the singer is to have the strategies necessary to mitigate the issue. It's also unlikely that this happens to entire sections at the same time, but it can sometimes happen to the more prominent voices in a section and present an issue. In any case, singing tenor can be inherently challenging.

Example passages

Example 6.2: Johannes Brahms, *Ein deutsches Requiem*, op. 45, "Wie lieblich sind deine Wohnungen."

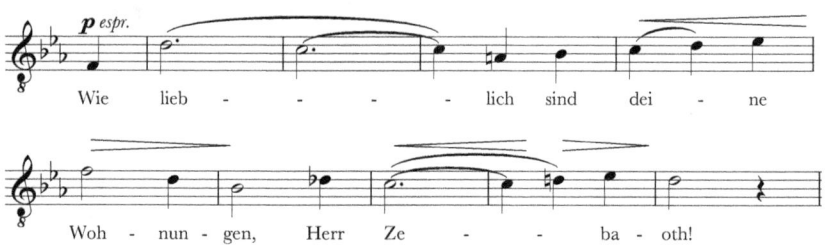

Example 6.3: Gabriel Fauré, *Requiem*, "Agnus Dei."

Example 6.4: Vaclav Nelhybel, "Estampie Natalis."

Copyright © 1976 Schott Music Corporation, New York, NY. Copyright renewed. Used by permission of European American Music Distributors Company, sole U.S. and Canadian agent for Schott Music Corporation, New York, NY.

Example 6.5: Francis Poulenc, *Quatre petites prières de Saint François d'Assise*, "Salut, Dame Sainte."

Published by Editions Salabert. International Copyright Secured. All Rights Reserved. Reprinted by permission of Hal Leonard Europe.

Chapter 7

Basses

...And for the bass, the beast can only bellow;
In fact, he had no singing education,
An ignorant, noteless, timeless, tuneless fellow.
— George Gordon, Lord Byron

General Range

Baritones

General range: A2 to D4
Trained range: G2 to F4

Basses

General range: F2 to C4
Trained range: D2 (and sometimes lower) to D4 (although many times E4)

Introduction

The lowest voices in the ensemble also have an unfortunate reputation as the troublemakers at the back of the school bus. They also have the unfortunate reputation of being the least trained, least musical, and least talented section in the ensemble. There is some truth to that, even in semi-professional choral ensembles. At least in North America, there are far fewer basses who are interested in choir or even exposed to it, and those low notes are precious commodities. Very often, conductors will make concessions or loosen standards when auditioning bass voices that they wouldn't allow for other voice parts. While there is truth to this reputation, it is not fair to the basses who have put in a great many hours of training and practice to achieve a high level of musicianship.

Basses, in general, are keener on their division than the other parts (including sopranos), so much so that they even have separate names. Rather than being called Bass 1 and Bass 2, they are called Baritone and Bass (Baritones being the higher voice part of the two).

The word bass comes from the Latin word for "low," which tracks as this was assigned to voices singing below the "held" tenor voice. This voice would sometimes sing drone, although later in Renaissance music the bass part would have been composed as an equal voice with the others. Through the Baroque period, as functional harmonies began to be more standard practice, the bass voice began to serve as the bass part and reinforced those functional harmonies.

Basses are written in the bass clef exclusively. There is no reason to use any other clef for basses or baritones. If you're writing parts with lots of ledger lines above the staff where you feel like it might make sense to use another clef to avoid so many ledger lines, you're writing too high for too long.

General Description

As one may guess, the low part of the bass voice is the most valuable. It also has a fair amount of power and a strong, robust timbre compared to other voice parts. This level of power is still modest and can't compete when other voices are in generous parts of their voices.

When a bass reaches the lowest part of their voice, however, the power and volume of the sounds drops off dramatically over the course of a few notes. For example, if a bass's lowest usable note is an E2, the E♭ will be about half as loud, and the D♮ will be about half as loud again. Some bass voices will have a slightly longer off ramp of low usable pitches, but maybe by a step or two. The volume of each low note drops off exponentially, as does its reliability.

Additionally, the very lowest parts of a bass's voice have limits regarding not just how loudly they can be sung, but how softly they can be sung. Phonating these pitches must pass a threshold of breath pressure and anything less will cause a breaking, uneven sound. It will begin to sound more like vocal fry than true phonating pitch. It's not so much a matter of a bass's voice being "on" or "off;" their lowest notes are just capable of a more limited amount of finesse and expression, noticeably less than the rest of their range.[1]

The middle part of the voice is very useful, but has a limitation regarding power, especially around E3. This part of the voice can balance well enough until a forte dynamic; afterwards it can easily sound pressed and overdriven if trying to compete with other voices in stronger parts of their respective voices. It's not so much that it has less power compared to the lower part of the voice; they have similar levels of volume. It's more that the growth of vocal power from low to high follows a different curve than most of the other voices do in my anecdotal observation.

The high voice can have the strength come back, and can take on a "roaring" character at loud dynamics and a sighing character in softer dynamics. Indeed, a great deal of power can come from the basses in the higher part of the voice but do be aware that this part of the voice can become taxed fairly quickly if maintained for too long. Additionally, it is a bit easier to sing louder in the high range than to sing softer. When composing in this range at a soft dynamic, basses will need to resort to singing in their head voice or their falsetto in order to try to execute in a reasonable, manageable way. Most trained basses will make this adjustment by default. The highest part of the voice can sound strained and squeezed, especially if maintained for too long or kept in excessively soft dynamics.

Many basses have a major break around B♭4 and C4. It's best to not leave them exposed in this register especially at softer dynamics. Singing louder helps mitigate the pitfall this break can become. Other breaks lower in the voice are a bit more manageable.

Agility

The bass section—for the most part—is not famous for being a section with a great amount of agility or dexterity. While historically there is plenty of

---

1   As a friendly reminder, while this is describing the low extremes of the bass voice, these same ideas can be applied to all voice parts in the extremes of their voices.

literature for basses to sing with a lot of dexterity and agility, it's very difficult for many of them, and one can argue that it never reaches the same level of accomplishment as any of their counterparts. In some ways, this is not without a reason as bass voices don't speak as quickly as the upper voices do and can have a much more difficult time with *coloratura* passages. And because they have a much more difficult time with *coloratura* passages, they don't universally practice them as often or as intensely, which makes them difficult for basses, making it a catch-22. One can compose passages for the bass section that call for some dexterity, but don't expect their ability, or the success of the passage, to be as pronounced as one of the higher voices.

Basses are capable of octave leaps but most untrained voices are not used to leaps beyond an octave. Mozart's quartet "Tuba Mirum" from his Requiem is a great example of a solo bass voice being asked to regularly leap up and down major and minor 10ths, but do not expect this from amateur bass sections. Even semi-professional bass sections will struggle with leaps larger than an octave.

Role in the Ensemble

For fear of stating the obvious, the main role of the bass section in the ensemble is to serve as the bass voice in the ensemble, very often singing the root of a chord. This voice adds a great deal of grounding—and almost cradling—to the rest of the ensemble and can bring confidence to the other voices when singing. Sometimes when the basses are tacet it can almost feel like the bottom has dropped out for the remainder of the ensemble. This section can also create strong overtones, which can help other sections unconsciously tune better.

Many audience members find themselves in awe of the extremes of range in the human voice. In the same way that the sopranos' highest pitches can be a showstopper, the same happens for the basses' lowest pitches. If prepared and voiced well, the basses' low pitches can provide this payoff with relatively little to no vocal toil. Plus, basses love showing off their low voices.

The bass section is also well suited to sing the melody, with the upper voices filling the harmonies in addition to singing counter melody. This is like giving the melody to the cello section in an orchestra. Basses will sometimes also sing the melody in canon with the soprano or alto section. This helps provide a contrast both in timbre and in register.

88 The Technique of Choral Writing

When duetting with the tenors, it can help provide a handsome change of timbre and adds a charming amount of supporting warmth to the tenors' brilliance. This is a very successful voicing combination.

Other Considerations

When most singers first wake up, they have lower voices than they do later in the day. This is due to the vocal cords swelling slightly during sleep and rest. As a result, their vocal folds are slightly thicker and will produce lower pitches than normal. As singers get moving through their day and start using their voice to speak, this effect diminishes, and their voices return to their normal ranges. Towards the end of the day and into the evening, their voices are usually the highest they will be.

Bass voices are no exception to this concept, but sadly losing lower notes through the day is less desirable for their voice part. Composers and conductors should keep this in mind when rehearsing and workshopping a composition during the day. The low notes that a bass may be able to sing with lots of resonance during a morning or even an afternoon rehearsal may not sound the same during an evening performance.[2] From my own experience, I can't tell you how many times I've been able to produce a beautiful, resonant low E during a rehearsal, but it isn't there during an evening performance. It feels like a heartbreaking betrayal.

Example passages

Example 7.1: Anton Bruckner, "Os justi."

---

2   The same can be true for altos.

Example 7.2: Frank Martin, *Mass for Double Choir*, "Gloria."

Example 7.3: Frank Martin, *Mass for Double Choir*, "Credo."

Example 7.4: Francis Poulenc, *Figure Humaine*, "Bientôt."

Published by Editions Salabert. International Copyright Secured. All Rights Reserved. Reprinted by permission of Hal Leonard Europe.

Chapter 8

Other Voices

We all sang, the boys in the field,
The chapels were full of singing.
— Ronald Blythe quoting Fred Mitchell

Sopranos, altos, tenors, and basses are now considered the standard voices that make up most choral ensembles. However, there are other, less common voices in choral music that require our consideration. These include countertenors, children, and cambiatas.[1]

Countertenors

Ranges

General range: A3 to D4
Trained range: G3 to E4

---

1 Singular is cambiata. Italian plural would be cambiati.

Introduction

Countertenors are male-assigned singers who primarily sing in their falsetto register and most often sing the alto part. These singers have an already beautiful and strong falsetto register—or Cricothyroid-Dominant Production (CDP)—and spend considerable training in that register. Renowned English countertenor Alfred Deller describes different types of countertenors this way:

> There are generally recognised to be two types of counter-tenor [sic] voice. The first, and more usual, is where the fundamental voice is baritone or bass, and the head voice, or so-called falsetto, is developed to the maximum range. My own voice is of this type. You produce this head voice naturally, and you work on it as you would on any other voice. . . The other type of counter-tenor is essentially a high tenor who can either dispense with falsetto entirely, or use it for the top fourth or fifth of the compass, without perceptible break.[2]

The second voice Deller describes sounds similar to what some would call an haute-contre, which put very simply is a very high-voiced tenor.[3] However, whether one is considered to be a "true" countertenor over the other type is less consequential to us as composers and arrangers. They do both yield slightly different qualities of sound in the middle to lower register, but for our purposes, we will simply consider these all one part as we have done with each of the previous voices in Chapters 4 through 7.

While these singers in the past have often been referred to as "male altos," countertenor is generally considered the most acceptable and preferred term. Countertenors have been singing alto parts since choral music began hundreds of years ago. This is where the term alto originates from; it was the highest-signing male-assigned voice, which sang above the tenor. Historically, these singers have been capable of singing bass, tenor, and alto parts which amount to *gamma ut*, meaning four pitches encompassing three octaves.[4]

Today, countertenors will very often sing opera roles originally written for a castrato, or castrated man. But it needs to be made clear: a countertenor is not a castrato. The institutional practice of castration for male-assigned singers

---

2 Peter Giles, *The History and Technique of the Counter-Tenor: A Study of the Male High Voice Family* (Aldershot, UK: Scolar Press, 1994), 188.

3 Some will argue that this description is reductive, which I wouldn't disagree with. I will leave the debate on haute-contre to others.

4 The term *gamma ut* is where the word "gamut" came from.

was outlawed in Italy in 1861 and the Roman Catholic Church ceased hiring new castrati in 1878. The last known castrato in Western music, Alessandro Moreschi, died in 1922.

In choral music, modern countertenors will most often sing in historically-informed performances of Renaissance and Baroque music. There is some amount of overlap in repertoire of this time period that would have been sung by a contralto, boy alto, castrato, or countertenor. They will also very often perform with church choirs of certain denominations that have a history of countertenors in performance. Countertenors will also sing in modern choral ensembles that perform new and contemporary music, but this is not a practice that is shared across choral traditions and depends on the ensemble. This practice occurs more often in Europe than in the United States or Canada, for example, but there are notable exceptions for both.

Countertenor parts should be written in treble clef, the same as altos.

General Description

The difference between the average countertenor, compared to the average alto, is that countertenors generally have a somewhat rounder, more "plump" sound. In Chapter 3, when discussing registers, I made the comparison between playing a specific pitch on a lower string versus on a higher string and how the quality of those sounds is different even though they are the same pitch. That same comparison could be made here with countertenors perhaps being closer to playing that pitch on a lower string.

The lowest part of the countertenor range can have a somewhat veiled quality and projection and power is relatively limited. The sound can also take on a somewhat croaky or hoarse quality as it skates along the very bottom of the CDP. Once out of the lowest few pitches and into the low register the voice quickly becomes more stable, although it still lacks some projection. It is worth noting that because the haute-contre is generally not working with the CDP in the same range they don't experience these same issues as falsettists.

As the voice ascends to the middle register, it gains a significant amount of power and projection and quickly takes on its distinct character. The higher the voice becomes, the more it gains intensity and brilliance. Here, the voice really shines and can prove a useful asset, whether in ensemble or solos. The voice in this register is also capable of asserting itself even against more robust accompaniment. Even countertenors near the beginning of their training will be able to find a great deal of this projection early on.

In high registers, their ability to sing softly will be limited and much more limited than female-assigned altos. Additionally, the brightness in higher registers is somewhat baked into the sound and flexibility becomes slightly more limited. In the very highest register, the voice can take on a strident, strained quality while maintaining almost all its intensity.

Countertenors can train their voices to have extraordinary flexibility and agility. A well-trained countertenor can perform coloratura passages with great success. Even as a section, countertenors can move together with great dexterity.

Role in the Ensemble

Countertenors play a similar role in the ensemble as the altos. They can have a great amount of influence on the overall tone and intonation of the choral ensemble. Their tone adds a great deal of roundness to the sound as well as depth. As discussed in Chapter 5, their voices lend well to duetting with neighbor voices and in octave doublings.

In some ways, the major issues with countertenors in choral ensembles mostly comes from within their own section. Some female-assigned altos—especially those who have little to no experience singing next to countertenors—can sometimes find it difficult to blend and tune with them. But in my own anecdotal experience I've heard some professional altos rave about singing with countertenors and others lament the experience. I have yet to identify any pattern following the two experiences.

Having said that, countertenors can provide a complimentary color and presence with female-assigned altos and sometimes fill in gaps in certain ensemble sounds. Some conductors have found success in only having countertenors sing second alto, while others prefer to split them evenly between first and second, or having fasettists sing first and haute-contres sing second.

Example Passages

Example 8.1: Bob Chilcott, "High Flight."

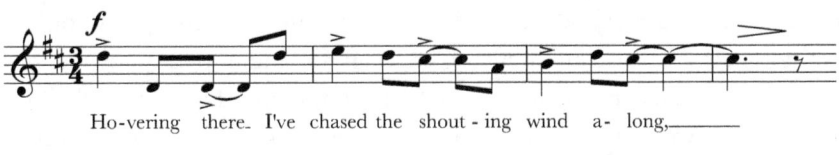

Music © Oxford University Press 2008.
Text 'High Flight' by John Gillespie Magee © This England. All rights reserved.

Example 8.2: Gabriel Jackson, "In all his works."

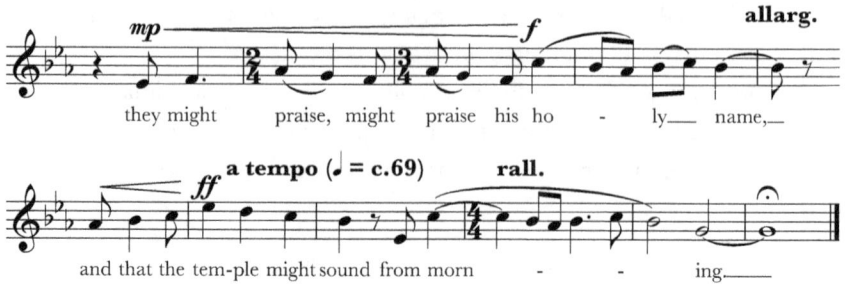

© Oxford University Press 2011. All rights reserved.

Children's voices

General Ranges

Young children (ages approx. 5-9) E4 to F5

Prepubescent (ages approx. 9-14) C4 to G5

Introduction

Never has a group of musicians been so misunderstood and underestimated as children. Different choral traditions will treat children differently. Very often in North America, but not always, children are seen and treated as marginally developed, over-stimulated, over-sugared hooligans. In some select British church choirs, children are auditioned quite young and regimented more like professional musicians in training. Their schedule is quite intense and advanced compared to what I've witnessed in other settings—sometimes at the expense of their childhood. There are other examples of children's choirs from East and Southeast Asia singing incredibly complicated music at a very high level. In summary, children are capable of quite a lot with the right instruction and fostering.

Another major misconception about children's voices is that they should be written in what is essentially an alto's range. Indeed, some readers may be surprised to see how much higher and more conservative the range I have listed is. In my study and experience, children will have lower pitches in their voices, however the register used to make these pitches is of a somewhat harsher, shoutier tone. Renowned educators of adolescent singers Irvin Cooper and Lynne Gackle[5] seem to agree that while the ranges may be larger, what is usable and suitable for music making is more modest.

Children's voices, especially children ages six to ten, should be written closer to what is a soprano's ranges. Prepubescent children are even closer to a normal soprano's range, albeit without some of their very low notes. Some children's voices are also capable of singing even higher than what is indicated here; however, I have kept these ranges more conservative for the sake of the lower common denominator.

Once children's voices are in the throes of puberty, their voices are generally divided and treated differently for two or three years based on the needs of those voices. Female-assigned children will very often begin singing repertoire for equal treble voices or they will begin to sing repertoire for sopranos and altos and generally work in the ranges of sopranos and altos straight away. Male-assigned children (if they are lucky) will transition to a Cambiata ensemble (see the next section) where they work in an ensemble of changing voices.

While these voices are still able to sing treble reasonably almost the same as they once did, they should begin to specialize in making music with multiple parts and harmonies. Cooper and Gackle suggest that rather than separating female-assigned adolescents into sopranos and altos they should instead be separated into equal part divisions and swap higher or lower parts from piece to piece or concert to concert.[6] In essence, leave voice classification for later as their voices continue to develop.

Some composers call for "boys" for example in Benjamin Britten's *War Requiem*. This was to try to create the English cathedral choir sound of "men and boys," which was very common in the Church of England. Today, these parts are sung by ensembles comprising more than just the one gender.

Children's voices should be written in treble clef.

General Description

As one can imagine, children's voices will sound young and very light compared to more grown voices. Like adults, children's voices have registers,

---

5   Don L Collins, *Teaching Choral Music* (Upper Saddle River, NJ: Prentice Hall, 1999), 130;141.

6   Collins, *Teaching Choral Music*, 129;140.

and most similar to a soprano's registers. In the higher registers the voice can sound quite sweet and have an almost floating quality to it. In the highest register the voices can also take on a somewhat piercing quality. In lower registers, especially quite low, the voice will lose quite a bit of power and take on a somewhat more speech-like quality.

As female-assigned students begin advancing through puberty many of them develop what is known as mutational chink, which is when the vocal folds fail to fully close between the arytenoid cartilages because of inconsistent growth. This failure of the folds to fully close results in a breathy sound that can sometimes take years to fully resolve. In some cases, there are exercises that a teacher can employ to help the student's muscles develop to help close the gap, but in other cases it's simply a matter of time and maturation.

Children can have a surprising amount of dexterity. Young children are capable of quite a bit of movement but save the real dexterity for prepubescent children. However, do not throw new singers into the deep end: save this singing for children who have received a little bit of training and practice. Also, don't expect it to be quite on the same level as a fully trained, adult soprano.

Strategies for Writing

Children's voices should avoid singing the extremes of dynamic ranges. If pushed too loud in the higher registers, the voices can sound strained and strident. In the lower register, the voice can sound shouty and pressed. It's also safe to say that intonation will be easily compromised throughout the range if children's voices are pushed too loud.

Young children's voices should also avoid singing outside of a conservative range. Prepubescent children's voices are slightly more resilient and begin to expand upon previous limits. However, children's ensembles should not be the place for demanding or extended techniques as one would do with an adult singer who specializes in new or contemporary music. It is our collective responsibility during a child's growth to be stewards of their voices before—and while—they learn how to be stewards themselves.

When composing for adolescent ensembles comprising female-assigned students, you should strongly consider composing in two equal parts rather than soprano and alto. As mentioned previously, during puberty the female voice can also go through changes, although less dramatically than male voices. Two equal parts will allow the singers to learn harmony without feeling stuck in one part of the voice and allow their voices to mature without worrying about having their voices classified before the voice has even settled.

Other Considerations

As a side note, texts that involve fewer words and more repetition are strongly preferred when considering texts for a child who is singing from memory. This is particularly the case with very young children. If they're singing from a score, lots of words are generally less of an issue.

Example Passages

Example 8.3: Benjamin Britten, *Friday Afternoons*, op. 7 "Fishing Song."

© 1936 Boosey & Co. Ltd. Reproduced by permission of Boosey & Hawkes.

Example 8.4: Benjamin Britten, *War Requiem*, op. 66 "Offertorium."

© 1961 Boosey & Hawkes Music Publishers Ltd © Renewed in 1991. Reproduced by permission of Boosey & Hawkes.

Cambiata

Ranges

Cambiata: A3 to A4

Adolescent Baritones: D3 to D4

Introduction

Cambiata is a term used for a male-assigned voice going through puberty, or what some scholars of adolescents refer to amusingly as "mutation." Cambiata was a term created by Irvin Cooper, borrowed from *cambiata nota*, or changing note, and used it as *cambiata voce* or changing voice.

In the early twentieth century, when a male-assigned singer's voice began to go through puberty, the prevailing idea was to refer to the child's voice as "broken"[7] and to banish them from singing till their voices have finished their evolution.[8] Some have reasoned that this is to avoid injury to the child's voice but also because the voice no longer serves the ensemble as before. For many years this was the prevailing paradigm for many boy choristers in the United Kingdom.

In North America, during the mid-twentieth century, several music educators such as Duncan McKenzie, Frederick Swanson, and Irvin Cooper attempted to challenge this "no-sing" theory and suggested that singing through puberty is not only safe but beneficial to the child.[9]

The most well-accepted theories come from Cooper and his Cambiata Concept. Cooper proposed that when male-assigned children begin puberty they go through two stages before their voices fully mature. He called these stages "cambiata" and "baritones" (which I will refer to as "adolescent baritones" so

---

7 This terminology has, of course, had negative effects on the child's mental and emotional well-being. This term should be abstained from entirely and replaced with "changing" and "growing."

8 Collins, *Teaching Choral Music*, 122.

9 Collins, *Teaching Choral Music*, 124.

as not to confuse with fully developed baritones). Cooper insisted that students going through mutation should not sing either alto or tenor, but instead should sing in a part written specifically for their limited ranges.[10] Swanson went a step further saying that these changing voices should be separated from female-assigned students, and instead make an ensemble all their own with music written for their specific ranges and needs.[11]

While these voices can come across as limiting, it should be seen as a challenge rather than a stumbling block. This is an invitation to be creative and imagine new ways to write for this oft-forgotten voice.

Cambiata should be written in treble clef, and adolescent baritones should be written in bass clef.

General Description

Without trying to sound too obvious, the general tone with both cambiata and adolescent baritones is partway between a prepubescent child and a fully grown adult. Cooper described the cambiata sound as "wooly."[12] Ranges will be severely limited for both cambiata and adolescent baritone voices. Tone and intonation may be uneven, but this is to be expected from changing voices.

Mobility in this voice will be somewhat limited for a time while the voice develops. Movement is possible, but coloratura, for the most part, is out of the question. Just give them a break; it can be a rough few years.

With good training, these voices can still sing with expression and with sensitivity. Above all, do NOT push the ranges of these voices or try to take them to extreme dynamics. Doing so can push these voices to strident and shouty sound relatively quickly. Additionally, singing in extremes during this transition can compromise the student's vocal hygiene. As stated previously, it is our collective responsibility to be stewards of their voices before—and while—they learn how to be stewards themselves.

Strategies for Writing

Because ranges are limited, one of the biggest mistakes you can make with cambiata voices or ensembles is to have everyone sing in unison or octaves.[13] Doing so will greatly limit your usable range. Instead, the best approach is to compose in harmonizing parts that can allow maximum use of their ranges.

---

10   Collins, *Teaching Choral Music*, 129;132.

11   Collins, *Teaching Choral Music*, 127.

12   Collins, *Teaching Choral Music*, 132.

13   Collins, *Teaching Choral Music*, 130.

Lest you believe that teaching a cambiata ensemble harmony is a tall order, remember that these students very likely have been singing previously. They've likely had some basic music training and done some part singing at the least.

Remember that cambiata ensembles will also very likely have pre-mutation students who can sing treble, along with cambiata, adolescent baritones, and in some rare cases, fully transitioned basses. Conservatively, there are three voices to employ in the part-writing.

Other Considerations

Roles keep changing in a cambiata ensemble as the school year continues. What makes this group of singers challenging to compose for is that the choir that you have at the beginning of the school year will be different than the group at the end of the year without making any roster changes. While changes might not be rapid, they can be unexpected. The director will make decisions about students who need to transition to the next part and when. After transitioning into tenors and basses, they usually rejoin the sopranos and altos into a mixed ensemble again, usually in high school.

Having said all of that, this group of singers deserves good repertoire and good writing. The quantity of music written for cambiata voices is woefully small. Perhaps this lack explains why boys often leave choral music.

Chapter 9

Various Choral Ensembles

The common singing-men in cathedral churches are a bad society, and yet a company of good fellows, that roar deep in the choir, deeper in the tavern.
— John Earle

Choral ensembles come in all different shapes, sizes, and combinations of voices, sometimes with drastic variation. The term "choir" doesn't refer to a single type of ensemble, but rather a family of ensembles. Each of them is valid and provides its own singular beauty. This is part of what makes choral music so compelling and provides continuing interest for even the most veteran choral musician. As a composer or arranger, it's important to be aware of, and sensitive to, all the members of this ensemble family. When you begin writing for a specific kind of choir, you need to know what those strengths, weaknesses, and needs are for the ensembles that typically occupy that particular vertical.

Additionally, when studying a choral score, it's important to understand contextually the kind of ensemble for which it was originally conceived. For example, studying a work written for a large symphonic choir is a poor way to learn what works best for a small chamber ensemble. The same applies to the inverse: studying a work for a small chamber ensemble won't necessarily be the prime way to learn how to write for a large symphonic choir. Studying a string quartet will teach you a great deal about string music, but it is different to studying a work for a string orchestra and understanding that difference is important. Treating choral ensembles as if they were the same will lead to multiple practical problems when bringing your writing to life.

Choirs are generally categorized by their size, their technical abilities, as well as their purpose, function, or the literature they choose to focus on. Almost all choirs can be described by these categories. For example, a choir may be the size of a chamber ensemble, be at a semi-professional level of ability, and also be a church choir. Other choirs may be a large ensemble, of amateur ability, and be a community choir. Some ensembles will be one-on-a-part, professional, and a touring ensemble. There are many interesting and exciting combinations.

It's important to stress that these are not value-based categories or terms. None of these differences make the specific ensemble more or less valid or valuable to their purpose. For example, being a large or small ensemble isn't good or bad; it simply describes what it is. Some in the choral community may have an affinity toward one type of ensemble over another, but that affinity doesn't diminish what every ensemble brings to the choral community.

In this chapter, we'll explore and describe these different categories of choral ensembles based on size, ability, and purpose or function. I will also attempt to share some details regarding the specifics of writing for these ensemble types by considering generally:

Ability or level of training
Vocal ranges
Division of parts
Vibrato use
Preferred repertoire choices

There may be other factors that may qualify these instructions, depending on each group. I will also provide the names in alphabetical order of some of the best-known ensembles in these categories at the time of publication. These lists are not meant to be exhaustive.

I will refrain from including repertoire lists for these ensembles; there are vast amounts of appropriate examples to include and narrowly selecting a handful from tens of thousands may be too difficult a task. I would encourage you, instead, to look up these ensembles and look through their programs and recordings for repertoire examples. Keep in mind that some ensembles—particularly those on the ends of the bell curve—will perform works that are specific to the ensemble. At times you will see different ensembles sharing a large cross-section of repertoire; these works will be valuable for providing not just contrast between ensembles, but also what works for multiple ensembles and what doesn't.

In some cases, there may be a significant amount of overlap between ensembles and how they operate or perform. Not all these things are mutually exclusive, but there are distinctions. Some readers may ask why a distinction is made in the first place. In some cases, the distinction may indeed be minor; in other cases, the distinction will be not just significant but existential. Because of this, some descriptions may seem to be repetitive. If you would rather consult a briefer explanation, I've made a matrix of all these categories of ensembles in Appendix A.

Finally, as you work with choral ensembles, you will find a few ensembles that may not fit neatly into one or two of these categories. You may even have the privilege of working with a few for a special project. Each is different and you may take exception to these generalized categories. Whenever you are commissioned, always consult with the ensemble about their strengths, weaknesses, and needs. No matter what I say here, the commissioning ensemble is who you should be composing for.

Choirs Based on Size

This choir metric is fairly straightforward and objective: one is simply counting voices. One pattern that will be repeated for each of these ensembles is that size is often not the primary indicator or determiner of the ensemble's ability, vocal ranges, divisions, or vibrato use. Other factors, such as the level of training for the average singers or the function of the group, will play a more crucial role in these matters. Even so, choir size does often determine the preferred repertoire choices of each ensemble.

In some situations, but not always, the size of the ensemble will influence the types of singers who staff these choirs. The number of voices in each ensemble can dictate several things such as ranges, divisions, solos, dexterity, stagger breathing, and vibrato use. While some may infer value based inversely on ensemble size (i.e. smaller is better or more impressive) there are phenomenal ensembles in each of these categories, and each will have its relative strengths or limitations.

One-on-a-part vocal ensembles

These are vocal ensembles where each part is sung by a single musician. These are typically comprised of professional musicians who have gone through a rigorous audition and vetting process. It's much less likely to have a one-on-a-part ensemble with volunteers, but you may find such groups in a collegiate setting.

There is a debate as to whether these ensembles are considered "choral," but for our purposes we will include them for two reasons: First, to allow us to explore the literature they typically sing, which can translate very well for choral writing, and second, so that we can learn their needs as an ensemble, which will translate to understanding the principles of better ensemble writing.

The ability of these ensembles—if they are post-collegiate ensembles—will almost always be comprised of very fine musicians with solid voices. They will also likely have had a significant amount of high-quality training and be of accomplished ability. If the group has been around a long time, perform regularly, or go on tour, they will be a very seasoned ensemble with a great deal of experience. Groups that have been around for less time may not have the same amount of experience with each other but will still probably be great musicians. If the musicians aren't that great, the ensemble won't be around for long.

Ranges, and vibrato use will be as varied as each ensemble. These will be determined by the composition of the ensemble and the repertoire they choose to perform. Some groups will be four singers performing SATB repertoire, but others will be SSATBB, SSAA, TTBB, AATBBB or any number of combinations. And as has been stated previously, two singers of the same part won't have exactly the same ranges. Ranges will be limited to whoever that specific singer is. For example, the soprano for one ensemble may be capable of floating high A5 all day at all dynamics. This may not be practical for another soprano in another ensemble or for sopranos in general. You may also find limitations based on that singer's passaggio. In many cases, taking the average singer's vocal registers into consideration will bypass most issues.

Even if the number and type of voices are the same, no two groups will be exactly the same: from season to season, membership will rotate, as will the nuances of a group's tone and ability. In most cases these changes won't matter for most compositions or arrangements. And in those few instances where it will make a difference, you will most likely be working closely with that ensemble to get it exactly right. It is much like tailoring a bespoke suit where the process of making a suit remains largely unchanged and only the measurements are different.

It should be obvious, but divisions within parts are not possible with this choir type. You should also keep in mind that these singers have no other colleagues to lean upon in case they need to take a quick catch breath or swallow saliva. If the musicians are all singing different pitches, stagger breathing is not possible. If a musician begins to fatigue during the performance, there is no other person who they can rely on if they need to tap out for a moment.

Most one-on-a-part ensembles will sing with limited or no vibrato; others will sing a mix of vibrato and no vibrato. Very few groups will sing with vibrato as a point of departure. In fact, most of these are quartets that will only exist for a specific concert or recording and not be a standing group. Groups that specialize in singing early music and/or modern music will usually sing with little to no vibrato. Groups that specialize in Classical or Romantic repertoire will more likely perform with a generous amount of vibrato.

These ensembles typically perform repertoire that is designed for one-on-a-part singing. Most often this means music from the Renaissance and early Baroque and more contemporary compositions including bespoke arrangements written for that specific ensemble. Occasionally this may include quartets from the Romantic period, but that is much less likely. These groups most often perform a cappella with occasional accompaniment.

Modern music for these ensembles is usually specific to the ensemble that commissioned it. For example, music written for the King's Singers will be written with two counter tenors, a tenor, two baritones and a bass in mind. When you see these works published, they will usually be sold as compositions for SATTBB, which can work very well for a mixed ensemble, but occasionally will need adjustments here or there.

One example of works written for one-on-a-part ensembles but that translate well for choral ensembles include the quartets of Brahms. These include opuses 31, 52a, 64, 65a, 92, 103, and 112. Keep in mind that these works were still composed for solo singers in a quartet and may contain some idiosyncrasies that don't work as well for choral ensembles. For example, in op. 64, no. 3. "Fragen," the soprano, alto, and bass sing in a trio and the tenor sings most of the movement alone. It's clear from the high *tessitura* and frequent solo passages of the tenor that this was composed with a solo quartet in mind rather than a choral ensemble.

Example 9.1: Johannes Brahms, *Drei Quartette*, op. 64, no. 3 "Fragen."

Similarly, in op. 92, no. 1 "O Schöne Nacht," each part gets its own opportunity to step out into the spotlight with significant solo passages that make a little more sense with a single performer than a group of singers. Still, this movement is very popular with choral ensembles and performed by them very often.

Many of these one-on-a-group ensembles will often balance their concert programs with somewhat lighter fare from crossover, vocal jazz, or a cappella genres. While the aesthetic of the music will change slightly and the vocal production may morph into a different technique, the principles of vocal writing will remain almost identical. Not only does this genre of vocal works deserve to include vocal writing of the same quality as classical writing, but this genre already contains a multitude of truly wonderful examples of excellent vocal writing. Composers and arrangers who consider themselves mostly in the classical space could afford to learn some of the lessons that crossover, jazz groups, and a cappella ensembles have learned over the years.

Examples include The King's Singers, New York Polyphony, The Real Group, Variant 6, and Voces8.

Chamber Ensembles

These are vocal ensembles where each divided part is sung by at least two and up to six singers per part (16 to 45 total singers). Depending on the context, groups this size are typically staffed with semi-professional or professional singers. Colleges and universities will often have their most advanced group in this size range. Because of the small size, hearing the timbre of vocal colors based on that specific group of singers can be endlessly fascinating to even seasoned veterans of choral music.

Keep in mind that a small community choir may be considered a "chamber" ensemble based purely on its limited size but not necessarily by its ability. Sometimes a church or community choir will find itself in the "chamber" category because of its size, but its abilities may be at the amateur level. If the word "chamber" is in the name of the group, they are typically aspiring to a high level of music making.

The range and technical ability of these ensembles will very much depend on the other factors surrounding the ensemble, but one can reasonably expect the ability to be on the more trained side. If the ensemble is auditioned, it's very likely the group will have singers with more trained ranges. This may change slightly from season to season.

Divisions are possible, but depend on one of two limiting factors: first, the ability of the chamber ensemble and second, the actual number of singers in the chamber ensemble. As stated above, not all choirs of this size will be of a semi-professional ability or above. Also, some ensembles in this category will not be evenly voiced when divided. You may have multiple singers on a part or you may have one part with two singers and another part with only one singer. And obviously, if the ensemble is comprised of 12 members, it's not possible to do a work that divides into say 20 parts.

These ensembles will mostly limit their use of vibrato, but this is not to be assumed. Vibrato use often correlates with the ability of the ensemble. The more accomplished the ensemble, the more likely they are able to adjust how much vibrato they use but will sing with less vibrato as a point of departure. Today's trend is to sing with less vibrato with a group this size. There will, of course, be some exceptions.

The typical repertoire of these choirs can be quite advanced and difficult (although not everything on their program will be of that same difficulty level). These groups typically perform a cappella or with light accompaniment such as a piano, organ, string quartet, etc. In certain cases, a very small chamber ensemble or baroque orchestra with period instruments may be possible, but anything more and these groups can easily be overshadowed. Music for these ensembles is not always ensemble specific. Occasionally you will find some ensemble specific works.

Examples include, RIAS Kammerkor, Roomful of Teeth, Seraphic Fire, The Sixteen, Skylark, The Tallis Scholars, and Tenebrae.

Large Choirs

These are ensembles that have several singers on each part—specifically on each divided part. Large choirs can vary in size between 50 singers and 100 singers (but sometimes more). Typically, they are choirs that have a variety of singers at different levels and different qualities. Some large choirs are comprised of singers who are trained, some amateur, and sometimes a mix. Because these choirs are larger, very often their sound can be quite bold, homogenous, and very attractive.

Large choirs will be able to move with a healthy amount of dexterity but will probably not be able to sing all virtuosic passages at breakneck speeds. The trade-off with these ensembles is usually getting large sounds and more flexible voicing, but at the cost of less dexterity and less clarity. However, it should not be interpreted that these groups are inherently sluggish.

These choirs will also be more likely to have expansive ranges in each section. This will not be the case with the average singer in each ensemble but rather with the outliers in each section. For example, in a large choir, it is more likely than not to have a bass with a low C, but the average bass in said ensemble is more likely to have a low F or E.

These choirs, in general, will be able to perform with standard and even extensive divisions without much friction. This may also include double choir music which may be somewhat easier here than in other cases. This will only be an issue if the choir is comprised mostly of less-accomplished singers.

Vibrato use in these ensembles will likely be more prevalent than with chamber ensembles, but depending on the ability of the ensemble, they will be able to sing with a great deal of flexibility in vocal color.

The repertoire of these choirs is typically one of larger works, and they can be very successful with light and moderate accompaniment including a modest chamber orchestra (provided the orchestration is on the lighter side). These choirs also do well with a cappella repertoire, and very often have repertoire that overlaps with chamber ensembles. These ensembles can excel with repertoire that involves extensive divisions, as well as *cori spezzati* or divided choirs (provided the level of proficiency is adequate). Music for these ensembles is not usually ensemble specific, but there definitely are some works that will be more successful with a larger ensemble like this.

Examples very often include large collegiate choirs like Harvard Glee, Michigan Glee, St. Olaf, and Westminster Choir. Also included are community-based ensembles like the Atlanta Master Chorale and the Los Angeles Master Chorale.

Extra-Large/Festival Choirs

These are vocal ensembles with dozens of singers on each part; they can vary in size, starting from 100 singers or so. These choirs are often staffed by singers with a variety of abilities from amateur to semi-professional or a mix. Occasionally, these ensembles will staff section leader positions with professional singers or have a professional core. Choirs of this size are less common and often only exist for special purposes like festivals or holiday celebrations. Very often, these choirs will perform with an orchestra.

Dexterity will in general be limited, as will clarity with groups this size. The point of these ensembles is not necessarily to be lithe, but powerful. Movement is still possible, but movement should be more modest. One will see groups this large putting on full performances of Handel's Messiah with moderate success. Take that as you will.

Because of the sheer size of the ensembles, broad ranges will be possible; however, their success is more dependent on who is staffing a choir this large. More likely than not, the musicians in these ensembles will range from respectable to very good. The bigger issue is being able to balance the ranges. The soprano section is very likely to be overstaffed, resulting in a very soprano-dominant sound. Additionally, choirs this size are likely to be singing with an orchestra resulting, at times, with sopranos being the main section that can be heard in the choir.[1]

Standard divisions within these ensembles will very often be completely fine. And extensive divisions can be made, depending on the ability of each individual singer. One might presume that with so many singers, the sky is the limit as far as divisions are concerned. And while this isn't a poor conclusion to draw, it neglects the principle that the ability of the singer will first dictate how extensive those divisions can be and second, as choirs get larger, the general tradeoff for power is at the expense of clarity. Yes, numerous divisions will be possible, but the clarity of those divisions may be obscured in an unsatisfactory way.

Vibrato use will be plentiful and, in some cases, expected. Very often, a rich vibrato is a natural byproduct of singing with a free and open sound with a plentiful amount of the singer's acoustic formant, which allows them to be heard over an orchestra. Vibrato is likely to be used less when singers are in lower ranges of their voices as well as at lower dynamic levels. While this isn't always a point of departure, one should compose with this in mind.

---

1 More on balancing with orchestras can be found in Chapter 13.

The repertoire of these choirs will usually be standard choral-orchestral repertoire as well as anthems for occasions like patriotic or regional folk songs. While a cappella singing is possible—and not out of the question—singing entire works without accompaniment is a little less common. Some ensembles this size will also perform with piano or organ accompaniment, although this will typically happen even less often. Additionally, a choir this size performing with a piano may sound overbalanced against the piano (as large as a piano's sound can be). In most cases, if one is putting together a choir of this size, it's probably for a large project that also involves an orchestra. But, as always, there are exceptions.

Examples include the BYU Men's Chorus, Estonia Song and Dance Celebration Choir, London Bach Choir, and the Tabernacle Choir at Temple Square (formally the Mormon Tabernacle Choir).

Choirs Based on Ability

Categorizing ensembles based on ability is not only subjective; it can also be somewhat controversial. The problem surfaces when one is determining the technical abilities of the choral ensemble and determining value thereby. We must take care when discussing choral ensembles based on ability because we shouldn't just value high ability alone.

Yes, we as a choral community should value and support professional level ensembles with tangible and intangible support. At the same time, we should value amateur-level ensembles because they provide an important musical and community value to those lay-musicians all over the world, even if the singers themselves are less-accomplished. By the way, these ensembles are not few in number.

Even if these ensembles don't provide high musical value, they possess other intangible values. Music written for and performed by amateur ensembles can have a great impact on the members of the ensemble and members of the audience. Some of those audience members may never have the opportunity or desire to attend a concert by a choir of higher ability, and yet will get great benefit from performances by amateur ensembles.

One would presume that ability can't be subjective (can you execute or not?). However, ability in music is tempered and altered by another question: "is it effective?" Its value has less to do with "can you sing that pitch?" or "can you sing this passage?" and more to do with "am I satisfied with the execution?"

Others in the choral community may feel differently about how to describe choral ability. Many choral educators will create grade levels based on ability. Correspondingly, many publishers will describe the difficulty of their sheet music with descriptions like "easy," "medium easy," "medium," "medium difficult," and "difficult." To avoid getting too much into the weeds and parsing too much into ability, the categories are simplified here into amateur, semi-professional, and professional. In theory, one can add more divisions and subdivisions into this section, but I will leave that granularity to others.

Additionally, as a composer or arranger, especially one starting out, you will certainly find yourself in a very competitive market if you're only looking to compose for choral ensembles of the highest ability. There are many accomplished ensembles in North America, but they only have so many resources to commission only so much new music. Meanwhile, other choral ensembles, which some may not consider virtuosic, are otherwise fine ensembles that are enthusiastic for new choral music, and have earmarked resources to bring them to life. Anyone who has conducted such ensembles can also tell you these amateur ensembles need good music to sing. They deserve good music, too.

You may be tempted to insist that less capable groups "just work harder" or "just perform better" and that your composition or arrangement is the encouragement they need to finally "be good." While that sounds inspiring, it's also very arrogant and not reasonable nor realistic. You must accept these groups for what they are when you find them and not what you think they "ought" to grow into. That is a journey for the ensemble to determine.

Amateur

These are groups of singers who love singing, but for whom singing may be a byproduct of the real goal of the ensemble. Other priorities may include social, educational, or ecclesiastical purposes. The singers who populate these ensembles range from people who have never been in a choir before to people who have been singing since childhood but may not have received formal training. These may include children's or youth choirs, school choirs, community choirs, and church choirs. Generally, these choirs will be based around an institution such as a church, school, or a specific region—a community choir. These choirs make up most choral ensembles throughout the world and provide immense value to the singers, the audiences, their sponsoring institutions, and the general community.

Even within this category, you'll find a pretty diverse range of skills and abilities. For most of these groups, dexterity won't be the best, and limiting your writing to brief moments of light movement will be helpful. It's not that movement of line isn't possible, but that it can sometimes eat up rehearsal time for the composition. Writing a piece with a large amount of vigorous movement is possible but understand that you're asking some of these less-accomplished groups to pay a big price to make it happen. Some amateur groups may decide that it is too big of a price to pay.

When considering ranges for these ensembles, one should stay contained to the untrained ranges listed in previous chapters as well as considering primarily the second soprano, first alto, second tenor, and baritone ranges.

For the most part, it is best to not divide parts when writing for an amateur choir as a point of departure. This will be dependent on a few other factors including the size of the ensemble and the relative experience of each musician. Some ensembles will have enough singers and experience to sustain brief divisions, and other groups may only manage to sing in two or three parts. If you must divide a part, it is better to divide the sopranos or altos rather than the tenors or basses. Again, when composing for amateur ensembles, dividing should not be a point of departure.

Vibrato use with these groups will mostly depend on the age. Young groups made up mostly of children will have less vibrato than groups with teenagers, adults, or senior citizens. But whether the group you're working with uses vibrato regularly in their sound or not, any direction you give will probably not matter.

There isn't any primary genre or period that amateur groups tend to gravitate towards, but I have noticed a bias towards new music of various genres. One will also find an abundance of arrangements of pop songs, folk songs, and religious anthems, as well as show tunes with an occasional classical work.

Because of the limited musical abilities of these singers, these groups will generally stick to music that is within their reach (although occasionally, you may find an over-zealous conductor). These choirs will select music from a wide variety of musical time periods but will try to stick to the more accessible works.

One can find numerous examples of these ensembles in every community across the world, although very few, if any, will pique international interest.

Semi-pro

These are choral ensembles of high accomplishment but still voluntary membership. These can include choirs from secondary and higher educational institutions, churches, and communities. Some semi-pro choirs include very talented singers and accomplish high levels of music making but are still unpaid (sometimes not by choice). Many semi-pro choirs could be professional if their organizations would actually make the choice to pay them. Many of these groups will give a regular performance schedule in their local community, perform at international conventions, competitions, and festivals, and even go on performing tours.

Since most of these groups are more accomplished and staffed by singers with some—or extensive—professional training, their abilities to handle more difficult music and singing will be greater. Many of these groups will be able to handle a greater number of *coloratura* passages provided they are not too demanding or extend for too great a period. Most groups will have the ability to handle some demanding passages without having to take up too much rehearsal time to make it happen. Some groups, like college choirs and community groups, will take on performances of late baroque music that features a significant amount of *coloratura* singing.

Consequently, the ranges that are possible within the choir will also be increased. Writing in the general range, but including all parts as written in Chapters 3-7, will be very successful for most ensembles in this category. With that said, you will find semi-pro groups who will be able to sing in the trained ranges of all parts written in previous chapters with great success. When working with an ensemble on a commission, it's still wise to consult with the director if you are in doubt about extreme ranges and what the group is capable of.

Standard eight-part division will probably be built into their audition and voicing process and their members would be able to handle them for extended periods. Many of the groups in question will be able to sing even more than the standard eight-part division. In some cases, semi-pro choirs will have their soprano and alto sections staffed with some outstanding and talented musicians, but the tenor and bass sections may be of a slightly lower standard. It's not a bad idea to consider having the sopranos and altos bear most of the divisions if appropriate and having the tenors and basses singing without division most of the time.

Vibrato use in these groups will vary, but many will lean on the side of moderate vibrato or less. The biggest difference between semi-pro groups and amateur groups is that semi-pro groups will be more flexible with their vibrato use and more able to add it or take it away with relative ease. You may, however, find some pushback from semi-pro groups, even more than professional ones.

These ensembles can be some of the most adventurous when it comes to repertoire selection and programming. Many of them will even commission new music for their choirs from composers of all stripes.

These choirs will also strive to sing works from as many different epochs as they can. They will also strive to find a balance between difficult and more accessible materials for both their singers and their audiences alike. These groups will often have a high level of enthusiasm for performing new works as well as new commissions. However, be careful: sometimes these groups will plead poverty and try to negotiate paying a smaller commission fee. If the group is a nonprofit in North America always do your due diligence and look up the financials before agreeing to a smaller fee.

Examples of these ensembles include the Atlanta Master Chorale, Dallas Symphony Chorus, The Holst Singers, London Bach Choir, Minnesota Choral Artists, National Youth Choir of Great Britain, New Zealand Youth Choir, Salt Lake Vocal Artists, and Phoenix Chorale.

Professional

This category is solely defined as an ensemble where the singers are compensated monetarily for their singing. Very often, in exchange for monetary compensation, you are rewarded with singers of a higher ability and very likely a great deal of formal training. The main focus of these ensembles is the musical product and sometimes very little else. The singers who make up these ensembles are generally seasoned musicians with a large amount of choral as well as solo experience.

Generally, these groups will be able to handle whatever virtuosic passages presented to them within reason. I say within reason because the human voice is capable of quite a bit, but not everything. There will be many groups in this category that specialize in singing music of the late baroque and eat coloratura passages for breakfast.

Ranges for these ensembles will all be in the trained ranges discussed in previous chapters. But keep in mind that some of the ensembles in this category include one-on-a-part groups that may be voiced differently than SATB. For example, the King's Singers is a group made up of two countertenors, a tenor, two baritones, and a bass. They can easily sing in all those ranges listed, but writing for this group as you would for any other SATB professional ensemble would be a big mistake.

Unless the ensembles in question are one-on-a-part or of a fixed number, these groups will be able to handle just about any divisions you can throw at them. Most of these groups will already be auditioned and voiced into the standard eight-part division because it's the most common. You can also assign singers into three-part (upper, middle, lower) as well as twelve-part divisions (upper, middle, and lower in each section). Very often, the repertoire will be selected by the music director first and a group will be hired to best suit that concert program.

Vibrato use in this category will vary, but many groups will probably sing with little to no vibrato as a point of departure. Some groups will use generous amounts of vibrato throughout; other groups will find a balance. In some ways it depends on the singers who are hired and the character of the group as well as the repertoire selected. In most cases, direction about vibrato use can be followed through (unless it's simply not possible or healthy for the singer's voice). You may receive some pushback from some groups either to add or take away, especially if they feel it's out of the character of that specific ensemble.

These choirs are very capable of doing anything they set their minds to. Many of these groups will sing a variety of music from each epoch, but at this level, you'll start to find some of these groups niche down and specialize in one or a few different epochs. Some pro groups will focus on early music (Medieval, Renaissance and Baroque), while others will sing a mix of Renaissance and Neo-Renaissance, and other groups focus only on new and experimental music.

Examples include the Ansan City Chorale, Conspirare, the King's Singers, the Los Angeles Master Chorale, New York Polyphony, Oregon Bach Festival, Santa Fe Desert Chorale, Seraphic Fire, Skylark, the Tallis Scholars, Tenebrae, and Voces8.

Choirs Based on Purpose or Function

Another way to categories choral ensembles is by their general purpose or function. The general purpose of these ensembles is to provide choral music for their community or to exclusively create recordings. Others will serve a much more specific purpose such as furnishing a worship service with liturgical music, or teaching music to children, young adults, or college students. Other ensembles will serve mostly as a social outlet for an ensemble or organization where music is the byproduct of the primary purpose.

A choir's purpose or function can be reflected in the music they sing. Some choirs will sing from a very narrow sliver of choral literature, other ensembles will try to find a wider spread of music representing several epochs for educational purposes. Inversely, choirs are also sometimes categorized by the literature that they sing. In some cases, this is easy to define: an early music ensemble or a new music ensemble. Other times, this can be more difficult to classify and especially subjective. There are choirs that sing well-established choral standards from the classical canon, choirs that sing crowd-pleasers, and choirs that sing what's popular in high school repertoire.

Some categorizations will have consistently higher levels of ability, such as early music ensembles, which very often require highly specialized knowledge and training. Some groups, such as children's choirs, will more likely have amateur ability with the occasional group of very high ability. Many of these categorizations will be a mix between amateur and semi-professional. A small number of categories will almost exclusively be professional. As with other categorizations, all these purposes and functions are valid and worthy of quality music. One purpose should not be seen as more noble or admirable than another. The following list of ensembles is by no means comprehensive.

Children's Choirs

These are ensembles that are most often not part of a school or other sponsoring organization (such as a church). The age of the children involved very often ranges from ages eight to 14 but will sometimes include children as young as six to as old as 17. (Outside of North America, the term "Youth Choir" is used to describe choir members ranging from 16 to as old as 22.) Children's choirs can vary drastically in ability: from absolute beginners to very accomplished musicians. Children's choirs are very often underestimated regarding their abilities, with some of them performing very challenging music.

The ability of these choirs to use divisions can vary widely and should absolutely be part of your discussion when writing for these ensembles. Younger voices can have a surprising amount of dexterity, and indeed can perform some very active choral parts. Just be careful how much you're demanding of this group if the group is mostly made up of beginning singers.

If you're working with a specific children's ensemble, make sure to find out the age range of the children in the ensemble to give you a better understanding about appropriate ranges. Whether you're working with prepubescent, cambiata, or teenage voices, age will be an important factor in determining ranges to be used.[2]

Some children's choirs can sing four-part harmony and beyond, while others can only handle one, maybe two, parts. If you're not sure, err on the side

---

2 For more information about the range of children's voices, see Chapter 8.

of fewer divisions. If you have a desire to write for children's choirs without being commissioned, consider it an opportunity to write the best music you can with just one or two parts.

Most children younger than 14 or 15 are not using a developed vibrato. Asking children to use vibrato can be detrimental to their natural and healthy vocal development.

The repertoire for children's ensembles can vary, but it very often focuses on new music as opposed to older standards. Some children's choirs will go out of their way to perform, and even commission, new music for their concerts. These choirs have the potential to be great collaborators for new commissions. Music for this ensemble is usually ensemble-specific, although they often also choose music typically written with soprano and alto voicings.

Examples include the American Boys Choir, Cantabile Youth Singers of Silicon Valley, Hong Kong Children's Choir, New Zealand Youth Choir, Singapore Symphony Children's Choir, and Texas Boys Choir.

Primary Education Choirs

These choirs are ensembles that are part of a primary school as a sponsoring institution. In the United States, primary schools are considered kindergarten through fifth or sixth grade (or six to eleven or twelve years old). Within these age groups, the size and ability of these ensembles can be drastically different from each other.

Sadly, because most schools in the United States are funded by local property taxes within a specific geographic region, it's not uncommon for schools in poorer neighborhoods to have less funding and resources for music programs than wealthier neighborhoods (this is before any extra donations from affluent parents). The disparity between the haves and have-nots can be quite evident in their respective music programs. While this isn't always the case, it unfortunately can be quite predictable based on the school's zip code and median household income.

The ability of children's choirs will sometimes be closely related to the quality of the music training they're receiving as well as how often they are receiving this training (the innate talent of the children will be even across the board). These children, especially fourth and fifth graders (10 and 11 year olds) are capable of some truly impressive ensemble singing with enough quality training.[3] Children's voices can be quite agile and lithe and capable of some dexterity and movement. However, a child's ability to sing in this way will still

---

3   Most of that excellence in children's ensembles will probably be found outside of the primary education setting.

be dependent on the quality and regularity of their training. In most cases, staying conservative and limiting your writing to brief moments of light, easy movement would probably be most successful.

Regarding divisions, keeping the writing to one or two parts is probably the best recipe for success unless you are working with a group that has told you they are capable of more. The ranges of these younger singers will be as discussed in Chapter 8 regarding children's voices.

As mentioned previously about vibrato use in children's choirs, virtually all the musicians you will find in primary school settings will not be capable of singing with a developed vibrato. Asking these singers to do so can build bad habits and be detrimental to their long-term vocal health and hygiene.

The repertoire for these ensembles can vary widely according to the age, size, and ability of each ensemble. Most often, newer music is chosen rather than older music. It's very often a balancing act trying to select music that will appeal to these young singers but also that will challenge and inform their music instruction. Very often these conductors will put more emphasis into choosing music that appeals to their students.

There are numerous examples of these ensembles throughout the world. Attempting to list accomplished choirs here can be tricky because leadership in elementary school choirs can rotate fairly regularly, and funding for school music programs is incredibly fickle in the United States. An excellent and accomplished grade school choir at the time of publishing may not be so excellent in the decades to come.

Secondary Education Choirs

Ensembles in this category will be part of a middle school (or junior high school) and high school choir ranging from sixth through twelfth grade (or twelve to eighteen years old). Grouping these ensembles into one category is a bit of a red herring because middle school choirs are very different from high school ensembles. For example, middle school is normally a time when male-assigned and females-assigned singers are divided into their individual choirs and not mixed except perhaps for a few concert numbers. The main reason for this division between male and female assigned voices is hormones, specifically with how they affect and alter male-assigned voices in dramatic— and sometimes traumatic—fashion.

Depending on their funding, class time availability, and limited number of male-assigned singers, high schools will sometimes maintain the divided choirs or have mixed ensembles or both. Nevertheless, when most choral musicians in the United States refer to a "high school choir" they are referring to a mixed ensemble unless they clarify otherwise. Similar to the issue of funding being tied to surrounding property taxes, the quality (or existence) of the music program in secondary education schools can vary widely. As previously stated, the innate ability of these students will be even across the board, but the amount of training will vary. With that, most middle school ensembles should be considered on the amateur level and high school ensembles to be somewhere between amateur and semi-professional. A few very talented high schools could fit into the semi-professional category.

Regarding dexterity, soprano and alto voices will likely have a greater amount of dexterity than tenors and basses at this age. In middle school, moderate passages of modest movement will be possible with sopranos and altos, while cambiatas will be capable of brief passages of light movement. In high school, all voices will be able to execute more, but writing extensive passages of virtuosic *coloratura* is not advisable. The ability of high school choirs to sing with great dexterity will most likely correlate to the ability to sing in divisions.

The ranges of singers in middle school will vary. Female-assigned voices will vary between children's pubescent ranges to conservative second soprano and first alto ranges.[4] Thankfully, while these voices are growing and developing, they don't experience the same change as male-assigned singers. The male-assigned singers found in middle schools will range from pre-pubescent children's ranges to cambiata voices.[5] Having a more developed tenor or bass in middle school post-cambiata stage is unlikely but not impossible. Most likely they would stay in cambiata ensembles until moving on to high school. The ranges of the singers found in high schools can follow the conservative side of the sopranos, altos, tenors, and basses. At that point, most male-assigned singers have graduated from their cambiata stage, but you will definitely find some late-bloomers among the freshmen.

In most cases, four-part writing will be perfectly adequate; with more accomplished choirs eight-part division will be possible. Some high school choirs can be very capable and venture to sing college-level repertoire. Be advised, however, that while many high school choirs can do such repertoire, this is not standard for most high school ensembles.

Vibrato use can become a tricky issue here as voices begin to show signs of a maturing and developing vibrato in high school. While this is exciting to many of the young people who experience this development, it can cause other singers to feel inadequate by comparison. In some cases, singers who

---

4 See Chapters 4 and 5 for more detail.

5 For more details, see Chapter 8.

have yet to develop a natural vibrato may begin to try to replicate the sound they hear with forced and unhealthy means. This can sometimes lead adolescent singers to singing with a bleating or wobbling sound. Additionally, these voices experiencing this new development of vibrato will still have lots of learn about how to sing with it naturally and healthily.

As a composer or arranger, it's beyond the scope of your work to discuss vibrato with any of these budding musicians. It's best to write without thinking of vibrato in mind or indeed asking for vibrato to be added or removed. Let the discussion of vibrato be had between the singer, their teacher, and their conductors, who should ideally be on the same page with each other.

The repertoire for these ensembles can vary widely given the age, size, and ability of each ensemble. Most often newer music is chosen rather than older music. It's very often a balancing act trying to select music that will appeal to these young singers but also challenge and inform their music instruction. Very often, these conductors will put more emphasis into choosing music that appeals to their students. Because of the emphasis on new music, some high school choirs (provided they have the funding) will often commission new music, especially for special or festival performances.

There are numerous examples of these ensembles throughout the world. Attempting to list accomplished choirs here can be tricky because leadership in high school choirs can rotate fairly regularly and funding for school music programs is incredibly fickle in the United States. An excellent and accomplished high school or middle school choir at the time of publishing may not be so excellent in the years or decades to come.

Higher Education Choirs

These ensembles are part of a college or university as a sponsoring institution and most often part of a school of music and its course work. These ensembles can come in all shapes and sizes. The size of the ensemble can vary between eight singers and over 200, but most higher education institutions will have at least one chamber choir of some sort. Likewise, the ability of these choirs can vary significantly with some ensembles including brand new singers and other ensembles with singers who are already at a professional level (with a handful already singing with professional groups). Overall, the ability and accomplishments of these choirs in North America have been increasing since the second half of the twentieth century. In the United Kingdom, certain collegiate ensembles have been singing at a very high level for hundreds of years.

As these college and university ensembles come in so many different sizes and abilities, there are just as many answers about divisions, ranges, and dexterity, etc. Some of these ensembles will be highly accomplished while others will have abilities similar to an average high school ensemble. However, if we're comparing flagship ensembles from the top tier music schools, we can get a bit more specific. Most of these ensembles will be able to sing moderate passages with modest movement. As can be supposed, the more accomplished ensembles can sing very demanding passages nearly on par with their professional counterparts.

When dealing with ranges, most choral ensembles will be able to handle the conservative ranges of each part just fine, with higher caliber ensembles with more trained singers being able to handle the trained ranges. In a few rare cases, some of these higher caliber ensembles will be able to regularly go beyond the trained ranges, but don't press your luck unless you are working on a specific commission with a specific case.

These ensembles were likely auditioned and voiced with divisions in mind and will make divisions with relative ease. Many of these higher caliber ensembles will be able to divide beyond eight parts with careful attention. Some of this might be dependent purely on whether the ensemble has the numbers or not.

Vibrato use will range widely through this category, almost more so than any other category listed (with perhaps the exception of religious choirs). Some university choirs will sing with little to no vibrato and other ensembles with all the vibrato, with some ensembles embracing both! It's really quite remarkable to witness how broad this specific characteristic can be in this type of ensemble. Many of the trained singers in these ensembles will have a more developed natural vibrato and have begun to hone this aspect of their voices much more than in high school. Having said that, you will still find a significant number of singers who will not have a developed or pronounced vibrato and still find the concept to be a mystery. In most cases, vibrato usage is something that you can inquire more about as well as giving direction in your music to either add it or reduce it. You may encounter some pushback, but it's not likely.

In most accomplished collegiate ensembles, an effort is made to not just sing the choral standards from most, if not all, musical epochs, but to perform some of the most challenging works from those epochs. Additionally, many collegiate ensembles will try to perform new music, and commission new works or even workshop student compositions. In general, these are historically some of the most successful and adventurous ensembles to partner with on new commissions.

Examples include BYU Singers; CSU Long Beach Chamber Singers; King's College, Cambridge; New College, Oxford; St. Olaf Choir; Trinity College, Cambridge; USC Chamber Singers; Westminster Choir; and Yale Schola Cantorum.

Religious Choirs

These are ensembles that furnish music to liturgical services of various faiths. It can't be overstated how different respective denominations and sects will play into the role, make-up, and ability of each of these religious choirs. Some denominations are more famous for their music culture than for their doctrines or practices. Even within denominations one can find a surprising amount of variation with choral ensembles and the role they play in regular worship.

The vast majority of religious choirs across North America will be staffed by volunteers of amateur to modest ability. With larger churches, you are more likely to have more accomplished volunteer singers. In larger cities and metropolitan regions, many churches will be staffed by at least a quartet of, and sometimes more, paid staff singers and section leaders. In the major metropolitan cities of North America, you can sometimes find choirs made up entirely of paid professional musicians, although this is rare.

These choirs are most often staffed by adults, but in larger churches you will also find youth choirs and children's choirs. In some churches, and more often in the United Kingdom, you can find religious choirs made up of children singing treble with adults singing alto, tenor, and bass. This configuration comes from the centuries-long English tradition of choirs made up of "men and boys." In the twenty-first century, this tradition is more widely viewed as inherently sexist and more institutions are departing from centuries-old traditions to welcome women to sing alto, and adolescent girls to sing soprano.

As stated previously, most religious choirs will be of amateur to modest ability. As such, when writing for these choirs in general, it's best to limit the divisions and keep the ranges to conservative, untrained ranges. And in the case of writing for no divisions, it's probably best to keep to the ranges provided for second sopranos, first altos, second tenors, and baritones.

Similarly, most of these ensembles will be better served by compositions and arrangements requiring light and modest dexterity. Predictably, ensembles with more trained singers will be able to execute more demanding passages of more vigorous movement.

The use of vibrato, as with higher education choirs, can vary dramatically from choir to choir. This is not only driven by the ability level of the choir, but often by the denomination and its surrounding culture. In some cases, you can make appropriate suggestions about vibrato; in other cases, you have absolutely no say in the matter.

The main purpose of these ensembles is to provide music for worship. Therefore, the repertoire for these choirs is almost exclusively religious in some way. Depending on the denominations, the choirs will sing religious music from nearly every period of music or just one or two. While some churches will exclusively use contemporary "praise music" for their services, many churches will have a separate contemporary service as well as a traditional one. Other churches will exclusively sing traditional music. Many other churches choose to have "blended worship" to try to please everyone. Discussing worship trends in modern Christianity in the United States is a topic for a whole separate book.

Music for these ensembles is not usually ensemble specific but more so denomination specific. As long as the music meets the choir's need to provide appropriate music for the services and the choir can pull it off, it's fair game. Certain denominations will have requirements regarding the music performed during services. In addition to stand alone anthems, some denominations require service music that is specific to their particular liturgy. Some denominations will only sing anthems and hymns, and very often anthems and hymns will be shared between denominations. Some denominations, including many Orthodox churches, require all their music to be a cappella with no instruments permitted.[6] These choirs will sometimes also offer concerts outside of a church service with music of their choosing.

Examples include the Cathedral of the Madeleine Choir (Salt Lake City), Choir of Westminster Abbey, Christchurch College Choir (Oxford), Emmanuel Episcopal Church of Boston, Grace Cathedral Choir (San Francisco), Kings College, Cambridge Choir, Marsh Chapel (Boston), New College Choir (Oxford), St. James in-the-City (Los Angeles), St. Thomas Church Fifth Avenue (New York City), Trinity College Choir (Cambridge) and Trinity Wall Street (New York City).

Community Choirs

These ensembles are simply made up of members from a community or region. The membership of these choirs can range from amateur to fully professional ensembles to a mix, but most often these groups are comprised of passionate volunteer singers of modest ability. What many of these groups

---

6   Although some Orthodox churches have departed from this restriction.

may lack in terms of singing ability, they make up for in other respects such as enthusiasm, a loyal audience, and community members who may be willing and able to donate funds for a new commission. Fully professional community groups, while rare, have many of these positives as well. For our purposes, most of this description will apply to the amateur and semi-professional iterations of this category as they are, by far, the most prevalent. For more information about professional community ensembles, see the section on professional choirs in the previous section.

As stated previously about amateur ensembles, divisions and ranges should be on the conservative side to be most successful. Semi-professional groups on the other hand are more likely than not to have some decently trained singers, can execute divisions in a convincing way, and sing with the trained ranges indicated earlier. Dexterity and agility will work in a similar way. Although, you will most often find these groups to be a mix of semi-professional sopranos and altos with well-trained singers and more amateur tenors and basses. This is something to keep in mind when working with most community ensembles.

Vibrato use may be as broad as that of other categories. You will find mild to profound amounts of vibrato and will be less likely to see little to no vibrato in singing here (although you will find it). In some cases, it would be appropriate to give some direction on this as desired, but there will be some ensembles where it may not be followed.

The repertoire for these ensembles will be as varied as their respective memberships, purposes, or missions. It's safe to say that there are community choirs of all shapes, sizes, abilities, and levels of enthusiasm for new music. While some may exist solely to sing music from the Baroque period (as one example), other groups are eager to commission and perform new music. Music for these ensembles is not usually ensemble specific.

Examples include Ansan City Choir, Kansas City Chorale, London Bach Choir, Los Angeles Master Chorale, Minnesota Choral Artists, Phoenix Chorale, Salt Lake Choral Artists, and Toronto Mendelssohn Choir.

Fly-in Choirs

These ensembles are most often found in North America and portions of mainland Europe. They are comprised of musicians who fly in from various locations for a few days of rehearsals and a handful of performances, then fly home. While some of these groups will fly in all the participating singers, some groups will fly in a portion of their singers and hire the remainder locally. Virtually all these choirs are comprised of professional singers (no exceptions come to mind). Because of the cost associated with hiring, transporting, housing, and feeding professional singers over the course of a contract, these ensembles will often be staffed by few singers —between 12 and 24 singers most often, but sometimes outsides of this range.

As virtually all these ensembles are staffed with professional singers, the average skill level for these ensembles is exceptionally high and they will be capable of quite a lot. Fly-in choirs are very likely to be the most flexible ensembles you encounter. Because they only meet for specific concert programs, they usually hire only the singers that they need and plan the roster around the music rather than the music around the roster. For example, if they decide they want to sing music that calls for very low bass parts, they will hire as many low basses as they need or are available.

In at least one case, for their summer festival program the Santa Fe Desert Chorale will have a concert program for its full roster, as well as smaller ensembles for their "cameo" concert programs. As an example, one summer there was one concert program for 16 singers, another concert program for nine singers, and finally another two programs for the full complement of 25 singers. This is one example of the ability and willingness of these ensembles to be flexible in their concert programming and roster selection.

These ensembles will be very capable of extensive divisions but may be limited simply by the size of the ensemble, which may vary depending on the project. Some iterations of these ensembles will be smaller or larger, depending on the concert program. Of course, larger ensembles will be more expensive to assemble and may mean that most of the concert programs each season will be on the smaller side.

Very often they will hire singers who specialize in whatever style of music they are choosing to perform. If the music is by Bach or Handel, they will hire musicians who can provide exceptional *coloratura* singing. If singing Russian music, the ensemble will make certain to hire as many *basso profundo* basses as they are able. Vibrato use will vary between ensembles, but more likely than not it is moderate to limited as a point of departure. Some ensembles will ask for no vibrato but will have the option as needed.

The repertoire of these ensembles can be quite broad and from many different periods but will often focus on works for smaller ensembles. These choirs will sometimes place a heavy emphasis on commissioning and performing new music. Some of these ensembles will emphasize performing in their respective regions, while others will make more effort to make recordings and tour other cities or regions. Music for these ensembles is not usually ensemble specific.

Examples include Bach Collegium San Diego, Conspirare, Kinnara, Oregon Bach Festival, Santa Fe Desert Chorale, Seraphic Fire, and Skylark.

Early Music Ensembles

There is an entire category of choral ensembles that dedicate themselves specifically to performing selections of older choral repertoire. Even though this sounds like niching down as an ensemble, there is still a surprising amount of variety in these groups including their size and the skill set of the musicians. Some are community groups, others are professional groups, some are part of a college or university.

With all this variety, it's still tricky to speak in terms of divisions, ranges, and vibrato use. For the most part, these groups will likely have the ability to recruit or hire the number of musicians necessary for the desired repertoire. Essentially, divisions and ranges are not as concrete as they can be in other ensembles.

Even dexterity and vibrato can still evade a solid answer. Some groups that specialize in Renaissance music will often perform with little or no vibrato in their sound. Other groups that specialize in the Baroque or Classical periods will sometimes sing with a moderate amount of vibrato. These groups will very often also be capable of incredible dexterity as the coloratura found in repertoire of this period can be extremely demanding.

The question that most often comes up with early music groups is almost always "how early?" Some groups specialize in Medieval music, others Renaissance, Baroque, or even Classical period music or some sort of combination. Each of these ensembles will have a different answer to that question. Some groups in this category have even performed music from the Romantic period. While there is some give and take as to what defines "early" music, each group will maintain a certain amount of consistency in the repertoire that they choose to program. For example, a group that specializes in Medieval music may also sing repertoire from the Renaissance because there's a great deal of crossover but wouldn't venture to sing Classical period music. Similarly, a group that specializes in music from the late Baroque period will also perform some Classical period music, but may not try performing Medieval music. Having said that, there's probably an exception to this principle.

Another caveat is that while some groups will only perform music from Mozart and earlier, some groups that otherwise market themselves as early music ensembles will also perform and even commission new music. When the Tallis Scholars, one of the best-known early music ensembles in the world, performed at the BBC Proms in Royal Albert Hall in 2014, their entire program consisted of music they had commissioned by John Tavener who had only recently passed away. There is a whole sub-category of ensembles that claim to specialize in Renaissance music and twenty-first century music in equal measure.

Examples of these types of ensembles include Alamire, Anonymous 4, Bach Collegium Japan, Bach Collegium San Diego, Blue Heron, Collegium Vocale Gent, The Hilliard Ensemble, The Monteverdi Choir, The Sixteen, and the Tallis Scholars.

Radio/Scoring Choirs

These are ensembles that primarily perform together for broadcast performances and recordings. Because of the intense recording and performance schedule of these ensembles, and the large amount of literature they perform, these ensembles are most often staffed with professional singers with exceptional sight-reading abilities. There are a few notable exceptions of ensembles in this category staffed by semi-professional volunteers.

As many of these ensembles are staffed with some truly exceptional professionals, they are capable of quite a lot, including extensive divisions, large ranges, and highly virtuosic singing. Even among the semi-professional groups, the level of training will be pretty high. Standard divisions and even extended divisions will be possible but would probably require hiring more musicians, making the session more expensive. However, if a studio is hiring an orchestra, they'll probably have the money to hire more singers for the divisions.

Vibrato use for many of these ensembles is very often the norm and a point of departure. Even among the smaller, chamber-sized ensembles, such as the BBC Singers, these choirs will traditionally perform with full-throated vibrato. Some of these groups will be able to limit their vibrato if requested, but that may not always be in the cards.

In the case of radio choirs, the roster is pretty much fixed with a rotating conductor in some cases or a principal conductor and one or two associate conductors. The repertoire chosen for broadcasts is usually chosen by producers and music directors for the needs of the broadcasts. Ranges should be pretty standard as the membership of these choirs is generally highly selective. Dexterity also will be high as these choirs need to sing a wide variety of repertoire. Vibrato usage will vary between ensembles with some using a sparing amount and others being exceedingly generous with its use.

In the case of scoring choirs, ranges, dexterity, and vibrato use will all vary depending on the needs of the score. Since each session choir is hired from scratch for each score, it's not out of the question to find and hire singers that match the sound needed. If your score sounds like it requires an opera chorus or a Renaissance motet, the choir can be built to accommodate that need. Vibrato use can vary widely depending on the needs of the score. A score like *Star Wars: The Phantom Menace* will require a robust sound with more vibrato, while a score like *The Abyss* will require a more translucent sound with less vibrato.

The repertoire of these ensembles can be quite broad to suit the needs of the broadcast. Very often the audiences of the broadcast will influence the programming of the ensemble. Overall, radio choirs will put a focus on choral standards from all periods and may not be ensemble specific. Some ensembles will have another emphasis such as new music, chamber music, or religious music. Scoring choirs, on the other hand, are mostly there to record the soundtrack for a film, television show, or video game and will be highly ensemble specific.

Examples include the BBC Singers, Danish National Radio Choir, RIAS Kammerchor, Swedish Radio Choir, the Tabernacle Choir at Temple Square (formally the Mormon Tabernacle Choir).

Touring Ensembles

The main purpose of these ensembles is performing in different locations across a country or indeed the world. They are usually comprised of a fixed membership that rehearses either one or a few concert programs and tours with the same material for weeks, months, or even years at a time. While other ensembles on this list may tour (and even tour quite a bit) if it isn't their main function it may not strictly be considered a touring ensemble. The membership of these ensembles is almost entirely paid professionals who have probably gone through a rigorous audition and vetting process.

As many of the ensembles are professionals, dexterity is likely to be quite high as far as ability is concerned. Ranges will be similar. Divisions will be less likely as many of these groups will also be "one-on-a-part" ensembles as described previously. It's less common, but there are groups with the ability to divide. Vibrato use will probably be limited but will be used for solos. Vibrato may not be appropriate with the style of music most of these groups sing.

The repertoire of these touring ensembles is particularly interesting because they usually need to serve a broad cross-section in each audience. These ensembles will often attract choir aficionados who are well versed in the choral art, and also the significant others of those aficionados who aren't well versed in the choral arts but got dragged along to the performance. Very often these ensembles will offer an eclectic mix of choral standards from the Renaissance, Baroque, and twentieth century, and more accessible pieces like choral arrangements of popular songs and folk tunes.

Music for this ensemble can sometimes be ensemble specific but will depend on the ensemble. For example, The King's Singers, New York Polyphony, and retired groups such as the Hilliard Ensemble and Anonymous 4, will perform concert programs with repertoire that includes music composed especially for them or music that fits their very specific voicing. Other ensembles, such as Chanticleer, Voces8, along with other groups that tour extensively like the Tallis Scholars, Tenebrae, Seraphic Fire, and the Sixteen, will sing programs that may include some music written especially for them, while the rest of the program music comes from a wide variety of sources.

Examples include Cantus, Chanticleer, The King's Singers, New York Polyphony, Seraphic Fire, The Sixteen, The Tallis Scholars, Tenebrae, and Voces8.

Opera Choruses

These ensembles serve the very specific purpose of staffing the chorus of any given production staged by the opera company. The ability of the singers depends very much on the opera company in question. In large houses in major US cities, these choruses are comprised of paid professionals, and sometimes even unionized musicians. In smaller or regional opera houses, they are very often volunteer singers of varying abilities. In Europe, depending on the house, many opera choruses will be salaried positions with benefits.

The ability and level of training for each of these choruses is directly related to the opera company staging the production. An "A" house will have a great ensemble, possibly on salary and unionized. A "B" house will probably hire contracted singers and will generally have a high level of training and ability. Smaller opera companies will probably have volunteer chorus members of varying ability but will probably lean more semi-professional. University operas will vary dramatically depending on the school of music putting on the production.

The specifics of a choir's sound will also depend on the opera being produced. A chorus in a Baroque opera will need a higher amount of dexterity while one in a Classical or Romantic period opera may not. A Romantic period opera may require very soft or very loud passages for extended periods of time and singers need to demonstrate a high amount of dynamic variation and stamina.

The music of each show can vary widely, but divisions are not as plentiful in this genre as they are in other choral genres. They are still present, however, especially in opera from the late Romantic period through to modern opera. Divisions in this music are more often dictated by the needs of the narrative rather than the musical needs.

Vibrato use is generous and highly valued from the individual singers.

Music for this ensemble is very ensemble specific. The literature can range from early Baroque opera to more recent contemporary musical theater, but more often than not, the opera staged will be from the Classical or Romantic periods. Some works originally written for an opera can sometimes be lifted for a concert performance. However, these ensembles themselves do not often perform outside of an opera performance setting. They may occasionally perform in a gala or festival setting, and will be hired for recording projects—usually recordings of operas.

As a friendly reminder, opera choruses will perform from memory in all staged performances. Naturally, these musicians understand this expectation and are ready to memorize a significant amount of music (depending on the opera). It's still a good idea to incorporate the strategies for memorized music discussed previously in Chapter 3 to help the musicians or at least not make their lives needlessly stressful. The musicians are already following staging, acting, and singing with good tone; having to struggle with music that is difficult to memorize will mean the rest of the performance will suffer.

It is worth noting that if you're writing an opera and not working with a pre-existing opera chorus, you have some flexibility to designate your chorus to be whatever style you want it to be. In most cases, an opera chorus' main distinction is that the choir goes through a staging process, but even that can be optional, as some productions call for opera choruses to be offstage and never seen by the audience.

Examples include the Metropolitan Opera Chorus (New York), Royal Opera Chorus (London), Teatro alla Scala Chorus (Milan).

Symphonic Choruses

These are vocal ensembles with dozens of singers on each part whose primary purpose is to accompany orchestras. These can vary in size starting from 100 singers or so. These choirs are often staffed with singers with a variety of abilities from amateur and semi-professional to a mix. Very often, the musicians in these ensembles will have a full-time day job and sing in a symphonic chorus as part of their music outlet. Occasionally, these ensembles will staff section leader positions with professional singers. Very often, the budget size and reputation of the corresponding orchestral ensemble will directly correlate with the ability level of the individual singer of the symphonic chorus, but not always.

Sadly, many of these ensembles are considered afterthoughts by the organizations that supervise them and the orchestral conductors who work with them. Case in point: the orchestras are staffed by well-compensated union players while many symphonic choirs are staffed by unpaid volunteers (or worse, must pay fees or dues in order sing in these ensembles). Even in cases where the chorus is staffed entirely with professionals who have a great deal of training and experience, they are often treated like plebs by their executive and artistic directors. There are few symphonic ensembles where the singers are members of a union like the American Guild of Musical Artists (AGMA).

The ability of these ensembles, as well as their vocal ranges, are often determined by whether the group is amateur, semi-professional, or professional. In general, ensembles are capable of a certain amount of healthy movement. However, a large size can prohibit these ensembles from being as truly lithe and dexterous as small ensembles. Thanks to their inherently large size, these ensembles are quite capable of dividing into eight parts and sometimes more, but this may not be the case with very amateur groups.

In general, vibrato use will be generous and, in some cases, plentiful. Non-vibrato use can still be an option, but stylistically it's not often called for. Do keep in mind that vibrato use with an ensemble of this size is less of a concern than it is with smaller ensembles as it's very often a desirable quality.

These choirs can have fairly ensemble specific repertoire and almost exclusively sing choral-orchestral repertoire. On the rare occasion when these groups are the featured ensemble of a performance, they will sing a few a cappella works, but most a cappella singing comprises passages in previously mentioned choral-orchestral repertoire. On occasion, you will find symphonic choirs where the roles are reversed and the choral ensembles are the featured ensembles and the orchestra plays the supporting role, but this is less-often the norm.

Examples of Symphonic Choruses include Atlanta Symphony Chorus, Chicago Symphony Chorus, Dallas Symphony Chorus, London Symphony Chorus, and the Los Angeles Master Chorale.

Continuing Study

Suggested Exercises

Short
- » Identify the basic types of ensembles based on size and list their approximate ensemble sizes.
- » Identify the different types of ensembles based on ability and discuss their strengths and weaknesses.
- » Identify the different types of ensembles based on purpose and identify what sort of repertoire would interest those ensembles.

Long
- » Find at least one recording from one of the ensembles mentioned in each category. Take note of the repertoire they are selecting for these recordings and how effective it is for each ensemble.
- » Compare and contrast recordings of the Fauré *Requiem* by the Atlanta Symphony Chorus (Robert Shaw), Choeur de l'Orchestre symphonique de Montréal (Charles Dutoit), and The Sixteen (Harry Christophers).
- » Compare and contrast recordings of the Bach motets by Bach Collegium Japan (Masaaki Suzuki), La Chapelle Royale & Collegium Vocale Gent (Philippe Herreweghe), and Nederlands Chamber Choir (Peter Dijkstra).
- » Make a list of at least five choirs in your community. See if you can categorize the kind of choir that they are and take note of what sort of music they are programming.

Suggested Listening

(in no particular order)
Silence and Music. Stuttgart Vocal Ensemble, Marcus Creed.
Brahms: Geistliche Chormusik. RIAS Kammerchor, Marcus Creed.
Figure Humaine. Tenebrae, Nigel Short.
Not No Faceless Angel. Polyphony, Stephen Layton.
Reincarnations. Seraphic Fire, Patrick Dupré Quigley.
J.S. Bach: Matthäus-Passion BWV 244. Collegium Vocal Gent, Philippe Herreweghe.
Grieg: Choir Music. Norwegian Soloists' Choir, Grete Pedersen.
Nielsen: Songs for Choir. Ars Nova Copenhagen, Michael Bojesen.
Lux Aeterna. Los Angeles Master Chorale, Paul Samlumonovich.
The Sacred Veil. Los Angeles Master Chorale, Grant Gershon.

Ansan City Choir, Shin-Hwa Park.
Requiem. Conspirare, Craig Hella Johnson.
The Origin of Fire. Anonymous 4.
Times Go by Turns. New York Polyphony.
Gleams of a Remoter World. BBC Singers, David Hill.
Euphonos: The Choral Works of Ily Matthew Maniano. The Philippine Madrigal Singers.
Nine Lessons & Carols. Choir of King's College, Cambridge, Stephen Cleobury.
Howells: Collegium Regale & Other Choral Works. Trinity College, Cambridge, Stephen Layton.
Rachmaninoff: Liturgy of St. John Chrysostom, Op. 31. Estonian Philharmonic Chamber Choir, Kaspars Putniņš.

Chapter 10

Divisions

*He set singers also before the altar,
that by their voices they might make sweet melody...*
— Ecclesiasticus 47:9

Music written for voices during the Renaissance and Baroque periods contains one part per staff for the vast majority of the time. Writing for two soprano parts meant writing those two parts on two different staves. We see examples of extensive parts written, even up to forty voices, in "Spem in Alium" by Thomas Tallis.

On occasion, there will be an outlier example of a divided part in a work from the Renaissance, but this is quite rare and only happens at external cadences. An example of this can be found in *Missa Cantate* by John Sheppard. Here, the work is for six voices (SATTBB) but there are six instances–three being found in the "Credo"–where Sheppard divides either the soprano or alto voice to add a seventh note. The instance in the "Sanctus" movement is found in the soprano part on the word "excelsis" at the cadence just before the "Benedictus" section.

Throughout the Baroque and Classical periods, one may find on occasion a division in the bass part, which happens most often at cadences if the bass part goes quite low. However, we don't see extensive or temporary divisions on the same part through the entire work until the early 1800s. A few examples of these divisions can be found in some of the a cappella choral works of Felix Mendelssohn, especially his setting of "Weinachten" from *Sechs Sprüche* op. 79.

Example 10.1: John Sheppard, *Missa Cantate*, "Sanctus."

Example 10.2: Felix Mendelssohn, *Sechs Sprüche* op. 79, "Weinachten."

In modern choral writing, divisions—even extensive ones—are used fairly freely, giving composers and arrangers a great deal of voicing options. The difference between a division and a separate part is sometimes only a matter of semantics. In general, a division is a single part that's divided and written on one staff, while different parts are written on multiple staffs. Sometimes, a division will temporarily be notated on an additional staff before being reunited in a single staff. In choral music with more than one singer on each part, this distinction is less important. What is most important is providing flexibility to the composer or arranger and notational clarity to the musician.

Deciding when to divide a part and when to write an entirely separate part on an additional staff can be subjective. If the music is mostly homophonic in character a division should do the job perfectly well. There are, however, some instances where a separate staff would be more ideal. These instances may include parts that are mostly polyphonic in nature, where there are more than two divisions or where there's a great deal of voice crossing. Your main objective should be providing a score that is clean and clearly shows your intention as a composer or arranger.

Dividing can yield richer, fuller sounds, but not all divisions will be a success. Sometimes more is just more, and other times less is actually more. Consider how much beautiful music has been composed with three parts, two parts, or even just a single part. That being said, some harmonies require more than four unique pitches and divisions will be necessary. When done correctly, divided voices can create especially beautiful and effective passages.

As a general principle, if you're working in a specific sonority—for example, a passage that is essentially four parts throughout—a momentary division into five parts should be kept to important moments, like a specific word or cadence. Having a random moment suddenly split into five or six voices can distract and the passage may sound inconsistent or uneven.

Standard Divisions

The standard division involves each part dividing into two parts: firsts and seconds. So, SATB can easily and regularly be divided into SSAATTBB. It's so standard that in many choirs, these voice parts are auditioned into these divisions as sections to always know what to sing. The mentality of many choral musicians is to be prepared for when the music divides rather than if the music divides.

Very brief divisions of any parts with amateur groups may be possible, but use sparingly if at all. Some novice choirs won't take on a piece with any divisions in it, let alone extensive ones. Groups that are semi-professional or professional can easily take on works with extensive eight-part divisions (provided the group isn't a "one-per-part" ensemble as discussed in Chapter 9).

When incorporating standard, eight-part divisions, it's important to remember that not every part needs to be divided simultaneously or evenly. You can divide the sopranos and altos and leave the tenors and basses unified or vice versa. As one example, in movement six of *All-Night Vigil*, Rachmaninoff has the altos divided while the sopranos and tenors are in octave unisons.

Example 10.3: Sergei Rachmaninoff, *All-Night Vigil*, "Bogoroditse Devo."

Dividing parts will spread voices out over multiple parts and result in those parts dividing their power and volume into two different pitches. This will affect the overall balance of the sound in the ensemble. Allowing one part to stay unified while dividing the other parts will cause the unified part to stand out from the other parts slightly. This is especially useful if you want to highlight a melody or line in one particular part.

Extensive use of eight-part divisions is possible, but make sure that if you're working on a commission that the ensemble is capable of handling it.

Example 10.4: Felix Mendelssohn, "Jauchzet dem Herrn, alle Welt."

Three-Part Divisions

One particularly interesting division in choral music is for the sopranos and altos to be split into three parts, for example SSA, SAA, or sometimes notated Soprano/Mezzo-Soprano/Alto. This division is a wonderful voicing option and possible even with some amateur ensembles. This three-part division doesn't always need to be notated on three different staffs.

Example 10.5: Herbert Howells, *Collegium Regale*, "Magnificat."

Copyright © 1947 (Renewed) Novello & Co. Ltd. International Copyright Secured. All Rights Reserved.

Three-part splits with tenors and basses into Tenor/Baritone/Bass are also a wonderful option and possible, but less so with amateur groups. As mentioned previously with sopranos and altos in a three-part split, tenors and basses divided into three parts will also need some clarifying direction about how you intend to have the sound balanced. Whether you desire the sound to have more of a tenor split, a bass split, or a more equal tenor/baritone/bass split, it's important to be specific. All three of these are valid and have their own merits, and each will yield a slightly different sound, especially in certain ranges.

These three-part splits allow choirs to be able to divide into other divisions such as SSATB, SATBB, SSATBB, or SAATTB, etc., which can yield surprisingly compelling vocal colors and an ability to manage a new level of voicing detail without being too overwhelming to either composer or musician.

Example 10.6: Healey Willan, "The Three Kings."

Whatever three-part split a composer takes on, it's important to be specific about how you want the division to sound. Many choral conductors will ask for their sopranos and altos to sing in a specific three-part split, where some second sopranos will sing first, and some first altos will sing second soprano. This division is done in an effort to produce a more balanced sound.

However, if the music is quite high, moving voices around to other parts may unfortunately be detrimental to a balanced sound and have too many singers singing higher pitches than they usually do, producing a somewhat top-heavy ensemble. Inversely, if the music is quite low and voices have moved to other parts, it may take away some needed power from the lower voices when they need it most. If you have in mind more of a soprano split without any voices moving to other sections or an alto split with no voices moving to other parts, it will be important to specify that as some directors will direct their choirs to sing a three-part split as default.

Double Choir Divisions

Double choir and poly-choral divisions have been a long tradition in choral music. Some of our first notated examples of this poly-choral style go back to at least the sixteenth century when the English were composing church music for the divided decani and cantori[1] and the cori spezzati practices at St. Mark's Basilica in Venice.[2] Considering the latter, composers like Gabrieli, Monteverdi, and Schütz would compose up to five choirs of singers and/or instruments.

The double choir division is the most common of the polychoral divisions throughout history and includes choral standards like four of the six standard Bach motets (BWV 225, 226, 228, and 229), Brahms' op. 109, Rheinberger's Mass in Eb, and Martin's Mass for Double Choir, to name only a handful.

Example 10.7: Johann Sebastian Bach, "Singet dem Herrn," BWV 225.

While very much a possibility, singing in double choir makes a large demand on choirs and is best suited for ensembles with at least semi-professional skill levels. As odd as it may sound, composing for double choir

---

1 Dennis Schrock, *Choral Repertoire* (Oxford University Press, 2009), 136.

2 J. Peter Burkholder, Donald Jay Grout, and Claude V. Palisca, *A History of Western Music*. (New York: W. W. Norton & Company, 2006), 282.

is noticeably different than writing for eight-part divisions. For some reason, singing SSAATTBB feels easier in ways than singing SATB/SATB. Part of it has to do with the fact that when performing double choir music in concert, choirs will often change formations with the first choir on the left side of the stage and the second choir on the right. The sections find themselves on opposite sides of the performance space and this causes them (sometimes unconsciously) to feel as if their forces are diminished.

SATB/SATB is typical for double choir divisions, but depending on the group, one could compose for SSAA/SSAA or TTBB/TTBB double choir. We can find fantastic examples of that in Holst's "Ave Maria" and Biebl's "Ave Maria."

Example 10.8: Gustav Holst, "Ave Maria."

In some cases, a composer may wish to treat a standard mixed SATB choir the same way they treat a double choir, with the sopranos and altos in one ensemble and the tenors and basses as the second ensemble. Some composers will compose their music in such a way that treats a mixed SATB ensemble with antiphonal passages. In at least one example by Trond Kverno, the double choir notation is explicitly notated.

Example 10.9: Trond Kverno, "Ave Maris Stella."

© 1976 Norsk Musikforlag A/S. All rights reserved. Walton Music Corp. admin. USA and Canada.

Some composers will write for divided double choir ensembles (SATB/SATB divisi), essentially 16 divisions in total. Again, while possible, be cautious about writing further divisions in double choir music, as it can take an already burdened ensemble and tax them further. This voicing is best suited for singers with a professional skillset or semi-pro singers who are almost professionals. Even then, consider limited divisions of this nature.

Example 10.10: Frank Ferko, *Hildegard Triptych*, "O vis aeternitatis."

© 2000 by E. C. Schirmer Music Company, Inc. (ASCAP), a division of ECS Publishing Group. www.ecspublishing.com. All rights reserved. Used by permission.

Extensive Divisions

Dividing beyond eight choral parts is possible and can provide even more voicing options and more depth, richness, and an even broader timbral spectrum. It can be common in secundal music for choirs to divide into as many as 20 different notes. Examples of this can be found in works by Ligeti, and more recently by Whitacre and Ešenvalds. These divisions are best used for brief periods of time and with groups that possess at least a semi-professional skill set. It can be very effective to write extensive divisions on an important word, or at important moments of a piece including (but not limited to) the climax of a work. Longer periods of divisions are possible, but usually only by choirs of a high skill level.

144 The Technique of Choral Writing

Example 10.11: Eric Whitacre, "Water Night."

© 1996 Walton Music Corp. All rights reserved.

Example 10.12: Ēriks Ešenvalds, "Vineta."

© Musica Baltica, 2009. Printed with permission.

Remember that with more extensive divisions, any attempts at stagger breathing will be compromised, and in certain cases not possible. If you have a 20-part division in smaller ensembles, several of the pitches are likely to be sung by a single voice and it will be quite noticeable when that voice tries to sneak in a breath. Even in large ensembles, one may have three voices covering a single pitch, but if one of those three voices has more presence than the other two, you may lose a significant portion of that sound—even half the sound—if that singers takes a breath.

Having said that, singers will put extra effort into being able to sing music with extensive divisions because they are willing to work for the reward they often feel with its execution. In general, a large portion of singers very much love to sing secundal music with extensive divisions. It creates a sonority and a sonic experience that singers can find very rewarding to create.

Extensive Parts

Occasionally, composers will ask for more parts beyond eight, such as twelve, sixteen, twenty-four or more. This direction is different from the previously discussed extensive divisions because these works are calling for more parts for the entire duration of the work and not just a brief moment.

Examples include "Mari" by James MacMillan for 16 voices, *Path of Miracles* by Joby Talbot for 17 voices, *Requiem* by György Ligeti for 20 voices, *A Choral Symphony* by Gabriel Jackson for 24 voices, and "Spem in alium" by Thomas Tallis for 40 voices.[3] Works like these are very often composed with the idea of having one singer on one part (except perhaps the Ligeti), and can have more flexibility to work from tutti forces and smaller sections–highlighting solos, duets, and trios–and to have greater control voicing larger chords.

Works like these are mostly tackled by ensembles of a professional or nearly professional caliber of musician. They can be very demanding on the individual musicians. When writing a work with extensive parts, consider every single part as if it were one-on-a-part (which is essentially what it is in some cases), their needs as well as their strengths, and give each ample time to rest.

---

3   A number of new compositions for 40 voices have been composed recently, specifically to be premiered alongside a performance of Tallis' "Spem in alium."

146 The Technique of Choral Writing

Example 10.13: Györgi Ligeti, "Lux Aeterna."

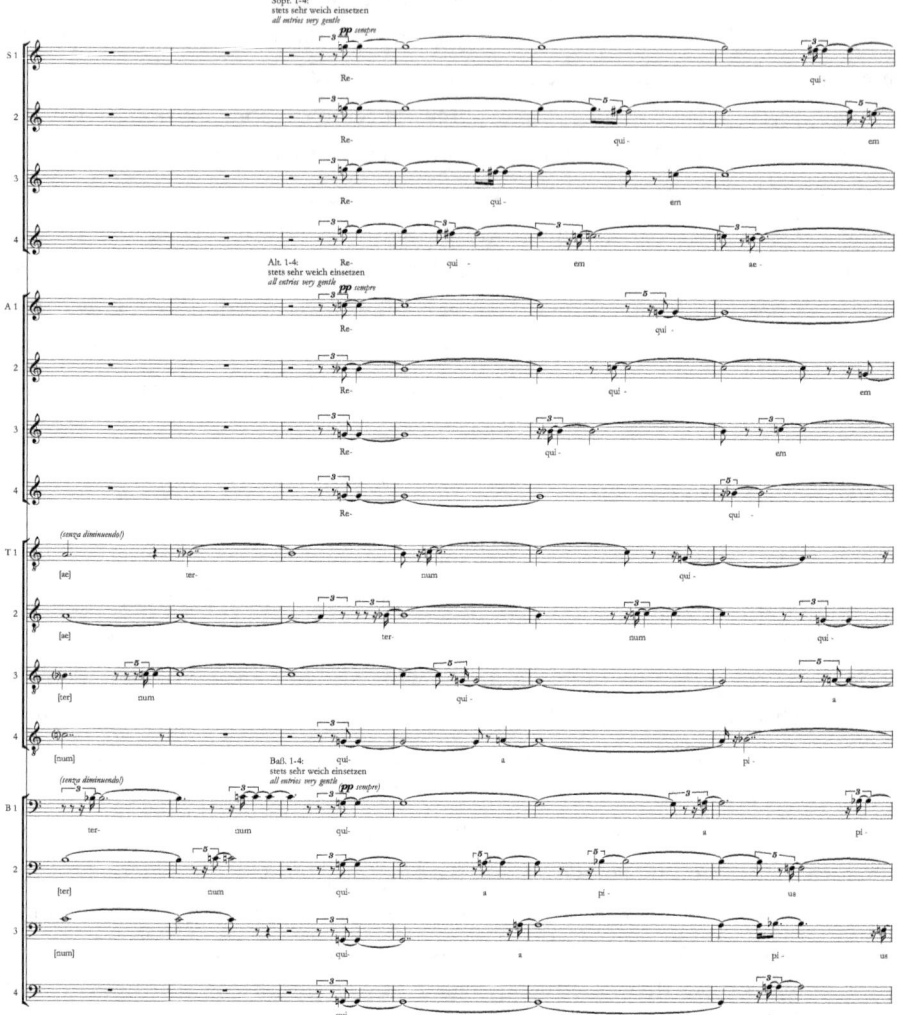

© 1967 Henry Litolff's Verlag. Reproduced by permission of Faber Music Ltd. All Rights Reserved.

Not every example of extensive parts is for mixed ensemble. A great example of extensive divisions for treble voices is "Ave Maria" by David MacIntyre.

Example 10.14: David MacIntyre, "Ave Maria."

© 1995 Cypress Choral Music. Used by permission.

Solos

Solos in choral music are a somewhat controversial but exceptionally effective way to write with contrast in choral music. As discussed previously in Chapter 3, the magic of the human voice is the ability to amalgamate so many various vocal colors into a completely new one. When you have solos in a choral work, you are essentially highlighting or isolating just one of those many colors and highlighting the contrast between pure and combined timbres.

Another benefit is that it also reduces the overall volume of sound down to a single voice, helping to provide greater dynamic range. It can help reset the audience's ears both to the full timbre of the choir as well as their full dynamic, and when a section or timbre is removed from a composition's tonal fabric, the listener can appreciate it more when it returns. This contrast helps create interest and when you bring the full choir back in, the contrast can make it sound larger and fuller than the audience may remember. It can sometimes give that effect of a "wall of sound."

A slightly less realized benefit is that solos can allow the other musicians to take breaks and can help with vocal stamina. Solos can essentially allow a large number of singers to rest their voices for a moment. This benefit isn't the primary reason for solos, but it is still a tangible service.

Choral solos can be extensive; for example, several verses of a strophic setting. However, this doesn't need to be the case for every solo passage. They can be shorter moments—or even just a measure—to help create a specific effect. "Gleams of a Remoter World" by Judith Bingham is one example, in which the work begins with a drone on E4 by the sopranos and altos and solo voices in trios sing the words "death and sleep" in Italian and German. These soli gestures are continued while the choir begins to build a larger, taller chord in the background. As a former member of the BBC Singers, Bingham is exceptionally skilled at seamlessly weaving and voicing soli ensembles with choral forces, producing a haunting, ghostly effect.

Example 10.15: Judith Bingham, "Gleams of a Remoter World."

© Peters Edition Ltd. Reproduced by permission of Faber Music Ltd. All Rights Reserved.

Another example can be found in MacMillan's "O bone Jesu." Here, MacMillan has asked for each note to be sung by a different solo singer in rotation. This direction accomplishes two things: first, it thins out the texture momentarily. Second, a wonderful effect is created when different voices with their own individual timbres are rotated through, creating a kaleidoscope of color with only a few voices at a time.

Example 10.16: James MacMillan, "O bone Jesu."

* each note and syllable should be sung by a different solo voice, rotating the order through each section

© Boosey & Hawkes Music Publishers Ltd. Reproduced by permission of Boosey & Hawkes.

Using solos for duets, trios and quartets is especially effective. An example can be found in the second movement ("Psalm 23") of Herbert Howells' *Requiem*.

Example 10.17: Herbert Howells, *Requiem*, "Psalm 23."

Copyright © 1981 Novello & Co. Ltd. International Copyright Secured. All Rights Reserved. Reprinted by permission of Hal Leonard LLC.

There are two aspects that make using solos in choral scores controversial: the use of vibrato and the hurt feelings of spurned singers.[4] The latter is not your problem as a composer or arranger. Regarding the former, the use of vibrato for a solo is a highly debated topic among choral conductors; some solos may be more effective with vibrato and others without, while for some solos it may not matter at all. If the use of vibrato is crucial in your mind to the success of a specific solo, you can ask for no vibrato with the Italian[5] marking *non vib.* or *senza vib.* or ask for it with the marking *con vib.* or *molto vib.* Otherwise, if no marking is given, the use of vibrato will be left up to the discretion of the musicians.

---

4   More common among vocal ensembles than it is among instrumental ensembles, but honestly not by much. Even among professional musicians, egos can run high.

5   As a side note, the use of Italian isn't required in your directions. Using the English no vibrato or with vibrato is perfectly acceptable, as well as your own vernacular.

Continuing Study

Suggested Exercises

Short
- » Discuss the pros and cons of dividing parts in a choral ensemble. Discuss the times when it's not possible or not advisable.
- » Discuss the pros and cons of double choir divisions.
- » Discuss the differences between extensive division versus extensive parts.
- » Discuss the pros and cons of using solos.

Long
- » Study "Os justi" by Anton Bruckner and take note of when Bruckner moves from undivided to divided parts.
- » Study movements 3, 6, 13, and 14 from *All-Night Vigil* by Sergei Rachmaninov and take note of when Rachmaninov moves from undivided to divided parts.
- » Study the BWV 225, 226, 228, and 229 and see how Bach works in the double choir voicing.
- » Study *Path of Miracles* by Joby Talbot and take note of how Talbot makes use of solo voices.

Suggested Listening

"Gleams of a Remoter World" - Judith Bingham
"Water Lilies" - Judith Bingham
"Os justi" - Anton Bruckner
In the Beginning - Aaron Copland
"Legend of the Walled-In Woman" - Ēriks Ešenvalds
"O Know to End, as to Begin" from *The Hourglass Suite* - Irving Fine
Requiem - Herbert Howells
Requiem - Györgi Ligeti
"Nunc dimittis" - Paweł Łukaszewski
"Màiri" - James MacMillan
"O bone Jesu" - James MacMillan
"Jauchzet dem Herrn, alle Welt" - Felix Mendelssohn
Sechs Sprüche, op. 79 - Felix Mendelssohn
"Nunc dimittis" - Arvo Pärt
All-Night Vigil - Sergei Rachmaninov
Three New Motets "in memoriam Thomas Tallis" - Steven Stucky
Path of Miracles - Joby Talbot
Spem in alium - Thomas Tallis
"When David Heard" - Eric Whitacre
"How They So Softly Rest" - Healy Willan

Part II

Chapter 11

Principles of Voicing and Balance

Without craftsmanship, inspiration is a mere reed shaken in the wind.
— Johannes Brahms

For my undergraduate education, I decided to major in sound recording technology, which was considered a music degree at my university. Besides learning music theory, history, an instrument, and participating in ensembles, I was privileged to learned about the art of recording. The principles I learned in recording translated extraordinarily well when I started learning to rehearse and compose for choirs.

One of the most important lessons I learned during our discussions about mixing theory was to think about your soundscape in three dimensions or on a physical stage. In this theory, controlling the volume of a track through the faders was the equivalent of bringing the sound to the foreground of the stage or putting it into the background. Controlling the panning of the track into the left or right speaker through the pan knob was the equivalent of putting a sound to the left, right, or center of the stage. The prevailing spectral frequencies of a track were the equivalent of the sound's placement in the loft of the stage: for example a low, medium, or high-pitched sound. The spectral frequencies could be tapered or accentuated to better fill the loft through the equalizer.

All this was to teach us that when you wanted to bring attention to a specific track—or a specific part of a track—you had to carve out a space in your mix for it. If you had a main vocal track singing with instrumental

Principles of Voicing and Balance

accompaniment, the conventional mixing method is to put the vocal track in the foreground of the mix, panned into the middle of the mix, and then fade, pan, and equalize the supporting instruments to avoid the space that the voice is in. In other words, leave a space where the voice is meant to be. There can be some overlap in the mix but sounds occupying the same space can create an overly opaque, dense, and otherwise unintelligible aural image. The same principles can apply to choral music: there needs to be a space created for each part, division, instrument, and solo in your composition.

Voice Strength and Balance

One aspect that is critical to idiomatic vocal writing is understanding how each voice balances with the others. As discussed in Chapters 4 through 8, different voices will exhibit different characteristics and different levels of strength in different registers. Understanding how these vocal characteristics interact with one another takes a lifetime of study and analysis. The voice isn't evenly strong throughout its range and as discussed previously, no voice part is equally strong in the equivalent places nor equally strong in analog to each other. Consider the motet "O Magnum Mysterium" by Hyo-Won Woo. Here she gives four declamatory statements of the word "jacentem." Each of them is voiced in slightly different ways and with voices in different registers with different strengths. Each of them is balanced, but will sound and resonate slightly differently to each other.

Example 11.1: Hyo-Won Woo, "O Magnum Mysterium."

© 2016 Walton Music Corp. All rights reserved.

Learning how these voices balance in relation to each other's strengths is a journey that cannot have a shortcut. Very often I will see composers or arrangers writing one or more voices in weak parts of their ranges and complaining that they are underbalanced in performance or they are in strong parts of their voices and are overbalanced.

There are some cases where imbalance is desired to bring out one voice over the others, but for almost all other instances, balance is the baseline. No matter the proportion, anytime the voices are taken out of balance should be intentional. Voice crossing will certainly compromise balance. There are times when it is warranted and even desired, but it's most advisable to keep those to moments rather than as a point of departure. More on voice crossing later.

Having a chord that is very spread out may sound great on a piano or in an instrumental ensemble but can be tricky to balance with vocal groups. It's tempting to put high voice into the stratosphere and basses into the deepest depths, but unless you have ideal conditions, the bass section is much less likely to be heard. Sopranos will almost always overbalance when up high if the other voices are too low. Sopranos above an E5 will almost never be softer than a mezzo forte (mezzo piano if you've got some really skilled singers). This imbalance can be mitigated somewhat by dividing the sopranos or having the upper voices at a softer dynamic, but there are still limits to how soft you can make the upper voices. Basses below a G2 will almost never be louder than a mezzo piano or a mezzo forte with some very trained voices.

One last word about chord balance: it's important to learn what works well and what doesn't as far as balance is concerned. It's also important to learn the difference between what is inherently balanced, what isn't but can be balanced later in rehearsal, and what is not able to be balanced within reason.

Chord Voicing Examples

Before diving into specifics of chord voicing, some basics of chord voicing as well as some defined terminology should be established. In most principles of common practice period writing, the upper voices of sopranos, altos, and tenors should not be further than an octave apart from each other. Basses, however, regularly can exceed an octave from the upper voices.

Additionally, the upper voices are sometimes categorized into "closed" and "open" spacing. In closed spacing, the upper voices are within a third or a fourth of each other and are within the space of an octave between the

Principles of Voicing and Balance

soprano and tenor (provided you have no voice crossing from the altos). In open spacing, the upper voices are within a fifth or sixth of each other and just larger than an octave between the soprano and tenor.

We could look at every chord in every key under the sun, but many similar chords would share the same descriptions as the ones listed here. Some slight variations may come up, but we will avoid unnecessary repetition. With that said, here are a few examples of voicing certain chords and how they will balance.

Four Parts in Closed Voicing

For this example, we will consider these chords in various voicing of C major.

This example will work in softer dynamic levels, perhaps mezzo piano and below. As most voices are in their lower registers, they will balance well with each other. The basses would be the exception being in their middle to middle-low part of their voices, which is more generous. However, even with basses in a more generous part of their voice, it will not overbalance with the other voices in softer dynamics. Because the upper voices are all in their lower register, the sound may come across as a little unfocused and perhaps even a bit aspirate. Louder dynamics won't be nearly as successful or balanced and with certain ensembles not possible. Having the soprano doubling the root with the bass will create a lovely color.

This example will work at many different dynamic levels—including mezzo forte—but especially on the softer side. The tenors and basses are both in medium low parts of their voices, and while not the most generous parts of their ranges, they are both in comfortable registers. The sopranos and altos are both in lower to middle-lower registers and will have less volume and power compared to the tenors and basses. Despite this slight discrepancy, balance will not be difficult from mezzo-forte and lower.

This voicing, like the previous, will also work well at many dynamic levels—including mezzo forte. The same discrepancy returns here but this time the tenors are in a stronger part of their voice compared to the others. Even still, this can balance well enough as the tenors are able to sing in this register at softer dynamics and thus able to balance with the other parts. Additionally, having the tenors in this stronger part of the voice can help brighten and lighten the sound slightly.

With the sopranos and altos in the middle to middle-high parts of their voices, they can balance very well with the tenors, now in a very strong part of their voices. In many ways, this voicing provides the most flexibility in dynamics and color. In softer dynamics, all voices can balance beautifully with each other, including the tenors in their head tone. At louder dynamics, this chord voicing will have a bright, ringing quality driven especially by the tenors.

At this point, however, is where you may start to hear the basses losing the ability to balance at louder dynamics. As other voices are in more generous and stronger parts of their voices, the basses remain in their middle-low register and will hit a wall in how much sound they can reasonable produce at louder dynamics. It can still be a sizable amount of sound, but it will not balance as well in very loud dynamics. This voicing will be possible at most dynamics.

This chord is possible at many dynamics, but especially louder ones. With all the upper voices in their stronger, more generous registers, this voice can have a bright, clear quality. Very soft dynamics will be less successful for the tenors and, in less-trained choirs, the altos as well. Professional and well-trained singers can make it work, but it's still a big ask.

As in the previous example, the basses will be less and less capable of balancing with the upper voices at higher dynamics—especially at fortissimo. In this chord, that loudness barrier is even more pronounced. Having the basses sing up an octave will balance much better.

This chord voicing will not work at any dynamics, and not just because the tenors are in an obscenely high part of their voices. The bass will be present but very much unbalanced in louder dynamics. The sopranos and altos in thirds here in their higher ranges can sound exquisitely beautiful but for less-trained voices it can be a reach, especially at softer dynamics.

Overall, this chord would be more successful if the tenors moved to the high G instead of the C, and the basses sang an octave higher. Doing so would take the upper voices out of closed voicing, but it would balance better and maintain recommended doubling.

Four Parts in Open Voicing

For this example, we will consider these C major chords in open voicing.

This example is similar to the second example in the closed voicing section in terms of balance. The timbre will change slightly by having the sopranos higher and tenors lower. This voicing will work well at softer dynamics, especially mezzo piano and lower. Each of the lower three voices are in low to medium-low parts of their ranges and will create a rich, warm sound. Having the tenors and basses in thirds in this somewhat lower register will lend a warm, rich, resonant quality. The sopranos will add just enough brightness to the overall color.

This chord voicing will balance well at almost every dynamic, except perhaps very loud dynamics. The sopranos are just starting to enter a stronger part of their voice and may over-balance at very loud dynamics. Otherwise, this chord will balance well. The basses and tenors being in fifths will provide an especially solid foundation and strong overtones.

This chord will balance well at many dynamics, even softer ones. Louder dynamics will also balance well, as the alto is just beginning to enter a stronger part of their voice where they can match the tenors and sopranos better. As discussed in previous examples of closed voicing, at this point the limitations of the basses to keep up with volume at louder dynamics will begin to become apparent in this chord. Having the basses singing up an octave will help them match in balance at louder dynamics if desired and having them double with tenors in unison will yield an especially vibrant, exciting sound. Having the bass up the octave at softer dynamics may not yield desired results.

This chord will balance fairly well at louder dynamics. The upper voices are all in higher parts of their voices and are able to lean into a broad, vibrant sound. The one concern with this particular voicing is that the sopranos may have a tendency to over-balance the rest of the ensemble. It's not inherently unbalanced, but it will be trickier for amateur or less-trained ensembles to execute. The basses will have the same issue as in the previous example, but more pronounced here. Again, their sound will be present but perhaps more felt than heard at louder dynamics. Having them sing an octave higher will absolutely balance at louder dynamics and yield a more robust sound from the whole ensemble.

Principles of Voicing and Balance

In Eight Parts

Voicing in eight parts sounds easier than it actually is. In some ways, having eight parts can prove somewhat unwieldy at times.

This chord will balance relatively decently in a small number of dynamics, mostly piano to mezzo forte. The basses and baritones here will be the limiting factor to balance at very loud dynamics. Forte and fortissimo will most likely yield less desirable results. Writing the basses and baritones in fifths is the bread and butter of this section for eight-part voicings. These fifths, especially in this register provides a solid foundation and a great deal of depth and richness.

The tenors are both in decently strong and flexible parts of their voices; The altos are also in generous and flexible parts of their voices. The sopranos are in generous and very strong parts of their voices and will be the limiting factor for balancing in very soft dynamics, but piano is reasonable for most semi-professional ensembles. Very well-trained ensembles may be able to balance decently well at pianissimo, but again that's asking a great deal from the first sopranos and may not be reasonable in all cases. At other dynamics it will be relatively easy to balance because the other voices are in more flexible parts of their voices and can balance well against the sopranos (with the exception of the second basses and the baritones to some degree).

Other Notable Examples

This particular example is quite successful in a number of applications, but especially in louder dynamics with brighter, more vibrant timbres. The tenors are in a very generous part of the voice and will be able to put out a great deal of sound and in a robust character. Having the tenors in this register with the root of the chord is a great boon.

The altos, while not in the strongest parts of their voices, will still be able to balance well with the tenors, albeit with a slightly less bright timbre. This disparity will actually be helpful to not overbalance the third of the chord.

The sopranos are also not in the most generous parts of their voices but are just on the cusp. They will also be able to balance well with both the altos and the tenors. It may seem like the tenors will overbalance the other voices, but in my experience that has not been the case; the tenors can ease up slightly if necessary.

The basses will probably have the most restrictive limit in this particular register. However, the amount of sound they can put out in this register before it gets shouty will be sufficient to help balance. This chord won't have the highest number of decibels, but it will be very vibrant and bright.

This example has all voices in very strong, very bright parts of the voices. It has the potential to deliver some of the highest decibels of loudness. Other keys (particularly D flat, C major, and B major) will be able to produce similar results but with a few minor differences. This chord will be most successful at higher dynamics, although I have also seen this chord used with a forte-piano and then a crescendo with great success. It would not be wise to have singers float this particular chord at a piano dynamic.

The divisions shown—with sopranos and tenors dividing—is the most preferable in this particular voicing. While some first altos and baritones may be able to sing an F sharp, the success rate for the entire section can be shaky even in professional groups, let alone less-trained ensembles.

This example has all the voices in low to very low parts of the voice. In these registers, the chord will have a warmer, richer character. The basses and baritones in fourths here particularly will add a lovely depth without obscuring or muddying the aural image. There may become a bit of an issue with having the third in both the undivided soprano and tenor sections; however, having both these voices in lower parts of their registers will help temper the third. The altos and basses being divided won't weaken their power comparatively as they are both in somewhat more characteristic parts of their registers.

Principles of Voicing and Balance

Problems with Chord Voicing

It is beneficial to point out at least one example of problematic voicing, so here is one example and why.

This chord has a number of issues—besides that it has too many thirds, which makes it difficult to balance. In theory, this chord should be able to balance well enough at softer dynamics, but it's a big challenge even for accomplished ensembles. The first major issue is that the second basses are in a very low part of their voice and a range that can easily be covered at most dynamics. The other part is that the first sopranos are too high compared to the tenors and basses. Sopranos, even trained ones, may struggle to sing this at a soft enough dynamic to not overbalance the rest of the ensemble. Dividing the soprano part helps, but it will still tend to overbalance. To compensate, most conductors will ask the basses to sing a dynamic or two louder than the other parts, which may or may not be possible depending on how many low basses comprise the section. If you have a robust enough section of low basses, that solution would help if the other parts are singing at piano or mezzo piano, but this option isn't as feasible at louder dynamics.

Additionally, the tenors are in a lower part of their voice, which has a limited amount of power. If the dynamics aren't too loud, it may not matter as much. The larger matter is that the first tenor is an octave away from the second altos. While this is still permissible in many part-writing guidelines, it's still a large gap between two chords of significant density. This may present some additional tuning issues, compounding the balance issues as the lower voices are all in lower registers with less power and direction in their sound, and the sopranos and altos are in higher, brighter, stronger parts of their voice. This voicing is great if sopranos and altos are singing on their own or if tenors and basses are singing on their own, but together, it's more challenging.

This chord works on a piano, but less so in choral forces. It's not impossible, and there are some changes that could be made to mitigate some of these challenges, but this example isn't likely to set up most choral ensembles for success.

Chord Spacing

The voicing of chords has been known to reflect the harmonic series in Pythagorean Tuning. The fundamental pitch is given a certain pitch, and the first harmonic is an octave above that fundamental pitch. The second harmonic is a fifth above that first harmonic and the third is a fourth above that and two octaves above the fundamental. The fourth harmonic is a major third higher, the fifth a minor third higher, and so on.

I had a theory professor postulate that the harmonic series should infer to us how to voice chords properly: more space and sonic distance between the lower voices and closer voicing in the upper voices. There is a great deal of wisdom in that maxim, especially when considering balanced chord voicing as a point of departure.

Very often, chord spacing has reflected this in either open spacing or closed spacing, with basses being written an octave or further away from the upper voices, while having the upper voices in general no more than an octave away from each other. This conventional spacing has proven itself time and time again to be effective for tuning and a generally pleasing aesthetic.

Notable Exceptions

Departing from this principle can yield certain effects that can be quite desirable. In Gabriel Fauré's setting of the requiem, several of the movements have the choir cadence to a slightly unusual voicing where the sopranos and altos are in thirds—or even in unison—and the tenors and basses in closed-voicing, four-part divisions. While counterintuitive to the spacing we see in the harmonic series, the voicing lends a lot of warmth and richness to these cadences.

Example 11.2: Gabriel Fauré, *Requiem*, "In Paradisum."

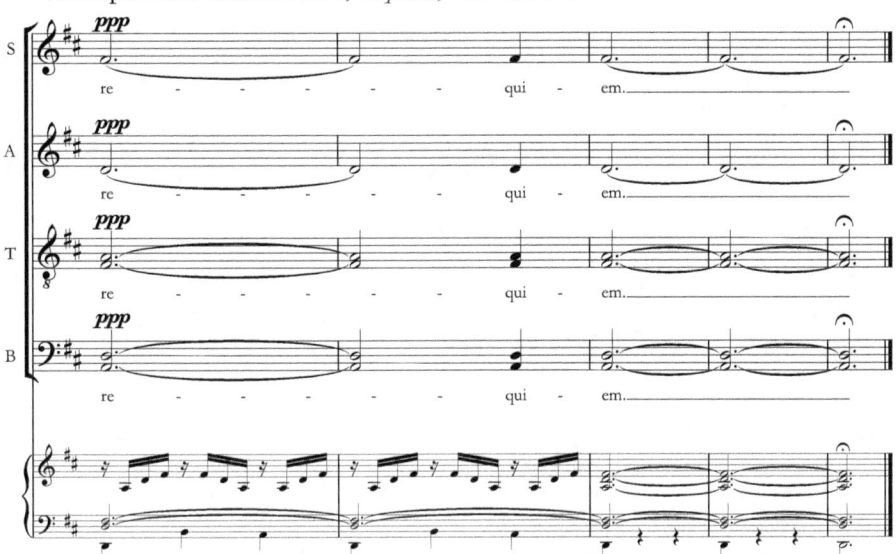

Indeed, having close voicing in the lower parts—even in relatively low registers—is noticeably more effective in the voice than it would be with certain instruments, especially if the lower voices are singing at a mezzo forte dynamic or softer. Of course, this does not mean that all your voice spacing needs to be as Fauré has written here. This decision is one of many perfectly acceptable choices a composer or arranger can make.

Another exception can be found at the end of Britten's part song "I lov'd a lass," in which he writes the sopranos and altos fairly high and the tenors and basses quite low, separating the tenors and altos by over two octaves. This huge gap between the two halves of the choir creates a peculiar aesthetic with such a large empty sonic space between and comes off a bit unbalanced. This particular voicing is meant to help emphasize the theme of alienation found in the text of this work.

Example 11.3: Benjamin Britten, "I lov'd a lass."

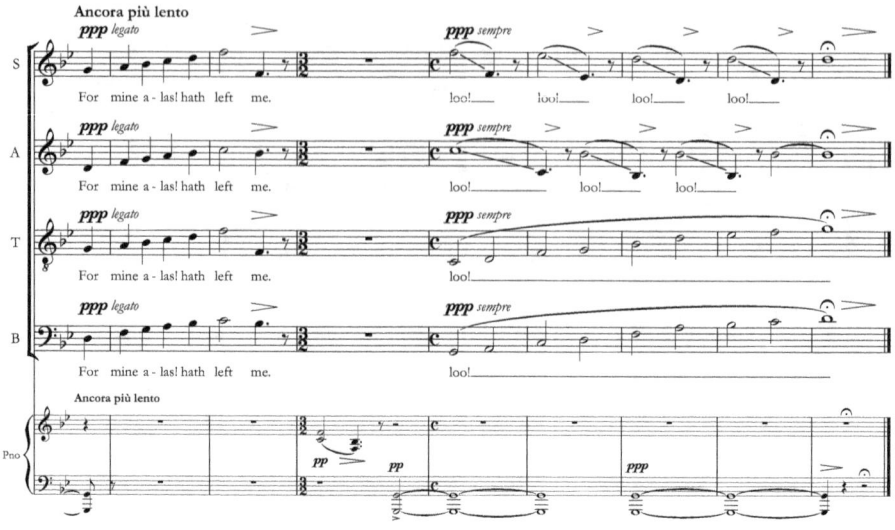

© 1934 Boosey & Co. Ltd. Reproduced by permission of Boosey & Hawkes.

Vibrato and Spacing

Vibrato can affect the way an audience hears and perceives different voice spacing and harmonies. For example, when an ensemble sings with a significant amount of vibrato, choral textures involving unison or octave doublings, as well as dyadic and triadic harmonies, are easier to perceive. But as harmonies become more secundal, and tone clusters and extended harmonies are involved, vibrato can obscure the harmonies. Many choral artists are aware of this perception and will tend to minimize vibrato during these closer, denser textures as they are able.

As a composer or arranger, this is something to be aware of in case you chose to write denser textures in high registers of the voice or at extremely loud dynamics. Remember that when singing in these high registers or at extremely loud dynamics it is somewhat easier and healthier for many singers to sing with vibrato. Writing those textures in those registers and at those dynamics may create an unnecessary, and frustrating point of conflict for the choral musicians. It may not be impossible to execute on its own, however, context can change how viable that request is.

Vowel Balance

In addition to register, another major factor in balance is vowel sounds. Certain vowels will inherently sound louder and brighter compared to others and will inherently stand out from the texture. The difference between vowel sounds will have a very pronounced effect on balance in the choral texture.

In the vowel chart, the vowels that resonate towards the front of the oropharynx have higher frequencies and stronger overtones and will be perceived as brighter and more present, compared to the vowels that resonate towards the back of the oropharynx. [i, ɪ, e, ɛ, and a] will all be perceived as brighter and more present while [ɑ, ɔ, o, and u] will all be perceived as darker and softer.

Knowing about the perceived brightness and darkness of each vowel can be especially helpful if you need certain voices to drop into the background and allow something else to stand out by contrast. This makes sense when one encounters an arrangement with a soloist and the remaining choral forces singing on [u], [o], or just humming. It allows a leading part or a soloist the ability to stand out without having to push their voice.

Anecdotally, I have heard at least one editor at a major publishing house for choral works say that they almost immediately pass on choral compositions or arrangements that feature sections with "oos or ahhs" supporting a solo line or leading section. Yes, it's been done a lot in the past, even overdone, but to me, hearing a composer or arranger saying they won't use "oos and ahhs" in their writing is like hearing a painter say they won't use the color purple anymore. It's been done a lot because it's very effective, and if it helps the work be more effective, one should feel free to use it. Why preclude yourself from using any colors at your disposal? Feel free to use it when you feel it is called for.

Other Chord Voicing Considerations

Adding non-harmonic pitches into major or minor triads should be treated similarly to thirds in terms of doubling and voicing. The root and the fifth should be doubled first before the third, and the non-harmonic pitches should be last. Additionally, with choral considerations, those extra non-harmonic pitches don't necessarily need to be in prominent or generous parts of the voices to be heard and appreciated. Consider the beginning of Lauridsen's "Lament for Pasiphaë" from *Mid-Winter Songs*, in which Lauridsen writes an E♭ major chord and adds an A♭ in the alto. The sopranos, tenors, and basses are all in very strong parts of their voices and can put out a great deal of sound on the pitches in the E♭ major chord. The altos, however, are not in an equally strong part of their voices. This combination of putting the non-harmonic pitch in one voice—and in a comparatively less strong part of the voice—is what helps balance this chord.

Example 11.4: Morten Lauridsen, *Mid-Winter Songs*, "Lament for Pasiphaë."

Copyright © Opus Music Publishers, Clermont, FL. Used by permission.

Lauridsen does the same in the first movement of *Madrigali*, "Ov'è, Lass', Il Bel Viso?" In the first B♭ minor chord, Lauridsen has the sopranos, altos, and basses all singing pitches from this triad but writes a C♮ in the tenors. While in this case the tenors can still put out a good amount of sound in this register, it's still not in the strongest part of the voice and is slightly tempered. This helps to balance this chord between harmonic and non-harmonic pitches.

Example 11.5: Morten Lauridsen, *Madrigali*, "Ov'è, Lass', Il Bel Viso?"

Copyright © 1987 by Southern Music Pub Co., Inc. Used by permission. All Rights Reserved.

Voice Crossing

While general voicing of the choral ensemble is pretty standard, with sopranos above altos above tenors and basses at the foundation, there are circumstances when you may want to have voices crossing for a specific color effect, in much the same way that you may want violas to play a melody above the pitches of the violins or have the clarinets play a higher pitch than oboes in certain chords.

One example of effective voice crossing can be found in Howard Hanson's "Prayer of the Middle Ages," when the altos briefly take over the melody for two measures while the sopranos sing a supporting line below the altos. The use of the altos rich, round sound in a higher, stronger part of their voices creates a beautiful timbre change.

Example 11.6: Howard Hanson, "Prayer of the Middle Ages."

Copyright © 1976 by Carl Fischer, Inc. Published by earthsongs. Used by permission.

Other examples of effective voice crossing can be found in the choral works of Francis Poulenc, who will often cross voices if the harmonies would otherwise call for static vocal parts. In the second movement of *Un soir de neige*, Poulenc writes a passage where the second soprano, altos, and tenors cross voices throughout, while the first sopranos sing above it all and the first and second basses below. The melodic lines of each of these inner parts doesn't really make sense as melodies and the harmonies remain relatively static, but because of these voice crossings, certain timbral shifts occur when one voices pops out of the texture only to be folded back into the very next beat. These timbral shifts caused by this voice crossing—especially at this soft dynamic—creates a somewhat shimmering or glittery effect that comes up throughout Poulenc's choral music. It also helps gives each voice movement and activity in a passage that otherwise would be uniform.

Example 11.7: Francis Poulenc, *Un soir de neige*, "La bonne neige."

Published by Editions Salabert. International Copyright Secured. All Rights Reserved. Reprinted by permission of Hal Leonard Europe.

While voice crossing is generally acceptable, this practice is best done sparingly or in limited instances for a special effect. Using this as a point of departure—for example, having the tenors' part consistently above the altos for the duration of the work—is less effective and yields a result that is often less desirable. This is before mentioning how this practice can be a challenge for amateur singers to pull off convincingly.

Unison Doublings

Unison doublings can amalgamate the timbre of two sections beautifully into each other. The characteristics and qualities of both sections are present and complement one another in a very charming way. However, the effect of unison doubling is largely for the voices that are adjacent to each other, for example altos being doubled with either sopranos or tenors.

Sopranos and Altos Doubled

This unison doubling is very effective. It has a way of beautifully amalgamating the brightness of the sopranos and depth of the altos. It creates a rich, almost creamy sound.

As a side note, I know that some directors in charge of preparing choirs for performances with orchestras will re-voice the scoring whenever there's a soprano or alto part singing on its own. In other words, if a composer has written a soprano line alone, some conductors will add altos to it, or vice versa, in an effort to have more sound and presence over an orchestra. More on that in Chapter 13.

Example 11.8: René Clausen, "Ubi Caritas."

Copyright © 2000 by Fostco Music Press, a div. of Shawnee Press, Inc. International Copyright Secured. All Rights Reserved.

Tenors and Basses Doubled

This doubling is also very effective. Similar to the sopranos and altos doubling, the tenors and basses combine into a beautifully balanced sound that is both clear and rich.

As mentioned previously, conductors may double sopranos and altos when preparing a choir to perform with an orchestra; some conductors will do the same with the tenors and basses. Again, more in Chapter 13.

Example 11.9: Maurice Duruflé, *Requiem*, "Introit."

Published by Editions Durand. International Copyright Secured. All Rights Reserved. Reprinted by permission of Hal Leonard Europe.

Altos and Tenors Doubled

This doubling can be very effective, especially if you have a tenor part going quite high. It can temper a brassy tenor sound with a more round, rich alto sound. It also uses one of the strongest parts of the tenor voice, as well as a generous part of the alto voice. It's not for constant use as it often has the tenors in a higher part of their voices for long periods of time.

Example 11.10: Francis Poulenc, *Gloria*, "Qui sedes ad dexteram Patris."

Published by Editions Salabert. International Copyright Secured. All Rights Reserved. Reprinted by permission of Hal Leonard Europe.

All Voices Doubled

There are a few moments when having all voices in unison on the same pitch can produce a very unusual but effective result. While it is possible to achieve that amalgamated sound between all the voices, it really only works for a handful of pitches (the ones surrounding middle C) and at softer dynamics (piano and softer). In a well-balanced, well-rehearsed choir it can create an unusually uniform tone in which every section can simultaneously be identified but also sound beautifully blended with the others.

One example can be found in the first and last movement of Dominick Argento's cantata, *I Hate and I Love*. Argento has every voice doubled on the middle C.

Example 11.11: Dominick Argento, *I Hate and I Love*, "1. I Hate and I Love."

© 1981 Boosey & Hawkes. Reproduced by permission of Boosey & Hawkes.

Another great example of this doubling can be found in an arrangement of the Christmas carol "In the Bleak Midwinter" by Abbie Betinis. At the end of the work, she has all the voices meet together on the B3.

Octave Doublings

Octave doublings don't amalgamate the sound of two sections the way that unison doubling does. Rather, it tends to accentuate certain characteristics of each section, which in many ways can be quite desirable.

Soprano and Altos in Octaves

This octave doubling can be very effective, creating a haunting quality. It emphasizes a fluty, floating quality in the sopranos, and a smoky, mysterious quality in the altos. If your soprano section already sounds somewhat thin, breathy, or brittle, it will unfortunately accentuate that trait.

Principles of Voicing and Balance

Example 11.12: Jean Langlais, *Messe Solennelle*, "Benedictus."

© Éditions Musicales de la Schola Cantorum, www.schola-edition.com.

Sopranos and Tenors in Octaves

This doubling can be highly effective. It emphasizes the brightness and piercing effect of both voices at loud dynamics while also emphasizing the floating quality that each voice can embody at softer dynamics.

Example 11.13: Sergei Rachmaninoff, *All-Night Vigil*, "Bogoroditse Devo."

Sopranos and Basses in Octaves

This doubling can be effective, but it very much depends on the octave used. One octave can be effective, provided that neither voice is in an uncomfortable range.

Example 11.14: Joby Talbot, *Path of Miracles*, "Burgos."

Copyright © 2005 Chester Music Limited International. Copyright Secured. All Rights Reserved.

Two octaves can be especially effective by emphasizing distance and loftiness between the voices. It can almost make the sopranos sound like they are singing higher than they actually are. It can also create an effect of exposure and loneliness but can have the soprano come off a bit mousy if used too extensively. One brief but effective example comes from "Cedit, hyems" by Abbie Betinis, which has the sopranos and basses doubling two octaves apart and the altos and tenors harmonizing in imitation.

Example 11.15: Abbie Betinis, "Cedit, Hyems."

Copyright © 2007 by G. Schirmer, Inc. International Copyright Secured. All Rights Reserved. Used by permission.

Another example of two octave doubling comes from the motet "O vera digna hostia" by Tarik O'Regan.

Example 11.16: Tarik O'Regan, "O vera digna hostia."

Copyright © 2003 Novello & Co. Ltd. International Copyright Secured. All Rights Reserved,

Most examples in literature of these voices doubling two octaves apart from each other almost always included a voice in the middle octave—whether a tenor, alto, or second soprano voice. This specific doubling is covered later in this chapter.

Altos and Tenors in Octaves

This doubling is not bad, but not ideal, either. Better to use other voices for octave doublings and save altos and tenors for unison doubling.

Altos and Basses in Octaves

This doubling can be highly effective. It emphasizes the rich and resplendent boldness of both voices, although it can come off as a bit too dark and possibly a bit dull compared to sopranos and tenors in octaves.

Example 11.17: Francis Poulenc, *Gloria*, "Qui sedes ad dexteram patris."

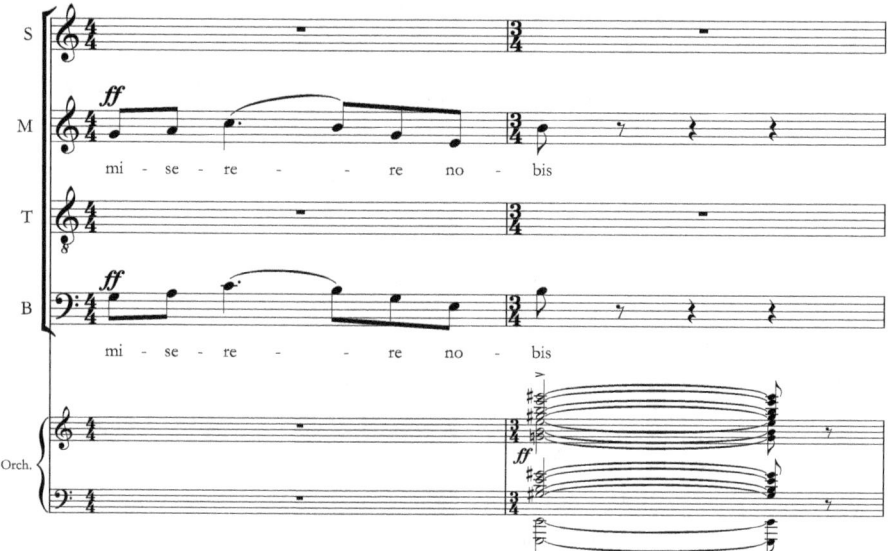

Published by Editions Salabert. International Copyright Secured. All Rights Reserved. Reprinted by permission of Hal Leonard Europe.

Tenors and Basses in Octaves

This doubling can be very effective, emphasizing the bright brassiness of the tenors, and the robust sound of the basses. But again, it can also accentuate some negative aspects of each section including accentuating excessive *squillo* in the tenors and gruffness in the basses.

Principles of Voicing and Balance 179

Example 11.18: Sergei Rachmaninoff, *All-Night Vigil*, "Voskreseniye Khristovo videvshe."

Sopranos/Altos and Tenors/Basses in Octaves

This octave doubling is very effective. It's very standard in choral music, especially when presenting or emphasizing a melody. It presents both the amalgamated soprano and alto sound and the combined tenor and bass sound in strong parts of most of these voices. Even when there are moments where it might be too low for the sopranos and tenors or too high for the altos and basses, the combination of these voices together helps make up the shortcomings of the other parts. It will, however, limit the range of a given melody one can reasonably present. Examples of this doubling can be found in numerous pieces, especially folk song or hymn arrangements.

Example 11.19: Mack Wilberg, "Arise, O God, and Shine"/"Rejoice the Lord is King."

© Oxford University Press Inc. 2002. Assigned to Oxford University Press 2010. All rights reserved.

Three Octave Doubling

This doubling is like soprano and bass octave doubling but with the inner voices filled. Does it ruin the effect of the sopranos and basses in octave doublings? Perhaps, but if you're using this doubling device, it's probably because the passage is a louder dynamic and not because you're looking for that same effect.

An example can be found in the climax of Gabriel Jackson's setting of "O Sacrum Convivium." Here, the top soprano part is doubled with the first altos and the basses in two parts of two adjacent phrases.

Example 11.20: Gabriel Jackson, "O Sacrum Convivium."

© Oxford University Press 2003. All rights reserved.

Divided Parts in Octaves

Having a divided part in octaves sounds reasonable enough and may work well enough in a very sparse texture, but more often it yields a less desirable result. The one exception to this would be baritones and basses, especially when the low basses are singing in a range that is too low for most baritones.

An example of this can be found briefly in Poulenc's cantata *Un Soir de Neige*, when the baritones and basses sing the melody in octaves.

Principles of Voicing and Balance

Example 11.21: Francis Poulenc, *Un Soir de Neige*, "Bois meurtri, bois perdu."

[Musical score excerpt for SI, SII, A, T, Bar., B voices with text "Un grand moment noyés" and "Un grand moment d'eau froide a saisi les noyés"]

Published by Editions Salabert. International Copyright Secured. All Rights Reserved. Reprinted by permission of Hal Leonard Europe.

"Wade in de Water" by Allen Koepke is another example where it is used very effectively to help anchor the arrangement's conclusion just before the final cadence.

Example 11.22: Allen Koepke, "Wade in de Water."

© 1998 Santa Barbara Music Press. Used by permission.

182 The Technique of Choral Writing

Continuing Study

Suggested Exercises

Short
- » Briefly discuss how voice strength in different parts of a singer's range affects balanced chords.
- » Discuss why the harmonic series is relevant to principles of chord spacing.
- » Discuss how vowels will affect a choir's ability to balance in a chord.
- » Discuss the pros and cons of the different types of unison and octave doublings discussed in this chapter.

Long
- » Using one of the following short melodies (or another of your choosing) complete the following harmonization exercises:
  - Start from unison and move to four-part harmony.
  - Start with four-part harmony and move to two-parts.
  - Start with unison octaves and move to eight parts at some point in the example.

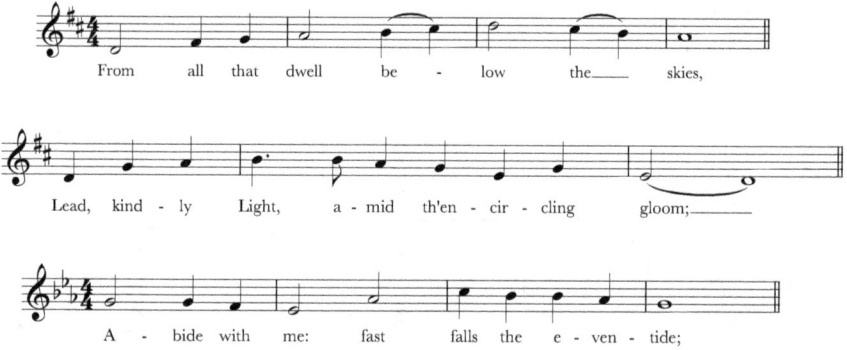

- » Find a melody or song that you enjoy and see whether it has already been arranged for choral ensembles. If it has, compare them to each other and see which ones you enjoy the most and why. If it hasn't, consider using it for an arrangement yourself.

Suggested Listening

Fest und Gedenksprüche, Op. 109 - Johannes Brahms
"Sing Ye Praises" from *Four Motets* by Aaron Copland
"Salus Aeterna" - Gabriel Jackson

Madrigali - Morten Lauridsen
Mid-Winter Songs - Morten Lauridsen
"O bone Jesu" - James MacMillan
Kanon Pokajanen - Arvo Pärt
"Nunc dimittis" - Arvo Pärt
"The Woman with the Alabaster Box" - Arvo Pärt
Messe en Sol Majeur - Francis Poulenc
Un Soir de Neige - Francis Poulenc
All-night Vigil - Sergei Rachmaninov
3 Geistliche Gesänge - Josef Rheinberger
Path of Miracles - Joby Talbot
Mass in G - Ralph Vaughan Williams
"O Magnum Mysterium" - Hyo-Won Woo

Chapter 12

Choral Textures

> *I am more and more convinced that music, by its very nature,*
> *is something that cannot be poured into a tight and traditional form.*
> *It is made up of colors and rhythm.*
> — Claude Debussy

After considering chord voicing as vertical moments, let's now consider choral texture or the horizontal, linear fabric of sound and how it relates specially to choral music. When discussing texture, we are referring to the different layers of activity and how they relate to one another. American composer and educator George Frederick McKay discusses some of these textures in his book *Creative Orchestration*, which this chapter will rely upon for discussion.[1] These layers are, of course, found in music of all genres and ensemble arrangements. The purpose of this chapter is not to discuss at length the textures themselves, but how they work in choral music and issues to consider, as well as examples of said textures from the choral canon.

In my experience, beginning students of composition have a somewhat limited perspective on the textures used for vocal music. Most often, I see students playing it safe and limiting themselves to harmony-focused textures like chordal or choral textures. Additionally, I see many writing for all available voices for most of the composition or arrangement.

---

[1] George Frederick McKay, *Creative Orchestration: A Project Method for Classes in Orchestration and Instrumentation* (Boston: Allyn and Bacon, 1969), 106.

I have sometimes heard of teachers inviting their students to learn orchestral composition by thinking of different sections of the orchestra as "choirs." This invitation involves thinking of the woodwinds as their own "choir," and the brass and strings as their own respective "choirs." While this paradigm can be helpful for beginning students, it can put them into the wrong mindset when they actually start composing choral music. Choirs are sometimes thought of as a section removed from a larger ensemble rather than as a whole ensemble of its own. This perspective might be one of the reasons why I've heard some composers and arrangers feel that writing for choirs is inherently limiting. We must approach the choral ensemble as already whole.

As discussed previously in Chapter 11 regarding choral voicing as it relates to sound mixing, we should, again, consider thinking about choral writing as if it were along three axes: what is in the foreground versus what is in the background; what—if any—spatial considerations can be made for possible antiphonal responses; and what are we considering with register and sounds of high frequency versus sounds of low frequency. Considering choral textures with these concepts can help us better understand how to creat more translucency or opacity depending on what the work requires.

In this chapter, we will consider density of texture, various musical textures with examples from the choral canon, how they are realized specifically in choral music, and how they can be devised or channeled in the choral idiom.

How Much Is Too Much?

When writing for choral ensembles it is very tempting, especially for beginning student composers and arrangers, to write for every voice, all the time. This tendency happens for two reasons: first, in the standard choral voicing there are only four voices, which can feel inherently limiting. Second, in their first few semesters of theory and composition, very often students will constantly compose four-part chorale exercises, and use J.S. Bach's chorales as examples and models.[2] But just as it's important to understand how to fill spaces of silence, it's also important to know when to leave those spaces silent.

When I was an undergraduate student still learning how to compose and write for choirs, I took a new composition to one of my theory professors. One of his (many) criticisms was that I composed for all the voices available

---

2   I don't write this to demean at all or to take away from the valuable lessons that can be found in writing these exercises or in the models found in Bach's chorales. There are very important lessons to be learned from that body of work. However, most compositions arguably will depart from a four-part chorale and it's important to look to other models as well.

too much of the time and that I should pull back and reserve writing for all the voices at the same time for special moments. He was mostly coming from an orchestral background where it's a bit easier to accomplish, but he told me to look at compositions by Josquin des Prez as my model, specifically Josquin's motet "Ave Maria virgo serena." The whole ensemble sings throughout but is only singing simultaneously for a minority of the time. In true Josquin fashion, canon is a major feature and opens this particular composition.

Example 12.1: Josquin des Prez, "Ave Maria Virgo Serena."

It's important to give your singers and your audience a break from certain sections from time to time to help create interest through contrast, to help with a singer's stamina, and to help the audience appreciate that timbre even more when it returns. Just as you don't have every instrument in a specific section playing all the time, one doesn't need to have every voice singing simultaneously through the work.

Even in William Byrd's *Mass for Three Voices*—specifically in the "Agnus Dei" movement—the composer doesn't have every voice singing at the same time. Not only has Byrd limited himself to three voices, but also there are moments in the last movement when he composes for only two voices to sing simultaneously. It's a masterpiece of using very little to say quite a lot.

Example 12.2: William Byrd, *Mass for Three Voices*, "Agnus Dei."

Choral Textures 187

Looking at another example from Willian Byrd, we find another great lesson in choral textures and restraint in the "Agnus Dei" movement from *Mass for Four Voices*. The movement is written in three major sections that reflect the three lines of the text. For reference, here is the text of the "Agnus Dei":

> Agnus Dei, qui tollis peccata mundi, miserere nobis.
> Agnus Dei, qui tollis peccata mundi, miserere nobis.
> Agnus Dei, qui tollis peccata mundi, dona nobis pacem.

The first section of this movement begins with two voices, soprano and alto, singing the first line of the text with imitative parts. While this passage is sparse, it doesn't feel incomplete. This section will be the shortest of the three lines of the "Agnus Dei."

Example 12.3: William Byrd, *Mass for Four Voices*, "Agnus Dei."

In the second major section—which sets the next line of text—we find that Byrd has written for three of the four voices: the two voices we haven't heard yet, the tenor and the bass, and again from the soprano. The three voices sing in a new point of imitation with slightly new material in a section that is also slightly longer than the first.

Example 12.4: William Byrd, *Mass for Four Voices*, "Agnus Dei."

For the third section—and the last line of text—Byrd brings the alto voice back into the texture, and all four voices are finally singing together. Here we find new imitative material and new opportunities for duetting not heard in this movement previously.

Example 12.5: William Byrd, *Mass for Four Voices*, "Agnus Dei."

This section is much longer than the previous two. One could argue that this last section is really made of two smaller subsections, each of them focusing around the two halves of the final line of text, with different thematic material in different points of imitation. This subsection—usually seen in combination with the previous section—serves to give us closure, not just to this movement, but to the entire mass.

Example 12.6: William Byrd, *Mass for Four Voices*, "Agnus Dei."

Finding success with limiting voices can be as simple as removing one of the outer voices and writing a section for alto, tenor, and bass or for soprano, alto, and tenor. Another solution is to write in duets, either for soprano and alto, tenor and bass, alto and soprano, etc. Using divisions within each voice is one solution that can make leaving out voices easier. For example, composing with divided sopranos and altos allows one to use only a portion of the choral forces, but still write in four-part harmony if desired.

There is, of course, a time and place for everything. There are some circumstances, either musical or extra-musical, where limiting or removing voices may not be the most prudent or practical choice. This may be due to a theme being in a weaker register for a particular section. Or perhaps when working with a more amateur ensemble with less training, certain sections may be understaffed, as is the case chronically with many tenor sections. There may be moments when having multiple sections doubling a theme or supporting harmonies will be more ideal or vital to the success of a composition. In any case, it's important to find a balance in what is too dense and what is too sparse.

Tutti Divisi

A related aspect of writing for every voice all the time is when composers divide every voice at every opportunity. Generally, given the normal SATB divisions, it could mean dividing to eight parts when it neither merits such division nor does that division make sense or balance well. This also happens in music for SSAA and TTBB; very often student composers will divide the ensemble into four parts throughout. One of the best pieces of advice I got was from a conductor of a TTBB chorus who said, "the problem with your writing is that every chord has four pitches for each of the voices. It's too much. It doesn't need to be four voices all the time."

I will admit that it can be especially challenging to limit one's use of parts in choral writing. I fear writing this as a hypocrite, as someone who is guilty of writing on the lusher side of voicing. Limiting the number of voices can sound underwhelming in certain choral ensembles and using more voices can be beguilingly beautiful. A useful attitude while composing for choir can be to follow the words of Antoine de Saint-Exupery: "Perfection is achieved not when there is nothing more to add, but when there is nothing left to take away."[3]

Texture Changes

One common question about musical texture is whether multiple textures are advised and if so, when are texture changes appropriate. Like many questions in choral music, the answer depends on several factors but there are some overarching principles.

---

3   Antoine de Saint-Exupery, *Airman's Odyssey* (Orlando: Harcourt Brace & Company, 1942).

Regarding shorter forms, it's not unusual for short octavos to use only one texture for the entire piece and use variants of that texture. Plenty of effective compositions and arrangements have done so. It's more commonplace to use only a few textures in a shorter work and incorporate variations of those textures. Too many, of course, may come across as inconsistent in tone or hyper-distracted.

In a multi-movement work, treating each movement like a shorter octavo is a worthy approach and one we see throughout the choral canon. These are, of course, guidelines and not hard-and-fast rules, and examples of exceptions to be found throughout the choral canon.

Very often texture changes will be guided by the text (if one is being employed). While the application depends on the text itself, some find that new lines, new stanzas, or new texts altogether are opportunities to change up the texture. But to be clear, these are opportunities, not directives. As stated previously, changing the texture might not be what the compositions needs to be most effective. Again, the point shouldn't be to try to incorporate everything under the sun.

Melody-Focused Textures

Monophonic

Monophonic texture comprises a single theme. Monophony can include doublings of any kind. As far as we can tell, monophonic texture is how Western choral music (post-antiquity) was first recorded. Even though it isn't prescribed on paper, it probably wouldn't be a stretch to imagine that this may be how the earliest humans experienced their first strains of music. Beyond the earliest examples we have of written music post-antiquity, including plainsong and chant, monophony is still found quite often in modern examples. Many of these modern examples of monophony comprise octave doublings of some kind. For more examples, please refer to the sections on unison and octave doublings in Chapter 11.

Monophonic writing is a large part of choral music, so choral musicians are well-practiced for this texture. However, having a very sparse texture where mistakes are very obvious can be a challenge for amateur musicians. Additionally, octave doublings in a cappella music can be tricky for intonation, so you might want to avoid extended passages with amateur groups. Semi-professional musicians and above should not have any major issues.

Example 12.7: Sergei Rachmaninoff, *All-Night Vigil*, "Voskreseniye Khristovo videvshe."

Example 12.8: Joby Talbot, *Path of Miracles*, "Roncesvalles."

Copyright © 2005 Chester Music Limited International. Copyright Secured. All Rights Reserved.

Polyphonic

Polyphonic textures are comprised of two or more voices that are independent of each other but complementary. While these voices are independent, they are related to each other in varying degrees of similarity. In the case of canon, these melodies will be exactly the same. In other cases, the lines will bear some resemblance or share a melodic contour.

Choral repertoire is replete with extraordinary examples of polyphonic textures and not just from the Renaissance. Most choral musicians adore singing polyphonic textures, especially those found in Renaissance music. There may be a number of reasons for this preference, including (but not limited to) ease of sight-reading, general ease of singing, an easier mastery curve, and the satisfaction of a panmodal harmonic language.

For all the ease it can be to both read and sing, polyphonic music still requires a certain amount of practice and confidence from the individual musician. The music is not well-suited to absolute beginners or amateurs with very little training, but more-experienced amateur groups with a good amount of practice and confidence can find success and satisfaction with performances of Renaissance polyphony.

Example 12.9: Giovanni Pierluigi da Palestrina, *Missa Papae Marcelli*, "Agnus Dei II."

The Baroque period—and especially the late Baroque period—also contains numerous examples of polyphonic textures. Many of these examples involve chromatic modifications as well as more demanding, virtuosic passages. While singers find some of these examples to be somewhat more challenging to sing, many singers really find satisfaction in taking on the challenge. Here's an example from one of Bach's motets of imitative entrances and a polyphonic texture of eight different voices:

Example 12.10: Johann Sebastian Bach, "Komm, Jesu, Komm," BWV 229.

There are also plenty of examples in later periods, including the late Romantic period and the early twentieth century. Some composers will take an approach closer to Renaissance aesthetics (as opposed to Baroque) but with Romantic harmonic language that many singers also find very enjoyable to sing. Some examples from the twentieth century adhere to a broader harmonic language and less common scales, which some singers can find to be somewhat more difficult to read and perform and, consequently, to enjoy.

Example 12.11: Josef Rheinberger, *3 Geistliche Gesänge*, Op. 69, No 3 "Abendlied."

194 The Technique of Choral Writing

Polythematic

Like polyphonic textures, polythematic textures include two or more contrasting themes. The most common example includes the double fugue which features two subjects. In choral music, these contrasting themes can be further distinguished by incorporating different texts for each theme. This is one way that choral musicians can capitalize on this texture over other instrumental groups. Multiple texts aren't necessary for polythematic textures in vocal music, but it's very often the reason why polythematic textures are used in the first place.

For most choral musicians, polythematic textures are viewed in a similar manner to polyphonic music: challenging but exciting to sing and perform. However, it seems to me that most examples of polythematic music are found in music that is moderately or very difficult for choral ensembles. This difficulty is perhaps colored by the examples that I have shared below, although it doesn't necessarily need to be the case. One can certainly write children's music—or other two-part music—using polythematic textures to great success.

One particularly famous example comes from the "Kyrie" of Mozart's immortal *Requiem*. The basses and sopranos sing the "Kyrie" theme in imitation while the altos and tenors sing the "Christe" theme in imitation, respectively.

Example 12.12: Wolfgang Amadeus Mozart, *Requiem*, K626, "Kyrie."

Another memorable example can be found in the "Sanctus" movement of a different requiem by Giuseppe Verdi. This double fugue has the first choir in imitative entrances using one theme and the second choir in imitative entrances using a second, contrasting theme.

Example 12.13: Giuseppe Verdi, *Requiem*, "Sanctus."

Polythematic textures, of course, need not be tied to a strict treatment like a fugue or canon. They can simply be contrasting themes in less formal imitative settings, such as this example from Pizzetti's "Il gardino di Afrodite."

Example 12.14: Ildebrando Pizzetti, *Due Composizioni Corali*, "Il giardino di Afrodite."

© 1961 Casa Ricordi Srl. International Copyright Secured. All Rights Reserved. Reprinted by permission of Hal Leonard Europe.

Heterophonic

This texture involves the simultaneous presentation of a theme as well as a variation of that theme and is somewhat rarer than the others. While this texture seems to be straightforward, it can be somewhat more challenging for amateur choral musicians in the learning phase. Amateur choral musicians very often rely on their surrounding colleagues to help give them confidence. It's a similar mentality to a school of fish that all move and retreat together. If one section is singing a slightly different version of a theme to what they are hearing from another section, they can sometimes begin to doubt their own execution and can come to an abrupt stop. It can be a struggle for amateur and even some semi-professional ensembles. Sufficient practice will keep this from being an issue during performances.

A great example of this texture can be found in Britten's anthem "Jubilate Deo," where the tenors and basses sing the simple theme, while the sopranos and altos sing with some slight variation and embellishment, respectively.

Example 12.15: Benjamin Britten, "Jubilate Deo."

Copyright © 1961 Britten Estate Limited. All rights administered by Chester Music Limited. International copyright secured. All rights reserved. Reprinted by permission of Hal Leonard LLC.

Harmony-Focused Textures

While melody-focused textures have been part of the choral canon for millennia, many contemporary listeners would probably now associate modern choral music with harmony-focused textures. And indeed, when polyphonic textures are not in vogue, choral music tends to become more harmony focused.

Chordal

This texture involves three or more voices that share exact or nearly exact rhythms. These chords move together and share the same note values. In choral music when text is involved, this can also mean that all voices are lining up with the text setting exactly (although there are a small number of examples where this may not be the case).

Choral musicians will very often have a strong affinity for this texture, especially for basking in certain harmonies at arrival points, climaxes, and cadences. There is a simple joy that can come from luxuriating in methodical, predictable, slow-moving chord changes, all moving together in unity. And it's important to point out that there is nothing inherently wrong or bad about this texture or about enjoying it. Choral music becomes a bore when chordal music becomes the sole texture in vocal writing.

Example 12.16: Jocelyn Hagen, *The Notebooks of Leonardo da Vinci*, "Perception."

Copyright © 2019 Jocelyn Hagen. Used by permission.

Bichordal/Polychordal

This texture involves two sets of chordal textures that overlap. This particular texture is especially effective for choral ensembles if the vowels of the text are different and not aligned between the chords. It can create a mesmerizingly blurred effect when done well. The slight variation in vowel overtones with such similar vocal timbres provides just enough contrast and unity, which can maximize this already beguiling texture. It's also one that singers really enjoy performing. Be aware that this texture requires a good amount of training and confidence from the singers. It's one that is best suited to very well-trained semi-professional groups and above. This texture works best in antiphonal settings, such as double choir formations, but can also work in normal formations.

Example 12.17: Caroline Shaw, "and the swallow."

© 2017 Caroline Shaw Editions. Used by permission.

Chorale

This texture, most often associated with the chorales of Johann Sebastian Bach, involves each voice using similar rhythms with allowance for variation and semi-independence between voices. This texture is very common in choral music, and probably the most common of all harmony-focused choral music. It is strongly associated with hymn tunes from different denominations of Christianity, especially Protestant ones. Singers will generally not have many issues with this texture as it's one that's most often associated with congregational singing in Christian denominations. Even amateur groups will be able to do reasonably well in this texture with sufficient practice.

Example 12.18: Johann Sebastian Bach, *St. Matthew Passion*, BWV 244 "Befiehl du deine Wege."

Gesture-Focused Textures

Ostinatos

One of the most common gesture-focused textures are ostinatos. These repetitions of short motifs can be very effective in a choral setting, either with texts or on some vocalises. The one caution about ostinatos in choral music specifically is that voices can sometimes have a difficult time executing quick repetitions if there's not a lot of places for the voice to rest and "reset," especially at higher tempos. This is particularly true with rapidly alternating neighbor tones (that are slower than a trill). What most conductors will do is divide those repeating parts between the firsts and seconds of a section.

A good example of putting this into the music—and indeed making the best out of a weakness—can be found in Carol Barnett's arrangement titled

"McKay," where she writes for divided altos to sing a rather quick repetition. Additionally, when the tenors have their own repeating theme, they are given a bit more time to "reset" and repeat the motif.

Example 12.19: Carol Barnett, *An American Thanksgiving*, "McKay."

Copyright © 2003 by Carol Barnett. Published by earthsongs. Used by permission.

Athematic

By strict definition, this is a texture that has no perceptible or recognizable theme or accompaniment without a melody. This texture can involve a combination of block chords, sustained notes, arpeggiation, and neighboring tones. The sky is the limit as far as what can comprise an athematic passage. There's not much about this texture that's highly specific to the choral idiom. However, this texture is suitable for text settings as well as vocalises.

Example 12.20: Tarik O'Regan, "O vera digna hostia."

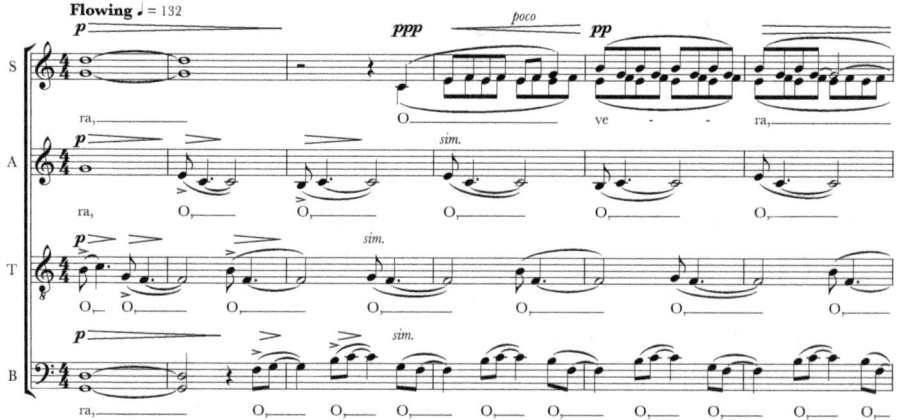

Copyright © 2003 Novello & Co. Ltd. International Copyright Secured. All Rights Reserved,

Choral Textures   201

Example 12.21: Judith Bingham, "Water Lilies."

[Musical score: Dreamlike, very mysteriuos ♩. = 50-55, with parts for S Solo, S, A Solo, A, T Solo, T, Bar. Bass Solos, Bar., and B, setting the text "Nymphaea."]

© Peters Edition Ltd. Reproduced by permission of Faber Music Ltd. All Rights Reserved.

Polyrhythmic

This texture involves the use of multiple rhythmic figures that are often repeated like ostinatos and is generally seen as similar to athematic. These most often appear as vocalises, but not always. What can make this texture special in choral music is the ability to vary the consonants used by the singers. Sharper consonants like [t], [k], [s], or [ʃ] can help accent the attack of the rhythm, while softer consonants like [l], [m], [n], and [b] can soften those attacks as needed. In most cases, it's not unreasonable to ask the musicians to go back and forth between these consonants as needed. Besides the wonderful example below by Whitacre, another great example of polyrhythmic texture is the above example of "Water Lilies" by Judith Bingham.

Example 12.22: Eric Whitacre, "Leonardo Dreams of His Flying Machine."

© 2002 Walton Music Corp. All rights reserved.

Onomatopoeic

This texture involves the use of non-musical sounds, very often those associated with animals, nature, or other extra-musical sounds. This texture is one that singers are especially successful at, particularly when it comes to mimicking animal sounds. The main challenge is intonation if the music is without accompaniment or has one or more sections maintaining pitch somehow. Depending on the music, having the musicians singing passages or gestures of indeterminate pitch can be a struggle when it's time to return to pitches. There are several examples in modern choral repertoire of this practice, including the works of Stephen Leek, who seeks to capture the spirit of the Australian bush.

Example 12.23: Stephen Leek, *Great Southern Spirits*, "Kondalilla."

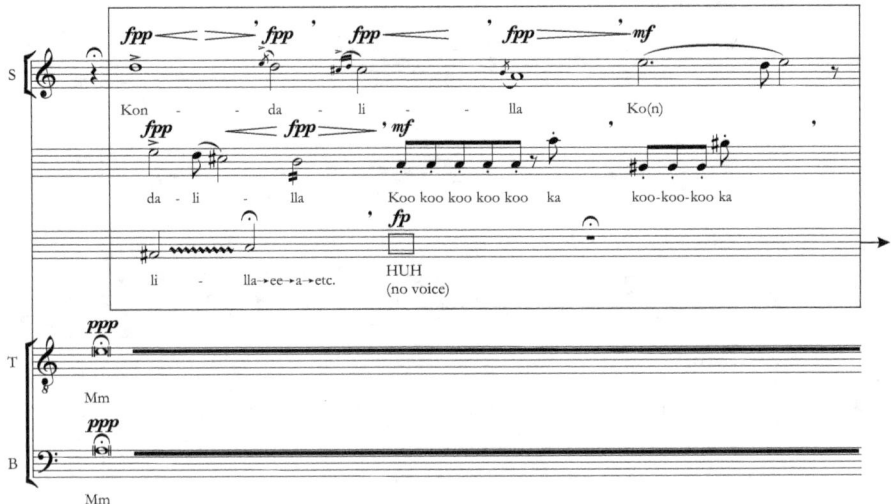

Copyright © Stephen Leek. Used by permission.

Variants

One of the joys of any composition is to find new, creative ways to combine and add variation to these different textures. Texture variants involve making changes within a texture's parameters or beginning to incorporate traits or characteristics of other textures; in other words, one texture finds a middle ground between one touchstone and another. For example, monophonic textures find variation by changing the voicing either through the section employed, the use of a solo, or a combination of different sections doubling in unison or at octaves. Each of these parameters, such as register, dynamics, voicing, and tempo, can be variants of any given texture.

Another example of a variant is found in planing, which is a variant of a chordal texture where the intervals are fixed either in diatonic or chromatic fashion. Even though planing is pretty clearly a chordal texture, it can often take on a quality that appears melody-focused instead of harmony-focused. In many instances, planing finds itself somewhere between the touchstones of harmony-focused and melody-focused textures.

Example 12.24: Gabriel Jackson, "Hymn to the Trinity (Honor, Virtus, et Potestas)."

© Oxford University Press 2006. All rights reserved.

In some of these cases, these textures find variants through different devices or treatments. An example of this is canon which is a variant of the polyphonic texture. This very strict treatment creates a very distinct variation for polyphonic music. An example of this is the Josquin selection found earlier in this chapter. Yet another option is the use of aleatoric constructs as a variation of athematic textures as well as a variant for onomatopoeic textures. An example of this is found in the Jackson selection in the next section of this chapter.

Composites

Texture composites involve combining two or more of these textures together. These can include textures within one focus or between multiple different focuses. These composites can create some truly singular musical experiences including some textures that are especially suited to—and that can maximize on—vocal ensembles. Other textural devices include ones covered more fully in Chapter 14 such as aleatoric or chance music.

Melody and Accompaniment

This composite is a combination of a melody-focused and harmony or gesture-focused texture. It is probably the most common composite texture in choral music and can be seen in many different variations and arrangements. In a cappella music, it can mean featuring a section or a single solo voice over the rest of the ensemble singing an accompanying figure, either with words or a vocalise. The thematic voice can be any section or solo voice from the ensemble. The latter can be seen in this example from the second movement of Maurice Ravel's *Trois Chansons*, which features a soprano and tenor solo.

Example 12.25: Maurice Ravel, *Trois Chansons*, "Trois beaux oiseaux du paradis."

One of the most common examples of this texture of melody and accompaniment involves the choir singing the melody in some fashion—either various sections in unison monophony or the entire choir in octave doubling—and accompaniment by some sort of instrument or ensemble of instruments. It is especially common in arrangements of hymns or folk tunes.

Example 12.26: Mack Wilberg, "Arise, O God, and Shine"/"Rejoice the Lord is King."

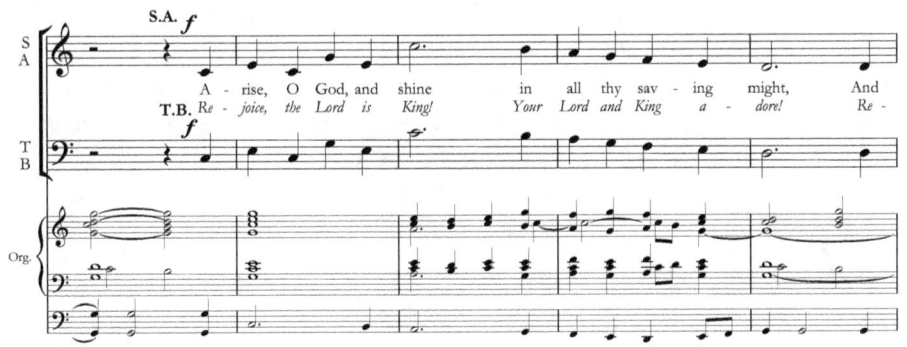

© Oxford University Press Inc. 2002. Assigned to Oxford University Press 2010. All rights reserved.

The accompaniment can take several different variants, including a variety of textures, in addition to the opportunity for different instrumentation. An example is found in the motet "Orbis patrator optime" by Gabriel Jackson.

There are three sections in this work where the sopranos have the main theme and the altos, tenors, and basses are singing an accompaniment. The first two times we have these sections, the lower voices are singing in aleatoric constructs as their accompaniment, which has a certain amount of soft haziness.

Example 12.27: Gabriel Jackson, "Orbis patrator optime."

© Oxford University Press 2007. All rights reserved.

For the third iteration of this section the lower voices are singing the same harmonies while the sopranos sing a new melody. However, the lower voices now sing with a staccato chordal texture, syncopated rhythms, and disjointed words. The harmonies in the lower parts are in a similar voicing as before but with drastically different, even opposing, textures.

Example 12.28: Gabriel Jackson, "Orbis patrator optime."

© Oxford University Press 2007. All rights reserved.

Other Composites

It's not within the scope of this text to discuss every composite or variation of the textures that are possible with choral music. Many composites can include being athematic simply by not having the presence of a theme. The examples we saw earlier from Bingham and Whitacre would fall under this category. However, it would be worth exploring a few examples of composite textures from some well-established classics in the choral canon.

From catalog numbers BWV 225-230, these six compositions by JS Bach are categorized as motets. Let us consider two examples from the first motet, "Singet dem Herrn ein neues Lied," which is a tour de force of choral texture from beginning to end. In the opening measures, we find a composition of a polyphonic texture in choir one and a chordal texture in choir two. The second choir then gives way to the polyphonic texture of the first choir before there's some antiphonal response and they start the composite again with the roles reversed.

Example 12.29: Johann Sebastian Bach, "Singet dem Herrn ein neues Lied," BWV 225.

Later, in the same motet, Bach creates another interesting composite of not just texture but genre. In the middle of the motet, Bach has the second choir sing what is marked as "Chorale" in a chorale style. The first choir, however, is marked as singing "Aria" with a variety of textures such as melody and accompaniment, polyphonic, and chorale textures with each voice getting a turn at singing the melody. I've heard many performances of this motet in which the Aria parts are sung by soloists while the Chorale parts are sung by the larger ensemble. It's a very effective and interesting combination.

Example 12.30: Johann Sebastian Bach, "Singet den Herrn ein neues Lied," BWV 225.

In addition to the Bach motets, it is worth discussing the wealth of different textures found in Martin's *Mass for Double Choir*. While the title indicates that it's meant for double choir, only parts of the work could be described as strictly adhering to traditional double choir, antiphonal writing. The work experiments with different textures and voicing ideas that are only made possible with a polychoral ensemble. The "Sanctus" in particular is a feast of different textures and ideas. The beginning features the altos, tenors, and basses singing an athematic texture in antiphonal response between the two choirs. Meanwhile, the sopranos from each choir sing a simple pentatonic scale, also in antiphonal response to one another, but at a separate rate than the altos, tenors, and basses.

Example 12.31: Frank Martin, *Mass for Double Choir*, "Sanctus."

In the "Benedictus" section of the same movement, Martin writes a composite of three basic ideas. The altos, tenors, and basses in choir two chant in a chordal texture but with a somewhat static variant with relatively few harmonic changes. The altos, tenors, and basses in the first choir also sing in a chordal texture but with a variant of planing and relatively more motion. Lastly, the sopranos sing in dyadic harmonies in antiphonal response high above the rest of the voices.

Example 12.32: Frank Martin, *Mass for Double Choir*, "Sanctus."

Continuing Study

Suggested Exercises

Short
- » Identify the basic categories of choral textures and some of the types of choral textures in those categories.
- » Discuss different types of variants for each of these textures.
- » Discuss different types of composites of different textures.

Long
- » Study the different settings of "Alma Redemptoris Mater" by Guillaume DuFay, Johannes Ockeghem, and Josquin Des Prez. Take note of their different approaches and the results.
- » Select one of the following short melodies (or another of your choosing) and practice arranging them using different textures.

Suggested Listening

Mass in B minor, BWV 232 - Johann Sebastian Bach
Motets, BWV 225-230 - Johann Sebastian Bach
"Gleams of a Remoter World" - Judith Bingham
"Water Lilies" - Judith Bingham
Fest und Gedenksprüche, Op. 109 - Johannes Brahms
Mass for Three Voices - William Byrd
Mass for Four Voices - William Byrd
Mass for Five Voices - William Byrd
"Ave Maria virgo serena" - Josquin des Prez
Trois Chansons - Claude Debussy
"Orbis patrator optime" - Gabriel Jackson
"Salus Aeterna" - Gabriel Jackson
Lagrime di San Pietro - Orlande de Lassus
O Antiphons - Paweł Łukaszewski
Mass for Double Choir - Frank Martin
"O vera digna hostia" - Tarik O'Regan
Missa Papae Marcelli - Giovanni Pierluigi da Palestrina
7 Magnificat-Antiphonen - Arvo Pärt
Figure Humaine - Francis Poulenc
Messe en Sol Majeur - Francis Poulenc
All-Night Vigil - Sergei Rachmaninoff
Trois Chansons - Maurice Ravel
3 Geistliche Gesänge - Josef Rheinberger
"Peace Like a River" - Ronald Staheli
Path of Miracles - Joby Talbot
Mass in G minor - Ralph Vaughan Williams
"Silence and Music" - Ralph Vaughan Williams
Requiem - Tomas Luis de Victoria

Chapter 13

Instrumental Collaboration

*Let but thy voice engender with the
 string
And angels will be born, while thou dost
 sing.*
  — Robert Herrick

*Join the great throng,
Psaltery, organ, and song
Sounding in glad adoration.*
  — Joachim Neander

As beautiful and transcendent as a cappella singing is, a full concert on its own can become monochromatic and the addition of instrumental collaborators can add new and fresh colors to a performance. It's not always necessary but instrumental collaborators can be very welcome additions to any choral concert.

Before we begin to consider each instrument or ensemble on its own, we'll consider a few things collectively first. Regarding balance, it should be noted that for every performance, the musicians themselves will have balancein the performance space as one of their main priorities. Conductors will generally ask the louder, more robust instruments and ensembles to always have their ear on the choral ensemble and to play half or a full dynamic lower than marked. With that in mind, when the choir is singing and the instruments are serving an "accompanying" role, it's important to almost always have the instruments marked a dynamic lower than what is marked for the singers. Choral ensembles, especially those that are staffed by singers who have less training, are easily overshadowed by their instrumental collaborators. Solo instruments can be marked at the dynamics they need and of course when the instruments take the lead role, they can be marked at whatever dynamic is necessary. It's always important to set up your musicians for success and to create a work that already helps them balance.

One aspect to consider with choral music is how to voice and arrange for choirs when singing a cappella versus how to voice and arrange with collaborative instrumentalists. Many principles will remain the same, but some things will need to be simplified or streamlined when instrumental accompaniment intensifies.

We will consider historic and common instrumental collaborators as well as a few unconventional ones. This chapter is by no means exhaustive regarding every possible combination of instruments or every possible writing consideration. As with any composing or arranging, there are some lessons that one can only learn by writing, listening, and evaluating. As you learn more, and workshop more pieces in person, you'll begin to gain more understanding of how to write in such a way that allows the singers to shine without them feeling as though they must holler and bellow to be heard.

Singer's Formant

In the voice's spectral frequency envelope, a number of different overtones are sounding above the fundamental pitch whose amplitude naturally diminishes the higher they become. Curiously though, within these overtones are a group of frequencies that actually increase in amplitude around 3kHz before tapering in amplitude again. This is what voice scientists and teachers refer to as the "the singer's formant." This envelope of frequencies is what allows a soloist to be heard in a large hall over an orchestra without amplification. The singer's formant is generally above the fundamental pitch of just about every instrument in the orchestra (except for a few instruments, including the cymbals). Part of a singer's training is learning how to boost this group of frequencies as much as their anatomy will allow.

Cymbals, whether crash or suspended, have a broad frequency spectrum and are one of the few instruments in the orchestra that directly overlaps with the singer's formant. With that information, be mindful that they will cover the singers' sound, even when the choir is singing at a very strong dynamic. A crash will only be momentary, but text intelligibility will be obscured. Suspended cymbals will be even more challenging.

While the singer's formant is there to give them a fighting chance to sing above an orchestra—and it will do a remarkable job—it should not be relied on entirely nor can it make up for poor writing. First of all, while every singer has this formant in their voice, most of them haven't been trained on how to boost these frequencies to their maximum potential. Second, even this boost in overtones might not be enough to overcome a large instrumental group with a variety of instruments playing at extremely loud volumes.

Piano

The piano has shown to be a very friendly companion to choirs through the centuries for the same reasons it has been used to accompany so many other soloists or ensembles. In practical matters, its ubiquity means that a piano will be present is almost any venue a choir will perform in—quality of piano aside. Additionally, so many different harmonies, soundscapes, textures, and effects can be provided by one musician rather than dozens that other ensembles would need. Musically, its huge range in terms of dynamics, registers, timbre, and texture possibilities provides enormous flexibility to composers. The piano is very capable of making significant adjustments regarding when to take a passive role, and when to step out and take the lead. Working with the piano can of course help younger or less experienced singers who may not be ready for unaccompanied singing.

Examples

Historically, the piano accompanying a choir is a more recent development relative to other instrumental collaborations. As we survey different examples of choral works with piano collaborations, we should also consider how the piano as an instrument has evolved over time. From modest beginnings, the instrument was a somewhat portable fortepiano with wooden frames, leather hammers, as few as 49 keys, and one string per key. Compare that to the behemoth instrument we have today in the modern piano, weighing up to 1,260 pounds (570 kg) with cast iron frames, felt hammers, at least 88 keys, and up to three strings made of tempered steel per key.

Among the first piano accompanied choral pieces are the accompanied part songs by Haydn, where the piano doubled the vocal parts for much of each song. Haydn's instrument was, of course, a smaller, softer instrument than what we have today. The singers would have had a much more assertive sound than the keyboard they were singing with.

Example 13.1: Josef Haydn, *Vierstimmige Gesänge*, "Die Warnung."

Working in the early and mid-Romantic period, we begin to see compositions with more robust, active piano parts as the piano itself begins to become a louder more reliable instrument. Works by Schubert, Schumann, and Mendelssohn are examples of piano parts of more assertive contribution.

Brahms wrote numerous works for vocal ensemble and piano, but many of them were conceived and intended as quartets with piano rather than larger choirs with multiple singers on each part. These were mostly intended as music for the parlor, involving small audiences in very intimate settings of private homes. Even so, we can learn something from the way that Brahms balances the vocal parts with piano.

Example 13.2: Johannes Brahms, *Zigeunerlieder*, "He, Zigeuner, greife in die Saiten."

The piano can double choral parts very easily, but as with any instrumental doubling, there is merit to preserving the timbre color of each part by avoiding doubling. Allowing each part their own independence can allow a translucency between each part of the ensemble. Of course, balancing between doubling and not doubling voices is also an effective strategy.

Example 13.3: Gabriel Fauré, "Madrigal."

Even somewhat denser and busier piano textures can balance beautifully with choral ensembles. An example can be found in a chanson by Lili Boulanger that features a fairly active and broad piano part. Even with this activity, the pianissimo dynamic helps to keep the piano in check and allows the choral texture to be supported, yet unimpeded.

Example 13.4: Lili Boulanger, "Soir Sur La Plaine."

A truly exemplary work of choral/piano collaboration in the twentieth century is found in Edgar Cosma's song cycle *Les Amours des Poètes*, specifically in the first of the three song cycles. Throughout this work, Cosma deftly crafts for the piano to leave room for the choral parts. For example, in the first movement, as the sopranos and altos sing "Douceur/En coeur," the piano part is written far above their pitches and a dynamic softer. This choice allows enough transparency for all the parts to complement each other and be heard with ease. It also gives this passage a previously unheard high register as well as a weightless, floating quality.

Example 13.5: Edgar Cosma, *Les Amours des Poètes*, "Quand vous voudrez."

© 1994 Éditions A Coeur Joie, 24 avenue Joannès Masset, F-69009 Lyon / www.EditionsACoeurJoie.com /

In the second movement, Cosma moves quickly between low and high registers at the recapitulation. When the piano plays an A major triad, doubling the sopranos and altos an octave higher, it provides a little sparkle and reinforces their first harmonic. Meanwhile, the tenors and basses are given a completely empty space allowing for their very wordy phrases to be unimpeded.

Example 13.6: Edgar Cosma, *Les Amours des Poètes*, "Rondeau."

© 1994 Éditions A Coeur Joie

218   The Technique of Choral Writing

The third movement has the piano playing several repeated chords in arpeggiation, sounding like a guitar strumming. This texture allows the sopranos and altos the ability to contrast this texture with long, sustained, sensuous lines. This contrast is a key technique that allows for choral and instrumental parts to be balanced and complemented. As the third movement draws to a close, the piano again plays high above the sopranos and altos to give a little goodnight kiss and cadence into a rich F major chord from the tenors and basses.

Example 13.7: Edgar Cosma, *Les Amours des Poètes*, "Les Roses de Saadi."

© 1994 Éditions A Coeur Joie

The opening of the fourth movement strikes a beautiful balance between having an active, flashy piano part and pausing to allow the choral parts to deliver text intelligibly without having to struggle to fight against an instrument. The pianist's part switches back and forth seamlessly between a more passive, supportive role, and then taking the lead.

Example 13.8: Edgar Cosma, *Les Amours des Poètes*, "Es-tu brune ou blonde?"

© 1994 Éditions A Coeur Joie

Organ

Often referred to as "the king of instruments,"[1] organs can have incredible breadth of range, from loud to soft dynamics and simple to complex sounds. The organ has advantages to the piano, in that organs have a huge galaxy of sounds, timbres, harmonies, and textures to offer—many more than the piano could dare offer—while again only requiring one person.[2]

The major disadvantages of the organ compared to the piano are first, that it may not be present in nearly as many venues as the piano is. Additionally, every single organ is different from the next. Every instrument will have a different set of pipes and therefore a different set of sounds to work with. In addition, while stops and ranks might share the same names, they will very likely be built in a different style, by a different builder, and will be voiced and tuned in different ways. And the organ in the venue is the organ you are stuck with. Even when you are working with the same organ, two different organists will have different opinions about how to register that instrument for your composition.

While this lack of consistency may be maddening to a composer or arranger who makes consistency a priority, this situation should be an opportunity to find enrichment in the different approaches that individual circumstances bring to your music. Not every choir will sound the same, and not every conductor will interpret your work the same. The organ should be seen in a similar way.

A Very Brief Overview

The pipes of an organ are organized by timbre into "ranks" which contain the full chromatic scale. These ranks can be turned on or off by the organist with a mechanism at the console called a "stop." Different stops can include sounds like "strings," "flutes," "choir," "tubas," etc. These stops are organized into different divisions. These divisions will be assigned to different keyboards called "manuals," and will have names like Great, Choir, Swell, Solo, et cetera. Some of these divisions can be combined with other divisions to a single manual by using what's called a "coupler."[3]

---

1 I have seen this quotation originally attributed to Mozart and Machaut.

2 Some compositions—and instruments—may require a register assistant, a page turner, or a third or fourth hand.

3 Ertuğrul Sevsay, *The Cambridge Guide to Orchestration* (Cambrdige: Cambridge University, 2013), 248.

Some of these pipes will be at different lengths and indicated on the stops. Eight-foot registers sound as notated. Four-foot registers sound an octave higher than notated. Sixteen-foot registers sound an octave lower than notated, and so forth.[4]

The selection of different stops to be played for a particular passage or a piece is called "registration." A single rank played is unmixed and will have a simpler, purer sound. Registration involving multiple ranks is mixed and will have a more complicated sound. Partials can be added above to create even richer, fuller sounds.[5] While registration suggestions can be made by the composer, the organist makes the final registration choices.[6]

If this sounds overwhelming at this point, that's because it is! The organ is a very complicated instrument to build and play. You now have a better understanding about why there are entire academic degrees dedicated to this instrument.

General Balance and Divisions

A well-trained organist will take great pains to maintain proper balance with any choral forces they are working with and adjust their registration as needed. Even still, as a composer or arranger, you can help set your performers up for success by being aware of a few general principles.

When organ registration is simpler and closer to a simple sine wave, like a flute stop, choral textures can be more easily heard. As more stops are added and richer, more complex registrations are chosen with stops like reeds and strings, choral textures are more easily covered, and again, one would write choral voicings in stronger, more generous parts of the voice that can compete with louder instrumental dynamics.

When accompaniment is light and on the softer side, extensive divisions can be easily heard, and textures are clear in every register of the singers. When accompaniments become medium loud extensive divisions may become covered or obscured, especially if voices are in lower or weaker registers. The standard four parts without divisions is better heard, especially if each voice is matching the dynamic and avoiding relatively weaker registers.

When accompaniments are loud and four-part harmonies are desired from your vocal forces, your writing will be most successful if all voices are in the strongest parts of their register. Otherwise, unison and octave doublings,

---

[4] Sevsay, *The Cambridge Guide to Orchestration*, 247.

[5] Sevsay, *The Cambridge Guide to Orchestration*, 250.

[6] Sometimes in collaborations with the conductor.

as well as dyadic harmonies, will be more successful. When organ textures are loud and robust, it's not a bad idea to pause the organ playing and allow a brief window for the choral voices to sing a cappella without any conflict or competition.

Examples

The segment of the choral canon with organ collaboration is overflowing with high-quality, memorable favorites among singers and audiences alike. There are many great composers who write for choir and organ, and several who made this genre their bread and butter, particularly in liturgical settings. Several of these composers, include Parry, Stanford, Howells, Vierne, Langlais, Rheinberger, Fauré, Duruflé, Dupre, Reger, Franck, Messiaen, and Willan to name a few. It doesn't hurt that many of these composers were themselves highly accomplished organists.

Some of the earliest records we have of organ use with choirs come from organs doubling the parts of choirs in religious worship. The first independent organ parts to accompany voices began when we see verse anthems towards the end of the English Renaissance and near the beginning of the *cori spezzati* tradition in Venice with *basso continuo*, where a bass line is given with figured bass for the musician to realize on their own. This *basso continuo* tradition continues for hundreds of years until we start to see fully independent organ parts in the Classical and early Romantic period.

In Tudor England, a genre of liturgical music was born called "Verse Anthems." This is a type of anthem that alternated between the "verses" with soloists and organ, and the "full," which included all the singers and the organ doubling the vocal parts. The verse anthem is in contrast with the "full anthem" which inspired the verse anthem. In an example by sixteenth-century English composer Thomas Tomkins,[7] we can see the organ part being slightly more independent during the verse sections (with some doubling still involved) and doubling the choral parts when the full chorus returns.

---

7 Is there anything more perfect than an alliterating name from sixteenth-century England?

Example 13.9: Thomas Tomkins, "My Beloved Spake."

Choral-organ music of the seventeenth and eighteenth centuries consists mostly of continuo accompaniment with a few exceptions. We begin to see more fully written out organ parts except in a few smaller masses by Josef Haydn and his brother Michael.

Example 13.10: Josef Haydn, *Kleine Orgelmesse*, "Credo."

During the nineteenth century, composers took the opportunity to write fully realized, independent organ parts when composing with a choir. Johannes Brahms' contribution to the choral/organ repertoire is small but memorable, particularly "Geistliches Lied." This short motet features sweeping lines when the organ is playing alone and then it takes a more supportive, passive role when the choir enters (in double canon).

Example 13.11: Johannes Brahms, "Geistliches Lied," op. 30.

The choral music of Herbert Howells is almost universally loved among singers, including his choral music with organ. Being an organist by training, Howells knew inside and out his niche of composing liturgical music for the Anglican tradition. As a result, some of his finest music includes the services that he composed. Of note is the *Collegium Regale* service he composed for the choir of King's College, Cambridge. Both the "Magnificat" and the "Nunc dimittis" contain a variety of choral and organ textures. There are both unison and octave doublings, balanced with four-part writing, divided parts, and a tenor solo. This is supported by an organ part that balances doubling the voice parts and its own separate part. It's a truly collaborative composition.

Example 13.12: Herbert Howells, *Collegium Regale*, "Magnificat."

Copyright © 1947 (Renewed) Novello & Co. Ltd. International Copyright Secured. All Rights Reserved.

Example 13.13: Herbert Howells, *Collegium Regale*, "Magnificat."

Copyright © 1947 (Renewed) Novello & Co. Ltd. International Copyright Secured. All Rights Reserved.

One of the best examples of organ collaboration with choir must be *Requiem* by organ virtuoso Maurice Duruflé. Much of the mass is based on plainchant from the requiem mass with impressionist harmonizations and lush organ accompaniment (and later orchestrated by Duruflé). This is a great example of not only Duruflé's endless imagination for organ writing, but also his venerable virtuosic ability.[8]

---

8   Because of the technical demands of Duruflé's *Requiem*, one should keep in mind how much practice and preparation needs to be made by the organist for a successful performance of this work. One of my organ colleagues in school told me that to hire her for this work, she would charge a premium in order to prepare it and would stipulate specific preparation time on the venue's organ before agreeing to the performance.

Example 13.14: Maurice Duruflé, *Requiem in D minor,* op. 9, "Sanctus."

Published by Editions Durand. International Copyright Secured. All Rights Reserved.
Reprinted by permission of Hal Leonard Europe.

Harp

While less common than piano or organ accompaniment, the harp can be a very effective instrument to pair with choral ensembles and one found in some very beloved choral music.

The harp has a naturally lower dynamic than the piano and is perfectly suited to accompany less-developed voices such as children or young adolescents. The harp can provide a very delicate, soft backdrop for choral ensembles to sing at softer dynamics with great effect. Conversely, when dynamics grow louder and parts divide, the harp remains a softer and supportive accompanying force that won't overshadow the choral textures. Instead, the harp allows more transparent sonorities, which lets the choral divisions be fully enjoyed instead of implied.

The obvious drawback with the harp is its relative lack of dynamic range and inability to be a truly assertive musical partner. While dynamics are possible, harps will never truly fill a concert hall the way a piano can, and certainly not the way an organ can. Additionally, the harp can find limitations in the character or mood it can bring to a work. The harp can sound heavenly, angelic even or sound like a pastoral instrument for shepherds and nymphs, but beyond those sounds, the timbral variations are limited. But not every instrument needs to be everything in all circumstances.

Examples

This instrument seems to come up most often in the repertoire for children's voices or for music focusing on Christmas or the winter season. A large amount of the repertoire for choir and harp is more or less of a conventional, perhaps traditional nature. The harp is an almost ideal instrument for this purpose as the instrument is set up to operate easily in diatonic scales. An effective example is Mack Wilberg's entirely diatonic arrangement of the American folk hymn "My Shepherd Will Supply My Need." While some very chromatic music isn't feasible on the harp, chromatic shifts in a reasonable period of time are possible and effective. An example is Stephen Paulus' Christmas piece "A Savior From on High."

Example 13.15: Stephen Paulus, "A Savior From on High."

Copyright © 2001 Paulus Publications. Used by permission.

Perhaps the best-known example of choral-harp collaboration is *Ceremony of Carols* by Benjamin Britten. This multi-movement cantata for treble voices and harp contains many examples of idiomatic harp writing including rolled chords, glissandi, and alternating hand work. This work is very popular among treble choirs, including children's choirs, and the harp balances especially well with those voices.

Example 13.16: Benjamin Britten, *Ceremony of Carols*, "Wolcum Yole."

© 1943 Boosey & Co. Ltd. Reproduced by permission of Boosey & Hawkes.

Example 13.17: Benjamin Britten, *Ceremony of Carols*, "Deo Gratias."

© 1943 Boosey & Co. Ltd. Reproduced by permission of Boosey & Hawkes.

Obbligato Instruments

Even the simple addition of one obbligato instrument can provide a great deal of interest and variety into an otherwise monochromatic a cappella composition. The additional timbre can be a very refreshing part of a choral concert. In the case of working with a single instrument, balance is not often a concern, except in the rare occasion of the choir overwhelming the instrument.

There are many good options to choose from and discussing every possible instrument is not practical or necessary for this particular text. As far as I can see from my study of the choral canon, there is no "wrong" instrument that can be paired with a choral ensemble, but rather more or less common choices. I will, however, present a few notable examples of different instruments as a point of departure and for inspiration.

Any string instrument will pair beautifully with vocal ensembles. In particular, the cello has become a favorite obbligato instrument to use alongside choral forces and it is self-evident to see why. Its versatility, between being a bass instrument capable of accompaniment as well as its ability to fit so well into a melodic character, makes it an almost ideal instrument to pair with choirs.

Example 13.18: Jocelyn Hagen, "See Amid the Winter Snow."

© Boosey & Hawkes. Reproduced by permission of Boosey & Hawkes.

Woodwind instruments are very popular to have perform alongside choirs, especially the flute, oboe, and clarinet. English horn is sometimes called upon, although less often (criminally so, in my opinion). Other woodwinds—such as bassoon, piccolo, alto flute, or bass clarinet to name a few—are rarely used as obbligato instruments, but that doesn't mean it isn't possible.

Example 13.19: Abbie Betinis, "Cedit, Hyems."

© 2007 by G. Schirmer, Inc. International Copyright Secured. All Rights Reserved. Used by permission.

Example 13.20: Howard Helvey, "O Quam Gloriosum."

© 2006 Boosey & Hawkes. Reproduced by permission of Boosey & Hawkes.

The most common brass instruments to appear with choirs as an obbligato instrument has to be the trumpet and the horn. Trombones and tubas are almost never called for as obbligato instruments. Again, that's not to say it shouldn't be done, but these instruments seem to be used more often in combination with others rather than appearing on their own.

One example of a horn instrument with a choral ensemble would be David Hamilton's ethereal and gossamer work "The Moon is Silently Singing" for two choirs and two horns. This piece celebrates everything antiphonal, as the choirs sing back and forth to each other while one horn is on stage and the other is offstage.

Example 13.21: David Hamilton, "The Moon is Silently Singing."

© 2005 Walton Music Corp. All rights reserved.

Less Common Instruments

As mentioned previously, there are many different instruments (outside of what one might conventionally find in a symphony orchestra) that one can choose to collaborate with choral forces. Again, there isn't really a wrong answer here; if you can make it work, it can work. That isn't to say that it will be immediately accepted by any given audience, but if you can write it convincingly, there's no reason to exclude one instrument or another.

One composer who has embraced using a variety of somewhat unconventional instruments is English composer Gabriel Jackson, who has written for soprano and alto saxophone, electric guitar, and marimba, among others, to perform with choir.

Example 13.22: Gabriel Jackson, "Ave Regina Coelorum."

© Oxford University Press 2011. All rights reserved.

Chamber Ensembles

Collaborating with chamber ensembles can be a wellspring of creativity, and one that is mostly underused in choral music.[9] There are numerous opportunities for innovative and unconventional instrument combinations.

The size and character of what constitutes a "chamber" ensemble can vary. It may be a string trio, woodwind quintet, marimba ensemble, french horn choir, gamelan, etc. There is no set definition about how many instruments constitutes a "chamber" ensemble, but it can range from two or three instruments to a small string ensemble consisting of six first violins, six second violins, four violas, three cellos, and a double bass.

With so many unconventional and unorthodox chamber ensembles, it's difficult to ask if there's any combination that doesn't work with choral ensembles. So far, my only thought is that if a composer can make that chamber ensemble work on its own, it can work with a choral ensemble. If it can't, putting it with a choir isn't likely to magically fix it.

In many cases, when the instrumental ensemble is small (three to five instruments) one can treat the instruments in a similar way to obbligato instruments by letting them have their moments to shine rather than thinking about them as only accompaniment. Many choral ensembles are capable of

---

9 One of the possible reasons for this being an underused form of choral music could be due to the extra costs and hassle associated with hiring instrumentalists. Managing a choir on its own can be a lot of work.

singing a cappella and don't necessarily need to be accompanied whenever instruments are present. Larger groups of instruments, however, generally favor an accompanying role with opportunities to step out into the spotlight.

General Balance

Voicing and balance will require a great deal of consideration as each kind of ensemble will have unique challenges not shared with other chamber groups. The overarching principle should be to make sure that each element of the combined ensembles has a space carved out for them. Some instruments can be easily covered by choirs and conversely, there are some instruments that can easily cover voices. This isn't to say that you shouldn't use any specific instruments in a chamber ensemble. However, be aware that it can cover the hard work you've put into your writing.

Strings, Woodwinds, and Brass

Writing for choir and string, wind or brass ensembles is very lovely, and these are mostly conventional ensembles to pair with choirs. It's reasonable to assume that these instruments will be available in many cases.

String quartets are a wonderful and versatile chamber ensemble to use in collaboration with choirs. The ensemble is capable of both serving as multiple obbligato instruments as well as serving a very helpful accompanying role if necessary. Additionally, string instruments can provide numerous timbral variations, from bowed playing, pizzicatos, harmonics, multiple stops, legato, marcato, tremolo, trills, and so on.

As with any choral-instrumental collaboration, it's key to write for all parts in a way that keeps all parts engaged. In many ways, it's easy to focus on the choral parts and have the string parts remain an afterthought by just doubling the entire time. It's important that the string players are also given parts where they can shine and be in the spotlight.

A somewhat recent example—and one that swept the choral scene in North America through the 2000s—is *Five Hebrew Love Songs* by Eric Whitacre. Originally composed for soprano, piano, and violin, Whitacre adapted several versions, including for mixed choir and string quartet. This very fine adaptation includes some luminous moments from the string quartet, especially in the texture-driven fourth movement "Éyze shéleg!" To compliment the aleatoric choral texture, spoken word, and soprano solo, the violins play harmonics in both long and short durations on a drone provided by the viola and cello. As the choir then turns to sing a vocalise on an [u] vowel, the quartet plays harmonized trills in a homophonic texture, creating a shivering quality.

Example 13.23: Eric Whitacre, *Five Hebrew Love Songs*, "Éyze shéleg!"

© 2002 Walton Music Corp. All rights reserved.

String orchestras by their nature will provide many further options for harmony, timbre, and texture to supplement a choral group. The main concern is making sure that the string ensemble is balanced with the choir, as adding instruments can easily overwhelm a very small vocal ensemble. In general, with well-trained voices[10] one can have an equal number of singers to modern instruments to achieve balance (1:1). Untrained voices will need at least a ratio of three singers for every two instruments to be adequately balanced (3:2).

Example 13.24: Tarik O'Regan, *Triptych*, "Threnody."

Copyright © 2005 Novello & Co. Ltd. International Copyright Secured. All Rights Reserved.

---

10 I don't consider the average undergraduate, collegiate singer to fall into this category, even for vocal performance majors, but I do with graduate-level voice students.

Brass ensembles are welcome additions to choral music. Very often, brass ensembles can be found in the liturgical music of several Christian denominations and are very often paired with an organ part. One should be cautious that even with one instrument on a part, brass instruments can still sometimes overbalance in certain registers. The brass-organ combination is a rich and stately one, appropriate for many liturgical occasions such as Christmas, Easter, Pentecost, and Christ-the-King. Of course, this combination is welcome outside of liturgical settings. Along secular lines, of note is "The Spacious Firmament" by Gabriel Jackson for choir, soli, brass quintet, and organ.

Example 13.25: Gabriel Jackson, "The Spacious Firmament."

© Oxford University Press 2008. All rights reserved.

Woodwind ensembles are somewhat less common, as these instruments have very distinguished timbres that seem best used for accents of color rather than as an accompanying ensemble. Most choral music would call for either one or two wind instruments rather than a quartet, quintet, or other ensemble. In fact, I had a difficult time finding examples for this section that called for more than two wind instruments (that weren't for full orchestra).

Even still, some would say that two woodwind instruments are simply two obbligato instruments and they wouldn't be entirely wrong. The timbres of many of these instruments have been designed with the goal of standing out. Perhaps one of the reasons why there are so few examples of woodwind ensemble and choir is that these instruments can be so different from each other, whereas strings and brass are somewhat more a unified color than woodwinds can be. It's not to say writing for choir and wind quintet is not possible, but the relative lack of examples for this instrumentation with choirs should say something.

Example 13.26: Eve Duncan, "Stars."

Copyright © 2016 Eve Duncan. Used by permission.

Percussion

Percussion players and ensembles are less common and somewhat unconventional but their collaborations have quite a bit of creative potential for composers and arrangers. We can also find some truly wonderful examples in modern choral literature.

On matters of balance there are no generalities to be made. Because of the variety of percussion instruments, each needs to be considered individually. Some percussion (both pitched and un-pitched) can cover a choir's sound: suspended cymbals, for example. Other percussion instruments will be softer and might be more easily covered themselves by a choir's sound (a possible example is a marimba). Still others will be heard well but won't cover a choir's sound easily, for example the glockenspiel.

The huge range of timbral colors available from so many different and varied instruments allows for an equally broad range of affects and moods with relatively little effort. Using certain percussion instruments with specific passages or movements of a choral work can very effectively create a variety of tableaus or vignettes.

One particularly good example of choir with percussion is *I Hate and I Love* by Dominick Argento. This cantata, based on loosely translated poetry of Catullus, explores a variety of moods and dispositions and reflects them in the percussion chosen for each movement. A different set of percussion instruments is called for from movement to movement. The first movement uses different sized suspended cymbals; the second calls for wind chimes and tubular bells; the third calls for wood block and temple blocks; the fourth calls for bell tree, triangle, and crotales; the fifth calls for timpani, tom-toms, bongos, and tambourine; and the sixth calls for four gongs and glockenspiel. The seventh is the most mercurial and frantic, calling for bass drum, tam-tam, glockenspiel, tubular bells, suspended cymbals, timpani, and gongs. The eighth movement—a repetition of the first—calls for suspended cymbals again.

Of note in this work is the constant callback of the choir singing the word "love" on an F augmented major 7th chord, punctuated by a tubular bell (marked as "chimes" in the score). This word on this chord with the tubular bell returns in different movements throughout the work. The tubular bell helps makes this callback more recognizable, especially in the movements that don't call for the bells otherwise.

Example 13.27: Dominick Argento, *I Hate and I Love*, "Let us live, my Clodia, and let us love."

© 1981 Boosey & Hawkes. Reproduced by permission of Boosey & Hawkes.

Example 13.28: Dominick Argento, *I Hate and I Love*, "You promise me, my dearest life."

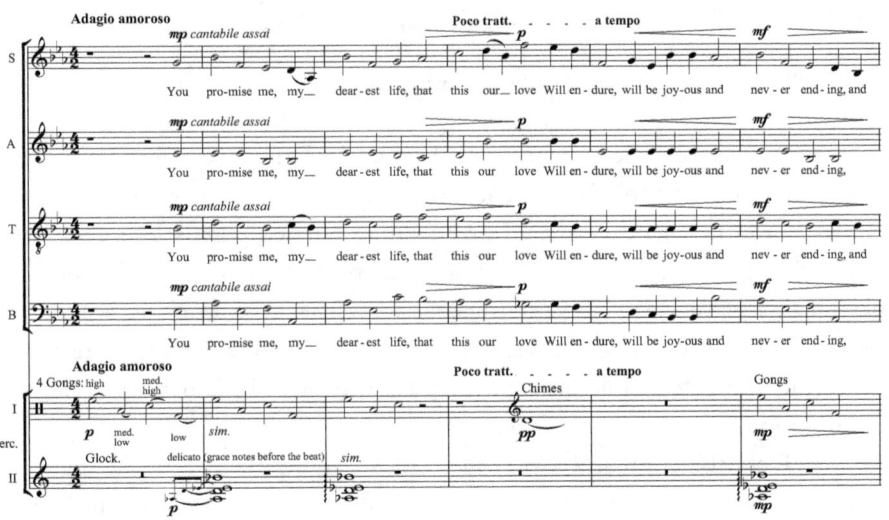

© 1981 Boosey & Hawkes. Reproduced by permission of Boosey & Hawkes.

Many of the percussion instruments are unpitched, which requires the choir to be more independent because the percussion can't be leaned on like a keyboard accompaniment would.

Example 13.29: Dominick Argento, *I Hate and I Love*, "Was it a lioness from the mountains of Libya."

© 1981 Boosey & Hawkes. Reproduced by permission of Boosey & Hawkes.

Another excellent example is "Vineta" by Ēriks Ešenvalds. In contrast to the previous example by Argento, Ešenvalds' work involves more pitched percussion rather than unpitched or indefinite pitched percussion. This work calls for vibraphone, glockenspiel, tubular bells, bass drum, suspended cymbals—presumably played by a single musician—as well as a few triangles among the singers. These instruments help create several tableaus of dramatically different color and character while also creating a sense of cohesion throughout the composition.

Describing a world lost at the bottom of the Baltic Sea, the maritime mood of this work evokes mystery, wonder, and simultaneously, the macabre.

Instrumental Collaboration 239

Example 13.30: Ēriks Ešenvalds, "Vineta."

© Musica Baltica, 2009. Printed with permission.

Example 13.31: Ēriks Ešenvalds, "Vineta."

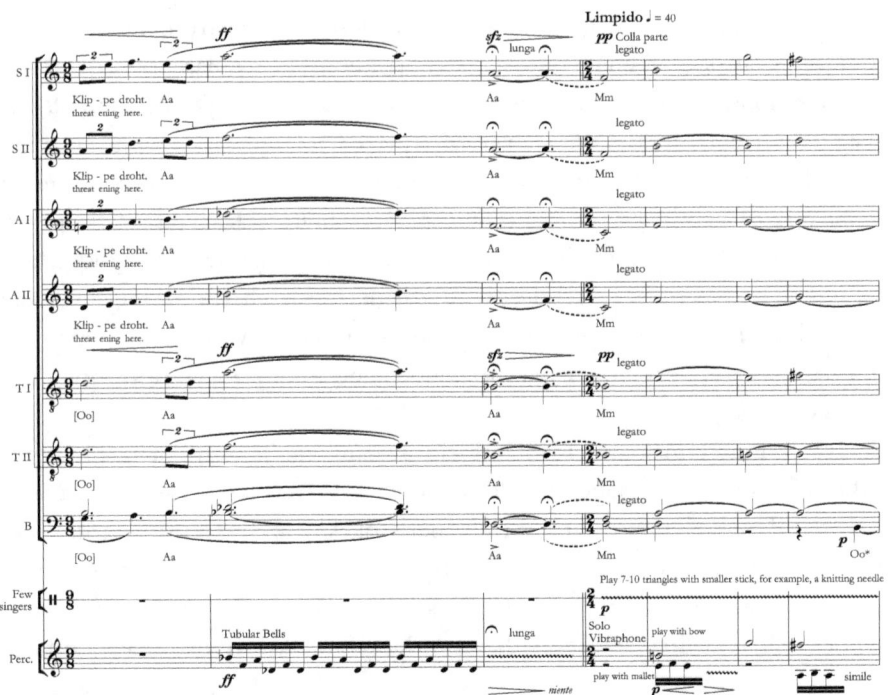

* Drone (bourdon) singing with possibly overtones' effect

© Musica Baltica, 2009. Printed with permission.

Example 13.32: Ēriks Ešenvalds, "Vineta."

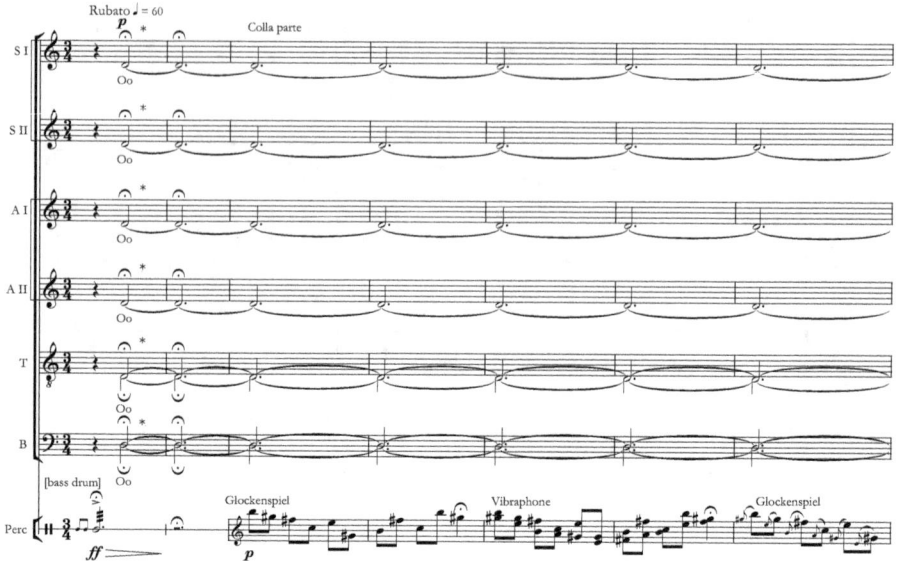

* Drone (bourdon) singing with possibly overtones' effect

© Musica Baltica, 2009. Printed with permission.

Bells and Glasses

Handbells and glasses are a category of instruments that are somewhat outside of conventional categorization but regularly part of choral collaborations. These are a series instruments where single instruments are assigned a single pitch, and the series is played by multiple people. In many cases, these instruments can be played by members of the ensemble themselves. In the case of handbells, sometimes this responsibility is delegated to a separate ensemble—a handbell choir—which specializes in handbell technique and literature. Bells can be a challenge to balance with choirs as they produce many different overtones, and their clappers can give a very sharp, percussive attack. They are very effective with louder, more jubilant compositions and arrangements.

Hand chimes are also handheld instruments like the bells. However, rather than being the shape of bells, hand chimes are shaped more like a large tuning fork or square tube and the clapper strikes from the outside rather than inside the bulb as with bells.[11] The clappers of the chimes are often made of softer materials, which lends to a less sharp attack. Hand chimes create a gentler, more mellow sound as they produce fewer overtones than the bells.

---

11 Venita MacGorman, "About Those Chimes," Accessed April 29, 2024. https://area9.handbellmusicians.org/about-those-chimes/

They have proved to be very popular with choirs as they are subdued, less percussive, and easier to balance with voices. They are effective for milder, more reflective compositions and arrangements.

The choice between these instruments is not always indicated by the composer, but the distinction would not be unwelcome.

Example 13.33: Bob Chilcott, "The Singing Heart."

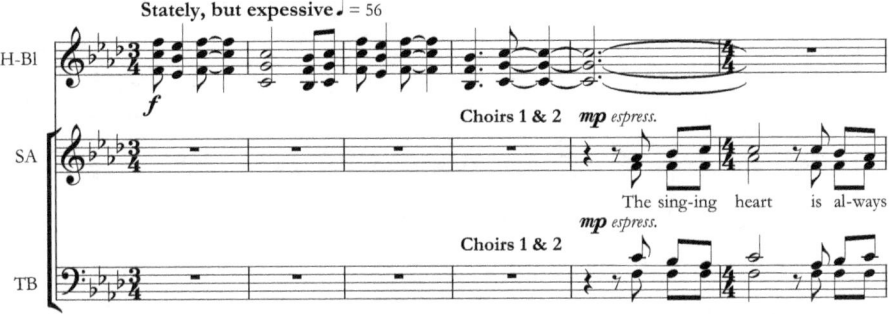

© Oxford University Press 2002. All rights reserved.

Tuned glasses—typically some sort of stemware—are a more recent addition to mainstream choral repertoire, made popular almost single-handedly by Latvian composer Ēriks Ešenvalds. Their sonorous humming sounds, produced by rubbing the rim of the glass with a wet index finger, can produce a shimmering, eerie effect. The amount of water in said glass will determine the pitch. In a notes of the word "Stars," Ešenvalds casually suggests "to ask your singers to check their kitchen at home." He also suggests not purchasing a set of glasses from the same manufacturer "as they might make the same sound."[12]

Regarding balance, Ešenvalds suggests 24 glasses—"4 glasses per pitch"—for a choir of 30 singers. A good rule of thumb would be to have a minimum of three glasses per pitch for small ensembles but each ensemble will have to make that balancing decision on their own. Even with many glasses, the sound is not likely to overpower the ensemble in any meaningful way.

---

12 Notes from "Stars."

Example 13.34: Ēriks Ešenvalds, "Stars."

© Musica Baltica, 2011. Printed with permission.

Other Examples

It's not possible to call attention to every possible combination of instruments for a chamber ensemble, but there are a few standouts. First would be *Fern Hill* by John Corigliano, which he composed for his high school music teacher during his undergraduate education at Columbia University. There are three versions: the original 1960 version was composed for piano, harp, strings; in 1965, Corigliano arranged a version for full orchestra; and in 1999 he again revisited the work and arranged it for chamber orchestra (flute, oboe, clarinet, horn, harp, strings).[13]

Of note is a work by Tan Dun called *Water Passion after St. Matthew* that was commissioned by Helmut Rilling for the turn of the millennium. The work for choir, two soloists, violin, cello, and three percussion players has found widespread acclaim from choral musicians who have encountered it. What makes this work so special is the use of water and other natural materials, such as stones, as a major percussion instruments.

A somewhat unusual but wonderful combination is found in *Walden Pond* by Dominick Argento, which calls for a harp and three cellos. The cellos provide some very compelling triadic harmonics and glissandi, while an arpeggiated harp imitates lapping water.

---

13 John Corigliano, "Fern Hill," Accessed April 29, 2024. https://www.johncorigliano.com/works/fern-hill-full-orchestra

Full Orchestra

Choirs have been companions to some form of orchestral ensemble from its conception around the beginnings of opera through its evolution to today's generally accepted modern form. As the composition and numbers of instruments—as well as the instruments themselves—have changed, so too has the role of the choir with these large instrumental ensembles. As orchestras have grown, and instruments have become louder, choirs have had to compensate with larger ensembles as well as a more robust singing aesthetic and technique.

Some of the following considerations will overlap slightly, but we will consider general balancing, doubling, text intelligibility, and choral divisions with regards to choral-orchestral writing.

Strategies for Scoring

It can feel easy to get overwhelmed when writing for choir and full orchestra, but it's important to not overthink it. The same strategies employed with writing for choir and keyboard instrument, or choir and chamber ensemble, can translate well to this application. The main difference is that orchestras provide a larger breadth of timbres and dynamic ranges that can easily cover the choral ensemble.

One approach is to compose "complete" orchestra parts and "complete" choral parts. In other words, if you separated the two halves from one another, they could stand on their own independently. This approach will of course result in nearly all the choral parts being doubled by some sort of instrument combination or section. This will yield good results, but just as with music that has excessive doubling, it may come across as dense and opaque throughout, as well as bring up some issues with balance. And while there are moments that call for this, as a point of departure it will be too dense too much of the time and each individual timbre won't be appreciated as much.

The opposite strategy is to not have any overlapping or doubled parts, but instead to carve out a space for the choir anytime the choir is singing. It's important to make space for the choir in what can be an easily overwhelming sonic landscape. This is a principle considered in orchestration generally before voices are added. If one wants to call attention to a specific instrument for a solo, or a section of the orchestra for any reason, it's important to leave room for that instrument—spatially[14], temporally, and sonically.

---

14 As the composer or arranger, you may not always have a say as far as space is concerned, but it's not unreasonable to give general spatial directions as other composers have done.

The downside with this approach is that choirs of lesser ability or training may feel unsupported without any instruments doubling their parts. It's not necessary to focus on one or the other alone; these two approaches can easily find balance. There is merit to having "overlapping" parts as well as instruments doubling with choral parts and merit in leaving space for every instrument without any doubling.

Nikolai Rimsky-Korsakov seemed to be of two minds regarding these strategies. He seemed to separate his strategies based on whether he was working with choirs or individual soloists. For choirs, he mostly approached the process with the idea of having the parts doubled: "Doubling choral parts by instruments is generally a good plan."[15] Regarding individual soloists, Rimsky-Kosakov seemed to advise against doubling for the most part saying, "In such a case the latter should not be doubled by the orchestra, neither should rhythmical figures be written for any instrument corresponding with those in the vocal part."[16] He goes on to add:

> Melodic doubling of voices by orchestral instruments (in unison or octaves) is of frequent occurrence, but incessant duplication for an extended period of time should be avoided; it is only permissible in isolated phrases... Uninterrupted or too frequent duplication should be avoided, not only because the operation deprives the singer of full freedom of expression, but also because it replaces by a mixed timbre the rare characteristic qualities of the human voice.[17]

Another strategy is to think of the choral ensemble as another section equal to the strings or brass. Yet another approach is to see the choral ensemble as essentially equal to the entire orchestra rather than just one section. The former will encourage the composer or arranger to have the choir as more of an afterthought or a supporting role to other parts, while the latter will call for the choir being front and center of attention. For example, perhaps the choir part is a vocalise and meant to serve as an effect in a film soundtrack. Or perhaps the choir is in an opera that is providing commentary like a Greek chorus. Either need requires different approaches.

---

15   Rimsky-Korsakov, *Principles of Orchestration*, 136.

16   Rimsky-Korsakov, *Principles of Orchestration*, 130.

17   Rimsky-Korsakov, *Principles of Orchestration*, 133.

General Balance

Modern orchestras can easily overpower voices, especially voices that are untrained or underdeveloped. There's a completely separate conversation to be had about how to staff and voice a choral orchestral performance to be successful, but most often, choral orchestral works—especially larger ones—require large to extra-large choral forces, as discussed in Chapter 9.

With well-trained voices[18] one can have an equal number of voices to modern instruments to achieve balance (1:1). Untrained voices will need at least a ratio of three singers for every two instruments to be adequately balanced (3:2). With Baroque or period instruments, one can have slightly fewer trained singers to instruments to be balanced. With untrained singers, one can have the same number of voices to period instruments (1:1) to achieve a balanced sound. One reason is because trained singers are very good at employing the singer's formant as mentioned at the beginning of this chapter. While the singer's formant certainly helps, it has its limitation, especially against certain instruments.

Each section of the orchestra has its own particular color and timbre that could compete with singers on their own. In general, the more sections of the orchestra are involved the more it has the potential to cover the choral textures. Rimsky-Korsakov confirms as much in his own writing: "It must also be remembered that a ff passage on an enlarged orchestra, comprising wood-wind in fours, and numerous brass (sometimes in threes), is capable of overpowering a large mixed chorus."[19]

In cases where the choir is somehow offstage, the orchestra should of course be brought down in dynamic to balance. Interestingly, Rimsky-Korsakov wrote this about offstage choirs: "A chorus in the wings requires as light an accompaniment as that employed for a solo singer on the stage."[20] One should also consider that having a choir off stage will limit that choir's text intelligibility, and in those cases, having few words, or simply vocalizing on pure vowels, is strongly recommended.

Even still, with all the care and attention made to balance in the writing process, certain balance issues still become apparent in rehearsals or performances. This is where some choral directors who are preparing choirs to

---

18 As noted previously, I don't consider the average undergraduate, collegiate singer to fall into this category, even for vocal performance majors. Graduate-level voice students are a different matter, but rarely does one find a symphonic chorus full of graduate-level voice students.

19 Rimsky-Korsakov, *Principles of Orchestration*, 138.

20 Rimsky-Korsakov, *Principles of Orchestration*, 138.

sing with orchestras take matters into their own hands regarding what's written in the score and will double a single part by adding on other sections. For example, if there is a soprano part by it itself, and it doesn't go too high, very often a choral director will instruct the altos to sing the part as well. This is similarly done with tenors and basses. Conductors will sometimes ask tenors to join on an alto part or add altos to a tenor part. This is done to throw as many voices onto a part as possible for presence and balance.

I remember sitting in a guest lecture with a conductor who spent most of his career with a major U.S. orchestra choir. During his remarks, he turned his attention to balance in Stravinsky's *Symphony of Psalms*. This conductor talked about their rehearsal strategy with the opening alto line by saying that they typically invite the sopranos to join. They went on to say that they even invite the tenors to join in as well, just to have enough voices on the part to balance with the ensemble, even though the part is only indicated to be sung at mezzo forte and the instrumentation is marked either mezzo forte or piano and honestly isn't very dense.

Example 13.35: Igor Stravinsky, *Symphony of Psalms*, Movement I.

© 1931 Hawkes & Son (London) Ltd. © 1948 Hawkes & Son (London) Ltd. U.S Copyright renewed.

This example is obviously a hyperbolic one, but it embodies the strategies that many choral conductors will employ to achieve balance, and to try to preserve some vocal stamina in repertoire that can be quite demanding on the voice. What should be gleaned from this anecdote? Perhaps that experiencing and expressing different vocal colors and their subtlety in voicing is best left for a cappella passages, and that when instruments are playing, subtlety with vocal timbres is not always feasible.

Doubling

Any choral parts being doubled by instruments should, of course, be marked a dynamic lower than the choir parts. If choral parts are divided, consider doubling with a single instrument. This practice can be seen in the

"Sanctus" movement of Verdi's *Requiem*. Verdi has written a double fugue for double choir and has the first oboe doubling the sopranos from choir I, while the second oboe is doubling with the sopranos from choir II. This doubling continues with the remaining choral parts doubling with single clarinet, bassoon and horn parts. Accompanying all of these are the string parts below in a softer run of sixteenth notes, which allows the singers to feel supported by the orchestra while allowing for balance and for text intelligibility.

Example 13.36: Giuseppe Verdi, *Requiem*, "Sanctus."

Text Intelligibility

I have some colleagues (composers, conductors, as well as singers) who joke that intelligibility is a lost cause in choral-orchestral repertoire, both in composing and performing. While text intelligibility is an issue in choral music in general, its pursuit should never be abandoned at any point in the creation of choral music. There are a few challenges with composing for choir and orchestra that end up compounding on each other. Each of these affect intelligibility of words.

When orchestration is dense and dynamics are high, balancing with the choir will already be a challenge, and naturally words will be less intelligible. The immediate solution is to have the choir sing in higher, stronger parts of their voices to balance. While singing in higher, stronger parts of the voice will allow the singers' sound to be better heard, it requires singers to modify their vowels to sing in a healthy, hygienic way.[21] These modifications usually come at the cost of intelligibility. More challenging still, many choirs that sing with

---

21 As discussed in Chapter 3.

orchestras—particularly very large choirs for very large orchestras—are often staffed by volunteer singers who may or may not have received adequate vocal training with diction technique.[22] There are, of course, notable exceptions where very large orchestral choirs are staffed by professional singers with extensive training, but this is very much the exception. These three compounding factors are an eternal struggle with some choral orchestral literature in particular.

One particularly tragic example of irredeemable text intelligibility is in the first movement of Ralph Vaughan Williams' *Sea Symphony*. Even while the work is an incredible triumph in the early catalog of Vaughan Williams and a leap forward for him writing in his newfound voice, the work is plagued with intelligibility issues. In some passages, these issues are simply beyond fixing in performance.

Example 13.37: Ralph Vaughan Williams, *Sea Symphony*, "I. A Song for All Seas, All Ships."

---

22   As discussed in Chapter 9.

While it is easy to lay blame on the dense and energetic orchestration, there are some fundamental problems in the vocal writing before we even consider the orchestration. For the moment, let's consider the choral part on its own. Vaughan Williams is setting a poem by Walt Whitman from his collection Leaves of Grass. While undeniably stunning poetry, the poem itself is written in a somewhat dense, free verse with many run-on statements:

> Behold, the sea itself,
> And on its limitless, heaving breast, the ships;
> See, where their white sails, bellying in the wind, speckle the green
>   and blue,
> See, the steamers coming and going, steaming in or out of port,
> See, dusky and undulating, the long pennants of smoke.[23]

Such poetry is difficult to set in a convincing way, and even still it can present an inherent challenge of immediate comprehension to the listener.

For the first few measures the altos and basses are singing in octave doubling, while the sopranos and tenors are singing an imitative part also in octave doubling. Within a few measures, each part is singing an independent part from the others in very sophisticated contrapuntal polyphony. This is where the intelligibility issues truly begin. Already, these voices are overlapping with one another and layering drastically different words on top of one another. In some cases, there are three words, with three different vowel sounds, being sung at once. The writing on its own will not allow for a clear understanding of the words, let alone their meaning.

Example 13.38: Ralph Vaughan Williams, *Sea Symphony*, "I. A Song for All Seas, All Ships."

---

23   Walt Whitman, "Song of the Exposition No 8," "U.S. Editions of Leaves of Grass." Accessed April 29, 2024. https://whitmanarchive.org/published-writings/leaves-of-grass/1881, 163.

Let's be clear, this vocal writing is actually quite good on its own and shows a very good understanding of the voice and how to write well for it. The error lies in having this kind of choral writing paired with this text. If Vaughan Williams were using this same vocal writing but instead setting one or maybe two repeating words, or if Vaughan Williams used this text with a more homophonic texture, intelligibility wouldn't be nearly as much of an issue.

The problems are only compounded once the orchestra is added in with its incredibly dense and active texture. Even though Vaughan Williams tries to pull the orchestra back by having specific parts play in mezzo piano or softer, it's not nearly enough. First, the sheer size and scope of the orchestration and second having too many instruments doubling the vocal parts and playing across the singers' register, make it difficult to allow the singers to be heard. Because the instrumentation provides so much competition to the choir—in addition to the parts being written in high parts of their range—the singers need to modify their vowels to sing that loud and that high in a healthy, resonant manner. As discussed previously in Chapter 3, modified vowels, while necessary, very often come at the cost of intelligibility. It also doesn't help that these parts are only doubling one other vocal part, so only half the choir is singing a specific part at certain points and only for a short period of time.

There are solutions to this issue. The first is to return to some principles of text setting regarding text intelligibility and Palestrina discussed in Chapter 2. For movements with fewer words—and where those words can be repeated—Palestrina composes in polyphonic textures because word intelligibility isn't a pressing matter. For the movements that have many more words, Palestrina composes mostly in strict homophonic textures because word intelligibility is a much higher need.

The same general principle should apply to choral-orchestra writing. If one has lots of difficult words to set, allow the choir the space to sing them without any significant competition and without having to do a great deal of vowel modification. And of course, consider more homophonic or even monophonic textures. Polyphonic textures will already obscure many of the words and adding lots of competing instruments will make it even more difficult. Additionally, avoid having one section sing on its own during these parts.

Let's consider another example by Richard Wagner, specifically in his opera *Tristan und Isolde*. Act I is the only act with a choral ensemble, with the chorus of sailors. When Wagner has a sizable number of words to get through with the chorus, he pulls the orchestra back to a handful of instruments in very soft dynamic, with a few flourishes that don't obscure the text. Wagner also has the choir singing in homophonic textures that make sure that the text is sung in an efficient and uniform manner.[24]

Example 13.39: Richard Wagner, *Tristan und Isolde*, Act One, Scene Two.

At other points, when there aren't as many words and orchestration is still light, Wagner can have the tenor and bass parts somewhat independent of one another. He still calls for a somewhat leaner orchestration because in many cases the choir is offstage.

---

24 It is worth noting that at this point in the opera the choir is offstage and would be covered quite easily anyway.

When there are even fewer words, Wagner can add more instruments at louder levels. In the last scene of Act I,[25] Wagner has the tenors and basses singing the repeated words "Heil! König Marke Heil!" Of course, Wagner will help balance the choir against the orchestra by having the tenors and basses singing in didactic harmony, without divisions, and at full dynamic and in very generous parts of their voices. For a measure they are being doubled by the woodwinds and some brass, but that doubling stops when the tenors and basses begin to divide again. The remaining orchestral parts are pulled back slightly and thinned out somewhat to allow the divided parts to be appreciated. Text intelligibility may still be an issue but in this case it's usually something that can be fixed in performance and is not irredeemable.

Example 13.40: Richard Wagner, *Tristan und Isolde*, Act One, Scene Five.

Divisons

Provided that the choral to orchestral balance is achieved as outlined in the previous paragraphs, one can then consider achieving balance through writing. As a general principle there is an inverse relationship between choral divisions and general loudness of the orchestration. In other words, when

---

25 In almost all productions, the choir is onstage at this point.

orchestral forces are soft and transparent, eight-part divisions are possible; however, when orchestral forces are loud or dense, divisions are less advised except perhaps at cadences.

In a cappella writing, most composers would find it conventional to have several divisions as one reaches louder or more climactic moments; in choral-orchestral music, the opposite is a smarter strategy. As the accompanying orchestral material becomes louder, the choral writing should not divide, but rather should stay undivided or consolidate.

At louder levels, as shown above, unison or octave doubling is very effective. Four-part harmony is possible at louder dynamics provided that each voice is singing in a stronger register. When accompaniments become medium loud, extensive divisions may become more easily covered or obscured, especially if voices are in lower or weaker registers. When accompaniments are loud, four-part (or further divided) harmony is most successful if all voices are in the strongest parts of their voice. Otherwise, unison and octave doublings, as well as dyadic harmonies, will be more successful. The standard four parts without divisions is better heard, especially if each voice is matching the dynamic and avoiding particularly weaker registers.

Extensive divisions beyond eight parts are probably less effective as many of the vocal colors present when singing without accompaniment will become harder to hear and appreciate even with light accompaniment. For example, in Vaughan Williams' "Serenade to Music"—a work written for 16 singers and orchestra—he has the choir divide into several parts with light accompaniment. But even with the lighter accompaniment, the vocal colors of this passage lose their clarity and warmth and it becomes somewhat lost in the texture, especially the basses and baritones. It doesn't help that the basses on a low D2 remain underbalanced. Additionally, the instrumental parts are overlapping the choral parts and providing contrary motion to what the choir is singing. It looks great on the page, but in person this choral passage isn't as impressive as it would be if it were a cappella.

Example 13.41: Ralph Vaughan Williams, "Serenade to Music."

© Oxford University Press 1938. All rights reserved.

I fear that having shared two poor examples of choral-orchestral writing from Vaughan Williams will convey the idea that I think his music is poorly composed for choir and orchestra. This is not the case but it's simply repertoire that I have closely studied. And to prove it, I'm going to share a good example passage from the same work.

Here, Vaughan Williams writes for the choir in unison octaves while the orchestra is playing at a fortissimo dynamic. When Vaughan Williams does have the choir divide, there are a few things that make it more successful than other efforts. First, all the voices are in strong or very generous parts of their voices and can balance better. Second, the sopranos and tenors are still doubling in octaves along with the altos doubling the basses. Third, the orchestra's pitches avoid, for the most part, overlapping with the choir's pitches. In other words, most of instruments have carved out a space for the voices.

Example 13.42: Ralph Vaughan Williams, "Serenade to Music."

© Oxford University Press 1938. All rights reserved.

For another example, let's return to another opera by Richard Wagner and observe how he divides choir with orchestra. Keep in mind that the singers for these parts are meant to be fully mature, well-trained professionals with big voices who have trained for decades to sing these staged works. In *Tannhäuser*, Act III, when the pilgrims begin to sing, the chorus is written in divided TTBB chorus with the orchestra tacet through most of it. Because most of this passage is a cappella, the choral divisions are heard clearly without anything to obscure them.

Example 13.43: Richard Wagner, *Tannhäuser*, Act Three, Scene One.

As the chorus reaches its climax and the orchestra begins to add instruments and increase the overall dynamic, Wagner pulls back on the divisions and has the chorus sing the melody in unison. In fact, the voices stop dividing and begin to sing in octave doubling by the time that phrase comes to an end. When the woodwinds and brass enter with a forte dynamic, the tenors and basses sing in unison.

Example 13.44: Richard Wagner, *Tannhäuser*, Act Three, Scene One.

The tenors and basses only return to their divisions once there is a break in the instrumentation and Wagner has a full bar of unaccompanied singing again. The tenors and basses remain in divisions as the orchestra begins to diminuendo.

Example 13.45: Richard Wagner, *Tannhäuser*, Act Three, Scene One.

As you continue to compose for choir and orchestra, you will continue to learn what works and what doesn't work as well and what you prefer as a composer. Another resource for studying choral-orchestral collaboration can be found in *Choral Arranging* by Hawley Ades, who focuses on texture and fabric of sound. Ades runs through several different examples of choral-orchestral collaboration and the principles that can be gleaned from those examples.

Wind Band

Wind bands—consisting of woodwind, brass, and percussion—are uncommon choral collaborators, but welcome ones. It's not necessarily an easy ensemble to collaborate with as the group can easily overpower and cover the choral ensemble, but there are ways to work around this issue and make this combination very attractive.

The same strategies used with choral-orchestral collaborations can also be applied to choral-band collaborations. Whether it be strategies to writing complete parts and doubling versus carving out space, placing the choir on equal footing to the entire wind ensemble, fostering text intelligibility, as well as balancing divisions, many of those same principles can apply here.

In addition to all these considerations, I've also heard some composers express that adding a choir to a wind ensemble can sometimes provide a similar effect as adding a string section to the ensemble. I'm sure some others would take umbrage with that sentiment that a wind band would need a string ensemble.

Balance

The composition of a wind band can vary between one instrument per part to several instruments per part. Nevertheless, a wind ensemble can still be tricky to balance with a choir, as wind instruments are still generally louder. Whether in one instrument per part or multiple instruments per part, with well-trained voices one can maintain a ratio of three singers for every two instruments to be adequately balanced (3:2). With untrained voices, it would be wise to maintain a ratio of two singers for every instrument (2:1).

The woodwind instruments will generally balance better than the brass instruments will, but the solution is fairly simple: mark the brass instruments a dynamic lower than the choir when they are singing and playing simultaneously. Additionally, as mentioned previously, allowing space for the singers—sonically, temporally, and spatially—will be especially helpful.

Examples

Among the first collaborations we see in choral literature is Schubert's *Deutche Messe*, which was published posthumously. It's a simple work; most of the instrumental writing simply doubles the choral parts, especially in the "Sanctus." Schubert is mindful when doubling to keep the instruments in balanced dynamics. When the horn and timpani sound on the cadences, Schubert is careful to keep those marked down a dynamic level.

Example 13.46: Franz Schubert, *Deutche Messe*, "Zum Sanctus."

The mournful dirge "Begräbnisgesang" by Johannes Brahms for choir, wind band, and timpani is a fine example from the middle of the Romantic period but relatively early in Brahms' career. Brahms is careful when doubling the choral parts to have the instruments a dynamic below when multiple words are being presented.

260 The Technique of Choral Writing

Example 13.47: Johannes Brahms, "Begräbnisgesang."

Although not for full wind band, Stravinsky's Mass, for double wind quintet, is another fine example of composing for winds and choir. Very often Stravinsky will mark the instruments to be a dynamic lower than the singers, or at least the very loud instruments. Other times, he is carving a space for the singers by keeping the instruments away of the singers' pitches for the most part or by allowing some windows of rest to let the singers' sounds pass through unimpeded.

Example 13.48: Igor Stravinsky, *Mass*, "Kyrie."

© 1948 Hawkes & Son (London) Ltd. Reproduced by permission of Boosey & Hawkes.

Example 13.49: Igor Stravinsky, *Mass*, "Sanctus."

© 1948 Hawkes & Son (London) Ltd. Reproduced by permission of Boosey & Hawkes.

Continuing Study

Suggested Exercises

Short
- » Discuss what makes a successful instrumental collaboration and what are some potential pitfalls.
- » Discuss the pros and cons of a piano collaboration versus an organ collaboration or harp collaboration.
- » Discuss general principles and strategies to maintain balance choir and instruments.
- » Discuss some text setting strategies when working with larger instrumental ensembles.

Long
- » Take one of the following short melodies (or another of your choosing) and create a short arrangement for choir and:
  - Keyboard instrument or harp.
  - An obbligato instrument of your choosing.
  - An instrumental ensemble of your choosing.

Suggested Listening

Piano
Peter Quince at the Clavier - Dominick Argento
Trois Chansons Bretonnes - Henk Badings
"In the Bleak Midwinter" - Abbie Betinis
"Soir Sur La Plaine" - Lili Boulanger

Instrumental Collaboration

Ein Deutsche Requiem (piano four hands arrangement) - Johannes Brahms
Liebeslieder Waltzes - Johannes Brahms
Les Amours de Poètes - Edgar Cosma
"Madrigal" - Gabriel Fauré
Airplane Cantata - Gabriel Jackson
Mid-Winter Songs - Morten Lauridsen
Zigeunerlieder - Robert Schumann

Organ
Chichester Psalms - Leonard Bernstein
"Jubilate Deo" - Benjamin Britten
Verse Anthems - William Byrd
Requiem - Maurice Duruflé
Verse Anthems - Orlando Gibbons
Collegium Regale - Herbert Howells
St. Paul Service - Herbert Howells
"In the beginning was the Word" - Gabriel Jackson
"I Was Glad" - Charles Horatio Hubert Parry
Berliner Mass - Arvo Pärt
Evening Service in G, op. 81 - Charles Villiers Stanford
Verse Anthems - Thomas Tomkins
"Jubilate Deo" - William Walton
"A Vision of Aeroplanes" - Ralph Vaughan Williams

Harp
Ceremony of Carols - Benjamin Britten
Three Nativity Carols - Stephen Paulus

Obbligato Instruments
"See Amid the Winter Snow" - Jocelyn Hagen
"O Quam Gloriosum" - Howard Helvey
"Ave Regina Coelorum" - Gabriel Jackson
A Procession Winding Around Me - Jeffrey Van

Chamber Ensembles
I Hate and I Love - Dominick Argento
Walden Pond - Dominick Argento
Water Passion after St. Matthew - Tan Dun
"Vineta" - Ēriks Ešenvalds
Requiem - Gabriel Fauré
To the Field of Stars - Gabriel Jackson
The Settling Years - Libby Larsen

Seven Last Words from the Cross - James MacMillan
Berliner Mass - Arvo Pärt
Passio - Arvo Pärt
Misa Criolla - Ariel Ramírez

Full Orchestra
Chichester Psalms - Leonard Bernstein
Ein Deutsche Requiem - Johannes Brahms
Fern Hill - John Corgliano
Requiem in D minor, op. 9 - Maurice Duruflé
Carmina Burana - Carl Orff
Belshazzar's Feast - William Walton
"Coronation Te Deum" - William Walton
Sea Symphony - Ralph Vaughan Williams
Dona Nobis Pacem - Ralph Vaughan Williams
"Serenade to Music" - Ralph Vaughan Williams

Wind Band
"Begräbnisgesang" - Johannes Brahms
Deutsche Messe - Franz Schubert
Mass - Igor Stravinsky

Chapter 14

Extended Techniques and Special Effects

*The lewd trebles squeak nothing but bawdy,
and the basses roar blasphemy.*
— William Congreve

Singing with words and syllables on specific pitches are only the primary colors of what vocal musicians can produce. As has been demonstrated by expiramental groups, and vocal ensembles of popular styles as well as other a cappella genres, the human voice is capable of a vast spectrum of sounds. These sounds have typically been at best underappreciated and at worst unimplemented by composers and arrangers in more classical styles of choral music.

There are countless ways to explore sounds that humans can make on their own and this list is by no means exhaustive. While I've done my best to gather all the techniques I am aware of in one place, there are likely to be others beyond my knowledge and indeed several effects and techniques that will need to be explored in the future.

Most of the techniques covered here are ones that are capable of being performed by the individual singer and, in theory, can be done by a larger ensemble. Some techniques and effects require multiple people, and thus can only be performed by a group of individual singers or the general ensemble.

I have attempted to be as inclusive as possible in this chapter. Consequently, some of these effects and techniques at the time of this publication may be considered gimmicky or passé and some conductors will not program music that includes some of these techniques. Listing them here does not at all indicate that these are all endorsed or even considered acceptable by the author. Please consider this caveat before incorporating them into your compositions.

While some of these ideas originated in vocal music, others did not but have found a home in choral music. For further study about techniques that an individual singer can explore, consider works by Luciano Berio for solo voice, such as "Sequenza III." Some of these may not be practical in a choral setting; however, these compositions certainly push the boundaries of colors and timbres to be used by singers and they are worth further exploration and discussion.

These various effects and techniques will be organized generally by production method. These will include pitched and un-pitched use of the vocal tract (from glottis to lips), techniques and effects that do not use the vocal tract, techniques and effects that require more than one musician, and other techniques. After being organized by their broader production, they will then be listed in alphabetical order.

Implementation

As discussed previously in Chapter 12 regarding choral textures, the question inevitably arises: how much is too much? This question could apply to both subjective artistic taste as well as practical matters.

Artistically, some readers may see the very existence of this chapter as too permissive. Others will be upset that I have relegated these ideas to a separate chapter, feeling that it sends the message that these ideas should be sequestered to the margins of what vocal music should be perceived as. Still others may interpret my cautions as too conservative or conformist. While I will give some cautions related to some specific techniques—as well as the overall use of them—these techniques should mostly be viewed objectively as any tool should be: appropriate for certain applications, less so for others.

For those who embrace a somewhat conventional point of view, less is often more. In their minds, special effects should be, for lack of a better word, special. The main idea is to avoid incorporating too many techniques or too much of one technique into a single composition. Overbalancing a single spice can ruin a dish, and overusing one effect or technique can tend to wear out its welcome quickly.

However, there are many instances where entire compositions based on unconventional techniques and effects have been immensely successful and effective. Creating a musical work outside of the traditional conventions of musical form and harmonic syntax takes an enormous amount of creativity, and often courage, to push against the norm. Why should I or anyone else hold anyone else back from experimenting in our art form?

Practically, some of these techniques require a significant amount of practice and training to execute. While it's important for singers to push the boundaries of what they can perform and grow in their techniques, it's also important to respect the amount of time that singers need for the rest of their practice. Singers, and indeed choral ensembles, may not have the luxury of using most of their practice time to master dozens of new techniques. Many of them are still working on mastering basic phonation and their time needs to be respected.

Additionally, the proficiency required for extended techniques can be a major consideration with any commissioning organization that you are working with. Some choirs will have the ability and willingness to take these risks while others will not. These issues should be a part of the conversation around your commission and the wishes and needs of the commissioning ensemble should be respected.

Intention should also play a big part of these uses. What is the intention behind the implementation of these techniques? Is it to further the artistic expression? Is it for shock value? Is it because it's trendy? All of these will have their merits, but maybe not all will be as valid. Some listeners will only be in favor of the first reason mentioned: to push artistic intentions and scoff at the rest. Some listeners just simply won't take many of these seriously and that's okay. Remember that pleasing everyone is not one of our goals as artists.

When we approach our proverbial canvas, we should consider all colors, all techniques, and all effects when creating our art. Part of that should include experimenting and that activity should come with a feeling of carefree play. How you chose to implement these techniques and effects will often come down to personal preference and taste. I encourage you to approach these ideas with curiosity but be open and willing to consider taking a step back if feedback from thoughtful, well-intentioned colleagues or mentors questions if you have overdone it.

Notation

Some of these extended techniques and special effects have become so ubiquitous that they have been codified into their own notation symbols. For example, trills (a technique we share with instruments) have been codified with a horizontal squiggle line. There are many other techniques and effects that have been codified somewhat with symbols that are not as ubiquitous as a trill. While they may be a very helpful shorthand, do not assume that every symbol will be immediately recognizable to every musician, and that you will probably need to provide a key explaining each symbol in a page before the score.

Many of these techniques and effects, however, will not have their own symbol and instead will rely on other means to convey their meanings to the musicians. Many of these will simply rely on instructions being written out, either above the staff or at the top or bottom margins of the page. Occasionally, the instructions will need a separate page—usually before the first page of the score—to fully explain. When writing these instructions out, take pains to be as clear and concise as possible. Also, make sure that you double check with a choral musician–either director or singer, but preferably both–that the instructions are clear and that your ideas are being conveyed in what is written.

Some choral techniques or effects can be notated through color coding or using colored markings to quickly relay information and ideas. This coding can be a very helpful method to convey certain needs, but consider a few potential drawbacks to this method: too many colors on a page can be distracting to read and can look confusing or intimating at first glance. Another obstacle may be that a music publisher will only print scores in black and white, and adding color can mean printing the scores will incur a cost the publisher won't wish to undertake. Cost is also something to consider if the scores are being printed by either yourself or the performing ensembles. However, this may not be an issue in the very near future as more and more choral ensembles are reading scores from electronic tablets.

Vocal Hygiene

All the sounds that humans can make both individually and collectively should be explored, cataloged, taught, and in many cases should be exploited much more than they currently are. Many of these techniques are relatively benign in their vocal demands, while others require heavy demands on the voice and are quite taxing and should be used sparingly, if at all. To return to the metaphor of tools: some tools are fundamentally harmless and others require words of caution regarding health and safety.

The vocal folds of the average female-assigned voice are 12 to 17 millimeters in length and between 17 and 23 millimeters for the average male-assigned voice[1]—about the length of one's thumbnail. These thin folds of tissue, while capable of some incredible sounds, can be quite delicate and can tire relatively quickly. Many singers will train for years—and in many cases decades—to hone a technique that allows them to sing big sounds for long durations in a sustainable way. It requires an equilibrium of physiological effort and airflow that some effects and techniques will almost certainly throw out of balance.

Within this chapter are many ideas that should be recorded and referenced, but with proper preparation and consideration. It is acceptable to ask for some of these techniques provided you understand that there is a price to pay, and you respect the sacrifice it takes. Listen to and respect any pushback from performers due to vocal hygiene. Please take any warnings about vocal health seriously and do not pressure a singer or group of singers to maintain unsustainable practices. While you may believe your composition or arrangement is a masterpiece, no composition is worth sacrificing the health, well-being, and longevity of a human voice.

Pitched Vocalizations

Animal noises and sounds from nature

This is the practice of imitating noises made by various animals or other sounds found in nature. Various animal sounds can be produced using a variety of techniques including pitched and unpitched vocalizations (although the examples shown all used pitched vocalizations).

This effect is very often used in arrangements of folk songs or in compositions about the natural world in an effort to sonically replicate a "wild" and "untamed" environment. This effect can lean towards being hokey or evocative depending on the desired effect.

---

1   Sataloff and Kost, "The Effects of Age," 63.

Example 14.1: Aaron Copland (arr. Irving Fine), "I bought me a cat."

© 1950 The Aaron Copland Fund for Music, Inc. Reproduced by permission of Boosey & Hawkes.

Example 14.2: Stephen Leek, *Great Southern Spirits*, "Kondalilla."

© Stephen Leek. Used by permission.

Buccal speech

Buccal speech is sometimes referred to as "Donald Duck" speech, named after the Disney character (originally voiced by Clarence Nash) who made this technique ubiquitous. This vocalization is made by using the vibrations of inner cheek to phonate rather than the glottis. I am not aware of any practical applications in choral music nor am I aware of any examples in the canon, but it's an option.

Chanting on pitch

This is where composers will designate a portion of text to be chanted at a natural speech rhythm determined by the performers. This technique is used regularly in the liturgical music of traditional Christian worship, in particular the chanting of psalms. The prevailing idea is for text to be performed in a declamatory fashion and to be highly expressive.

Example 14.3: Claudio Monteverdi, *Vespro della Beata Vergine*, "Dixit Dominus."

Example 14.4: Claudio Monteverdi, *Il quarto libro de madrigali a cinque voci*, "Sfogava con le stelle."

Falsetto

This is the highest register in male-assigned voices and is the register used regularly by countertenors. This sound is produced by singing in Cricothyroid-Dominant Production (CDP).[2] Walt Disney famously used this register to produce Mickey Mouse's voice. Navigating in and out of this register is part of the training that male-assigned voices practice on a regular basis. Trained tenors and basses will have been taught to use personal discretion if their part is written too high and too soft to reliably use a lower register.

Nevertheless, direction can be given to ask tenors and basses to sing a phrase or section in falsetto for a specific timbre. All male-assigned voices can be asked to sing in this register and can help extend the range of these lower voices into much higher ranges than they would normally sing.

One example of a composer's use of falsetto can be found in Ravel's *Trois Chansons*. In the first movement, "Nicolette," Ravel has the tenors sing the melody in falsetto and in a very high range to imitate the sound of the pre-pubescent page whose voice has not yet matured.

Be aware that not all these low voices use this register regularly and singing in it for extended periods of time may cause more fatigue than normal.

Example 14.5: Maurice Ravel, *Trois Chansons*, "Nicolette."

Flutter tongue

Flutter tongue is the rolling of the [r] consonant by gently placing a relaxed tongue on the alveolar region of the mouth and focusing air flow to allow it to vibrate. This technique is closely related to flutter tonguing that we find in flute music. The main difference is that in choral music it is voiced and

---

2 McCoy, *Your Voice*, 68.

pitched rather than just releasing unvoiced airflow. This sound is a distinctive characteristic in some languages, particularly Spanish and Italian. Keep in mind, however, that this rolled sound is sometimes difficult to pick up for speakers outside of those languages and may require more practice.

Forward and back placements

The human voice is capable of so many different colors, and much of that can come from the forward and back "placement" of the voice. It isn't that the voice is physically moving to these physiological regions, but rather that the sound waves produced by the vocal folds are resonating in different parts of the oropharynx and nasopharynx.

When very far forward, the voice can have a bright, pitched, nasal quality. When very far back the voice can sound round, dull, and swallowed. In between these two extremes, one can find so many different color gradients of useful timbres. Most singers and voice teachers will spend a considerable amount of time finding the ideal balance in their voice placement and singing from that place as a point of departure.

Composers and arrangers can and should feel at liberty to ask for "bright" or "warm" affects in certain lines, and even asking for extreme vocal placement if the music warrants that effect. You may also use the term "ordinary phonation" or "normal phonation" to clarify when you need the ensemble to return to their normal phonation (it's not necessary to say "balanced" or "normal phonation" otherwise). If the effect only needs to apply to one or a small group of notes, a bracket indicating the pitches can be very helpful for the purpose of clarity.

Example 14.6: Jaakko Mäntyjärvi, "Pseudo-Yoik."

© 1995 SULASOL. All rights reserved. Walton Music Corp. admin. USA and Canada

Glissando

A glissando is when you allow the voice to slide between either ascending or descending pitches. These slides can be done quickly or slowly over a variety of ranges and on vowels as well as voiced consonants. Where this can be tricky is when a slide is over an octave as well as over major breaks in the voice, especially from the head voice to the chest voice in female-assigned voices, and from the falsetto into the head voice for male-assigned voices. It's possible to navigate these breaks for trained voices and at slower speeds, but it just requires a bit more practice.

Example 14.7: James MacMillan, "O bone Jesu."

© Boosey & Hawkes Music Publishers Ltd. Reproduced by permission of Boosey & Hawkes.

Extended Techniques and Special Effects

Hand wah/Oscillation

This practice entails singing while covering the mouth with the hand and opening and closing the hand. This oscillation can be executed rapidly or at a slower speed. It is like a hand technique used by harmonica players to get a wah-wah effect on their instrument. This technique was made popular in the opening credit music for the HBO series *The White Lotus*.

A word of caution: this technique has also been used to mock and ridicule traditional vocal techniques used by Indigenous people of North America. Continuing this practice of mocking these Native peoples is highly offensive, and any use of this technique should be as far removed from that practice as possible.

Humming

Humming is sound made by closing the airflow out of the oropharynx and mouth and allowing the air to escape through the nasopharynx and nose. While humming is usually created by closing the mouth like an "m" consonant, it can also be created by closing the mouth with the tongue like an "n" consonant. Some composers will choose to notate humming with directions like "mouth closed." An example can be found in "O Magnum Mysterium" from *Quatre Motets pour le temps de Noël* by Francis Poulenc who notated with the phrase "bouche fermée."

Example 14.8: Francis Poulenc, *Quatre Motets pour le temps de Noël*, "O Magnum Mysterium."

Published by Editions Salabert. International Copyright Secured. All Rights Reserved. Reprinted by permission of Hal Leonard Europe.

Other composers will choose to notate humming by writing in the underlay "hum," "mm," or "hmm" depending on which they prefer.

Example 14.9: Andrew Maxfield, "For the Future."

© 2018 Walton Music Corp. All rights reserved.

One popular variation of humming is to sing with the alveolar [n] consonant instead of the bilabial [m]. While the sound is like humming, it has a slightly brighter, "buzzier" sound (even though the sound is still quite veiled and muted overall). Singers have also expressed being able to hear better when making this sound compared with humming because of the way it vibrates in the skull. This may be a better alternative to humming in a few situations and some conductors will ask their singers to use this alternative when presented with humming in a score.

Lip quaver

This technique involves phonating normally and using one's finger to oscillate back and forth between the upper and lower lips. This creates a cartoonish sound, giving an effect of singing under water with sound being made through water bubbles. Vowels and words can still be distinguished with this technique, although the intelligibility will be significantly marred. This technique is fairly specialized and may not prove useful in most scenarios.

Lip vibration

This technique simply requires forcing airflow through "motorboat lips." This can be done with or without phonating with the vocal folds. Without phonating, the sound produced will be just the lips vibrating against each other. With phonation these vibrations produce a humming, vibrating sound. Variation can be achieved depending on the speed of one's airflow as well as the tightness of one's embouchure. This technique is more useful during warmups to help singers balance their phonation, but it should still be presented as an option. The practicality of this technique in choral writing will be limited.

Microtones

Microtones involve singing intervals that are smaller than a half step. These can be approached by asking a singer to begin singing on a given pitch and then singing a microtone above or beneath that given pitch. Asking a singer to sing a microtone from a leap (as opposed to a step) is significantly more challenging and not advised.

In some ways this technique should be one of the most easy and ubiquitous for a singer to use, and yet it is hardly ever used even in modern choral music and rarely taught. As a result, it's not in the mainstays of many singers' techniques and somewhat difficult to incorporate even for professionals. That's not to say it's unreasonable to call for, but you should be aware that it may require a significant amount of practice.

Mainstream choral music is mostly bereft of microtonal usage, but one example of microtones in choral music can be found in Todd Kitchen's highly progressive work "Refraction Sacrée" for choir and organ. In the first section, a tenor solo is directed to glissando a quarter step above G3 and then glissando back down. Different sections of the choir then imitate with their own G natural to G quarter step to G natural motif.

278 The Technique of Choral Writing

Example 14.10: Todd Kitchen, "Refraction Sacrée."

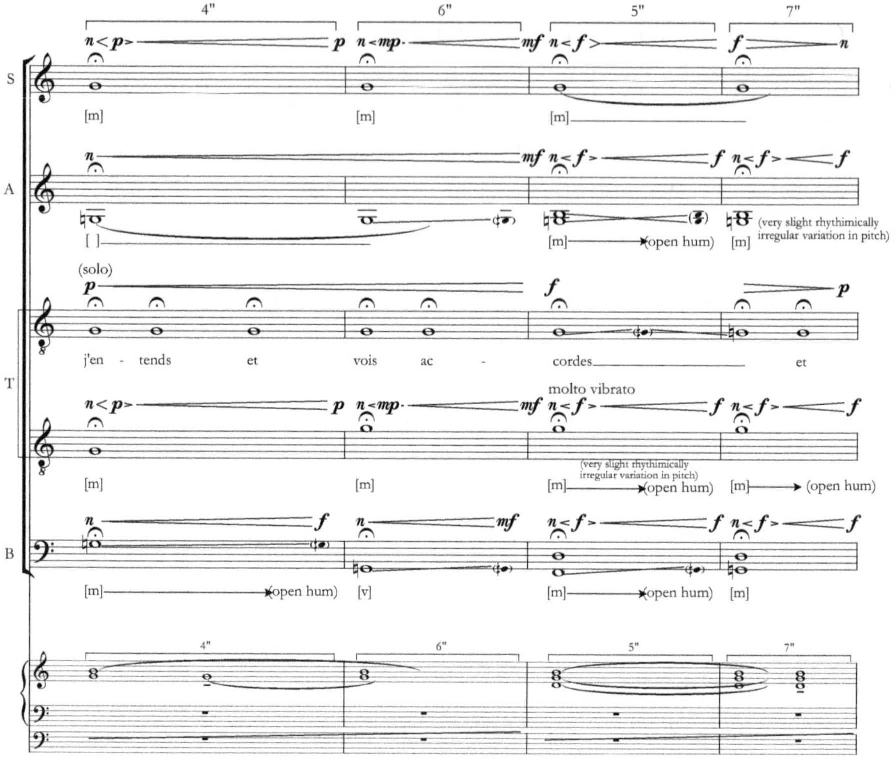

Copyright © Todd Kitchen. Used by permission.

Overtone singing

Overtone singing is the practice of manipulating certain overtones to be amplified while attenuating others. The sound of the voice is made up of a fundamental pitch followed by numerous overtones of varying strength and amplitude found in the harmonic series. By changing the shape of the inside of the mouth, we can alter the strength of overtones produced, which we recognize as different vowel sounds.

Extended Techniques and Special Effects

Overtone singing is done by migrating between an [u] vowel, which amplifies the lowest overtones, and an [i] vowel, which amplifies the highest overtones. Migrating very slowly between the two vowels allows one to voice the pitches between. It's a technique outside of conventional vocal instruction and takes a fair amount of practice.

The sound of the overtones can take on a ghost-like, whistling quality. With very practiced singers, the overtones can sound very pronounced, even more so than the fundamental, and can move through overtone scale with relative ease. This technique is possible but requires training and a hefty amount of practice. Additionally, the practice required can be considered obnoxious to outside listeners and is advised to be done in isolation. With reasonable practice, many singers are capable of overtone singing.

While its use is more limited than most techniques, overtone singing has been finding more popularity in choral music and concert halls. Some of the best-known uses of overtone singing can be found in the music of Australian composer Sarah Hopkin, particularly her pieces "Past Life Melodies" and "Honour the Earth."

Example 14.11: Sarah Hopkin, "Past Life Melodies."

© 1991 Morton Music

Trill

Trill is the use of quick, wide vibrato oscillating between two neighboring pitches. In practice of the 1700s and 1800s, this technique would have been used frequently as an ornamental signal in preparation of a cadence. Its use outside of cadential material was limited. Now, the trill is primarily used for timbral effect.

Trills are generally executed by individual singers, but in Baroque practice there are plenty of examples of choral ensembles singing trills as an ensemble. Keeping it together can be a real challenge, so its use is often relegated to brief instances; it's a technique generally undertaken by more trained singers. Still, asking for trills as an aleatoric feature, without any intention of keeping them together, can bring an interesting texture to a composition. Extended uses of trills are rather difficult to sustain.

Example 14.12: Judith Bingham, "The Drowned Lovers."

© 1997 Peters Edition Ltd. Reproduced by permission of Faber Music Ltd. All Rights Reserved.

Trillo

This technique, used most often in Baroque vocal music, is sometimes referred to as a "Monteverdi trill" or a "goat trill." This technique is a tremolo-like, rapid onset of phonation; it sounds like a machine gun of a repeated pitch. This technique is almost always used as a cadential ornamentation in vocal music from the Baroque period. Often it starts slowly, speeds up, and then slows down, almost like an agogic *messa di voce*.

While common in contemporary performances of Baroque repertoire, you may not see it actually notated or called for in the score. Even though this technique is used most often in Baroque vocal music, it need not stay exclusive to that epoch. One example of a trillo in modern music is Whitacre's "Leonardo Dreams of His Flying Machine." Here, trillo is called for in the solo found in measure six and notated in the following manner.

Example 14.13: Eric Whitacre, "Leonardo Dreams of His Flying Machine."

© 2002 Walton Music Corp. All rights reserved.

Ululation

This vocal technique is associated with African, Middle Eastern, and South Asian music and celebrations. It is produced by phonating a somewhat higher pitch, with the tongue extended between the lips and oscillating horizontally from one corner of the mouth to the other. Most often the speed of this oscillation will be as rapidly as possible. It's important to remember that this technique is specific to the practices of cultures that should be respected.

Voiced fricatives

This is the practice of singing on a voiced fricative rather than an open vowel. These voiced fricatives are consonants that have air passing through articulators in the mouth as well as phonated sound through the vocal cords, which can produce a buzzing sound. Variations of this buzzing sound are determined through the placement of certain articulators. The voiced fricatives are [β] [v] [ð] [z] [ʒ] [z̺] [j] [ɣ] [ʁ] [ʕ] and [ɦ], but the ones you will most likely be working with are [v] [ð] [z] and [ʒ].

An example of this technique can be found in the last movement of *Five Ariel Songs* by Frank Martin. Here, Martin indicates that divided sopranos and altos should sing on a "w" character. If we consider that Martin had moved to Amsterdam prior to composing this composition, it's very likely he meant to have the "w" following the Dutch pronunciation. This seems to indicate a sound that most closely resembles the [v] consonant, imitating the sound of buzzing bees.

Example 14.14: Frank Martin, *Five Ariel Songs*, "Act V, Sc. 1."

© Copyright 1968 by Universal Edition A.G., Zürich

Whistle tone

Whistle tone is the highest register in female-assigned voices. The sound is produced by singing very high pitches with CDP where the vocal folds never completely close and can produce higher pitches than normal production may allow. The resulting tone is a very high, piercing sound and can often have a noticeably breathy affect as the vocal folds are not coming together completely. This technique is probably best known because of its use by pop singer Mariah Carey and, more recently, Ariana Grande. Its use in choral music is limited but still viable.

Whistling

This technique entails passing air through puckered (and slightly wetted) lips to create a fluty and sometimes piercing sound. Skilled whistlers can create this sound using exhaled or inhaled air. Whistling can create an interesting mood depending on the context. Whistling can add folksy charm to an upbeat folk tune arrangement or composition in that style. It can also create a windy, haunting sound in something slightly more ghoulish or macabre.

Example 14.15: Carol Barnett, "Cindy."

Copyright © 2001 Transferred to Colla Voce Music www.collavoce.com. Used by permission.

Example 14.16: Jeffrey Van, *A Procession Winding Around Me*, "Look Down Fair Moon."

© 1994 Walton Music Corp. All rights reserved.

Yodeling

In most Western vocal instruction, the goal of the instruction is to minimize the breaks, or passaggios, in the voice moving from one register to another. Yodeling, however, is just the opposite. This singing technique is about maximizing—and indeed glorifying—the major break in the voice between Thyroarytenoid-Dominant Production (TDP) and CDP.[3] The style capitalizes on this major laryngeal mechanism shift by singing rapid leaps between low and high registers.[4]

Yodeling is often a featured and highly stylized technique of a few genres of folk music from Switzerland and the United States. It can be difficult to incorporate the technique into other vocal music because it is so tightly connected to those genres. The International Western Music Association still awards a "Best Yodeler" Award each year.

Again, I'm not sure if there are any practical applications in choral music nor am I aware of any examples in the canon. However, there is a whole new field of avant-garde yodelers taking yodeling into new and interesting directions.[5] The opportunity is there.

Unpitched Vocalizations

Audible breathing

Audible breathing can come in many different forms including, but not limited to, panting, shallow breathing, open throat breathing, expelling air through slightly relaxed lips, and ujjayi breathing, among others.

It should be noted that the sound level of moving air is directly proportional to the velocity of the moving air as well as the size of the opening for said airflow. For example, blowing air slowly through puckered lips will not be as audible as blowing air quickly through the same puckered lips. Additionally, air moving through a large opening will not be as loud as air moving through a smaller opening.[6] Generally, louder sounds come through faster airflow and smaller openings.

---

3   McCoy, *Your Voice*, 65-66.

4   Bart Plantenga, *Yodel-Ay-Ee-Oooo: The Secret History of Yodeling Around the World* (New York: Routledge, 2004), 12.

5   Plantenga, *Yodel-Ay-Ee-Oooo*, 280.

6   One of the principles taught to us in sound recording theory was that when building the air conditioning system in a recording studio, removing the vents and leaving the openings as large as possible to help reduce air conditioning noise.

Extended Techniques and Special Effects

The usefulness of this particular effect may not come up very regularly. And yet, breath is so foundational to a singer's sound production. Expelling air through slightly relaxed lips causes the air coming out to sound with more noise and creates a quasi-ocean wave sound as seen here in "The Sounding Sea" by William Eric Barnum.

Example 14.17:. Eric William Barnum, "The Sounding Sea."

3. Blow through lips as if blowing up a balloon, with pressure. Start off with a bit of a 'pff' and continue with a 'ff' sound through the diminuendo. It is a beat early, as if the waves are cresting.

© 2009 Walton Music Corp. All rights reserved.

Beatboxing

Beatboxing is a form of mouth percussion found widely in more contemporary genres such as a cappella or vocal jazz groups. While this technique is mostly associated with contemporary hip-hop, it can be a very useful technique that could be considered for applications in choral performances (although virtually no examples in use could be found for this text).

One of the easiest ways I was taught a very basic kick, hi-hat, and snare sound was to say the words "boots and cats" with the consonant sounds exaggerated and the vowel sounds eliminated. I will defer further study of this technique to the many "how to" videos that can be found on YouTube.

Chomping

This technique of chomping the teeth together, giving a unique percussive quality, is probably more effective when done by larger groups of singers rather than a small group or individual. Usage is very rare. Be considerate of those who may have sensitive teeth, or you may receive a letter or two from singers with cracked crowns or caps.

Coughing

This is the sharp exhale of air through partially closed vocal folds and can be manipulated by the articulators. Be warned, forced coughing can lead to actual coughing, which can lead to coughing spells. This effect is probably not a good idea in a post-Covid world.

Gasping

A quick inhale of air, that causes a sharp, rushing sound of indeterminate pitch. This sound is most often associated with surprise, shock, or distress from an inability to breathe. Depending on its context, it can provide a certain drama or comic relief. The sharp sound associated with rushing air in gasping can dry out the throat and negatively impact the singer's voice if done too much without enough hydration afterwards. The suction from the gasp can also cause stray saliva droplets to find their way past the epiglottis and into the larynx, which will cause a violet coughing spell. This technique can be notated with a simple cross note head and the word "gasp" in parenthesis.

Example 14.18: Carol Barnett, "Cindy."

Copyright © 2001 Transferred to Colla Voce Music www.collavoce.com. Used by permission.

Glossolalia and mumbling

The word glossolalia comes from the Greek words for "tongue" and "speech" and refers to speaking in an unknown language. This practice is usually associated with worship practices, particularly those found in the Pentecostal denomination. The idea is to utter syllables that resemble a language—and may incidentally share a word or phrase—but is not meant to be a known language.

Mumbling is slightly different but closely related to glossolalia as both involve the use of random syllables. The main difference between the two is that mumbling involves more voiced consonants and fewer vowels, appearing to come across as less intelligible. On the other hand, glossolalia comes across as having conscious articulation and may appear to at least resemble real words.

At lower dynamics glossolalia may resemble what many consider to be mumbling. I'm sure there is someone who will contend that these are not the same thing, but for our purposes we will consider them related techniques.

Glottal stop

A glottal stop is when glottal pressure is applied to stop the air flow through the glottis. This technique can be used to immediately and abruptly stop a vocalist's sound. Conversely, it can be used to have an immediate and abrupt onset of a vocal sound and is often called a glottal onset. In general, most vocalists spend hours practicing to avoid glottal onsets in favor of a more balanced onset. With that said, there are some moments when a glottal onset is required. For example, towards the end of the fourth movement of Beethoven's *Symphony No 9*, the syncopated entrance on the words "Alle Menschen" almost certainly requires a glottal onset at the tempo and character required. In Beethoven, there's no mention of the glottal stop in the score; it's simply done by the singers. Any intentional use outside of textual scenarios such as this one could be notated using an asterisk or other symbol.

Grunting

Grunting is the forcing of air through a stopped glottis. This technique is similar to a glottal onset but different in that grunting doesn't require a determined pitch or even a vowel sound to follow. Most often, a grunt is made with a voiced consonant sound like [m] or [n].

Example 14.19: Jaakko Mäntyjärvi, "Pseudo Yoik."

© 1995 SULASOL. All rights reserved. Walton Music Corp. admin. USA and Canada

Hiccup

The quick, sharp, almost violent inhalation of air that imitates a hiccup almost has a popping quality to it. Sometimes these fake hiccups will have a squeak added to the inhalation, almost like a quick, small glissando. This effect is often used in choral music whose texts discuss indulging in libations.

Moaning

A combination of a somewhat slow and drawn out high to low glissando of indeterminate pitch with either an open or closed mouth. The main difference between moaning and humming is the use of determinate pitch. Moaning is meant more for aleatoric applications with indeterminate pitch.

Sighing

A combination of a high to low glissando of indeterminate pitch with an aspirate phonation, this effect is meant to convey resignation or disarming relaxation. While singers often sigh as part of their warmup routines, it comes up only rarely in the canon of literature. It's mostly seen as a somewhat silly, kitschy effect, but there may be appropriate uses in more serious applications.

Singing the lowest or highest pitch possible

This effect is pretty self explanatory. Every singer has their own lowest possible pitch or highest possible pitch. What makes this technique interesting is that each performance of this effect will be unreplicable. Each ensemble is made up of singers with different low and high notes specific to that group. Even from season to season, or day to day will yield a different performance as the margins of the voice can change slightly between iterations.

Shouting or screaming

A sound comprising overdriven phonation of indeterminate pitch where the vocal folds are brought together with intense sub-glottic pressure. Use sparingly, only on a word here or there. Just like people don't like to be shouted at in real life, most audiences don't like to be shouted at for extended periods of time.

Shouting is very fatiguing on the voice and can be harmful in even small amounts. Because every musical moment needs preparation, every shout will have to be rehearsed, so even if it's only "a few instances," the choir may have to shout each instance several times over several rehearsals. Proceed with caution.

Example 14.20: William Walton, *Belshazzar's Feast*.

© Oxford University Press 1931. All rights reserved.

Speaking

Speaking is the use of natural speech performance with inflections and contours managed by the singers themselves. The composer can choose to dictate the rhythm or can decide to let the singer speak with their own natural rhythm (in a specific time frame if needed).

The use of speech in a choral composition can be very effective in a variety of applications. Whether the application is meant to be humorous, exasperated, angry, shocked, or several other emotions, speech can be helpful for diverse scenarios. Its use can provide contrast with normal singing and can punctuate a rhetorical idea. It can help cover a lot of text or exposition necessary for a narrative your composition may be conveying.

Gabriel Jackson has several examples of having one speaker, a section, or the entire choir speaking, in strict rhythm or freely.

Example 14.21: Gabriel Jackson, "Rigwreck."

Music © Oxford University Press 2015. Text © Pierre Joris, used by permission. All rights reserved.

Example 14.22: Gabriel Jackson, *Airplane Cantata*, "Newsreel/Narration."

*From within the choir. More than one speaker may be used for successive phrases, if desire. Slight amplification may be necessary.

© Oxford University Press 2011. All rights reserved.

Sprechstimme

The word "sprechstimme" literally translates to "speaking voice" and is a particular speaking effect in vocal music. While very much associated with normal speech, this technique is different in that the approximated pitches, as well as the pitch contour, are dictated by the composer rather than left to the singer's discretion. Additionally, the rhythms here are fixed and exact, where in normal speech that may or may not always be the case.

The practice of sprechstimme was pioneered by German Expressionists such as Arnold Schoenberg and his students, Alban Berg and Anton Webern. The most notable example of this technique is found in Schoenberg's groundbreaking song cycle, *Pierrot Lunaire* for Mezzo Soprano and small chamber ensemble. In choral applications, examples can be found in the choral music of Einojuhani Rautavaara.

Example 14.23: Arnold Schoenberg, *Pierrot Lunaire*, "Nacht."

Tongue or palatal clicking

This technique is created by the tongue being placed against the roof of the mouth and pulled down against suction from the back of the mouth. This clicking sound is made of a combination of two sounds: the breaching of the suction and the tongue hitting the floor of the mouth. This technique creates a very percussive, resonant popping sound reminiscent of wood blocks.

Changing the shape of the vocal tract into different vowel shapes will cause the tongue click to resonate differently. For example, clicking the tongue with the mouth shaped for an [a] vowel will sound different from clicking with an [o] shape and [u] shape. Even more variations can be found through slight differences in tongue placement.

Its use in choral music is somewhat limited. However, it's effective, easy to execute, and can be done for extended periods if needed.

Example 14.24: Peter Gritton, "Dry Bones."

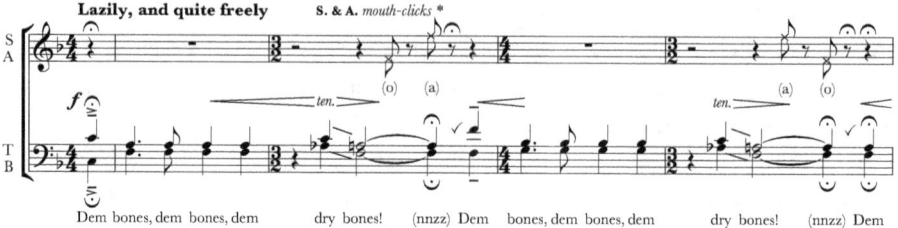

© Oxford University Press 2004. All rights reserved.

Unvoiced fricatives

Like voiced fricatives, this is the practice of keeping airflow through an unvoiced fricative rather than an open vowel. Unvoiced fricatives are consonants that have air passing through articulators in the mouth, but unlike their voiced relatives have no phonated sound through the vocal cords. This technique creates sounds that occupy very high frequencies and sometimes sound like spectral portions of white noise.

The unvoiced fricatives are [ɸ] [f] [θ] [s] [ʃ] [ʂ] [ç] [x] [χ] [ħ] and [h] but the ones you will probably use the most are [ɸ] [f] [θ] [s] and [ʃ].

Example 14.25: Andrew Maxfield, "The Door."

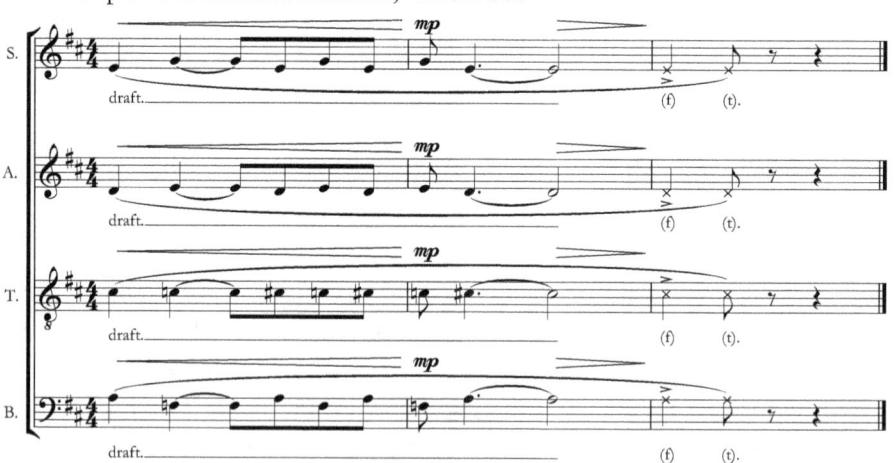

© Andrew Maxfield. Used by permission.

Vocal fry

Vocal fry involves using the lower registers of the voice with the slowest possible airflow. When the vocal folds are vibrating at such a slow rate the vibrations are pronounced yielding a gravely, croaky sound. This tone appears constantly in modern speech among millennials and has been the subject of several articles on healthy speaking habits.[7]

While not called for very often in vocal music, its use is still a possibility and can add a very useful sound. You may find it not very useful for extended periods of time nor will you find many singers eager to use this technique for extended periods. As many of those articles point out, it can be taxing on the voice and cause issues with vocal hygiene.

Whispering

An unphonated sound of indeterminate pitch where the vocal folds are left open and the air passing through is made into vowels using articulators in the oropharynx. This technique creates an aspirate, ghosty sound that can be very effective at low volumes. This sound is easily covered and it's important to make sure that any other accompanying sounds aren't above a piano dynamic level.

A fairly ubiquitous misconception about whispering is that it's easier on the voice than normal speech or singing. This belief is not true. Whispering can be fatiguing for the voice and possibly lead to chronic incomplete glottal closure and muscular tension dysphonia.[8] In addition, the passage of continuous air over open vocal folds dries out the vocal folds. Returning to phoning sound can sound scratchy and rough initially and it takes a few moments to get the voice back in proper working order. Additionally, prolonged and extensive whispering will affect the vocal hygiene of the singer. Use sparingly and proceed with caution.

---

[7] Lee Akst and Kristine M. Pietsch, "Is Vocal Fry Ruining My Voice?," accessed 26 June 2024.

[8] McCoy, *Your Voice*, 120.

Example 14.26: David Hamilton, "The Moon is Silently Singing."

© 2005 Walton Music Corp. All rights reserved.

Non-Vocal

Body percussion

Body percussion is its own art that is derived from the dance traditions of various countries and cultures throughout the globe. The objective is to treat one's body like an idiophone and create different sounds by striking the body in various places and in different ways.

One particularly important point to consider with body percussion is that in most cases these motions require one or both arms to be used, which could make holding music prohibitive for the singers. It requires singers to either perform from memory or to sing from music stands (which is sadly not common in North America).

Take care when attempting works with body percussion in primary education choirs (or even secondary), as rehearsing such techniques could result in absolute chaos.

Choralography

The word "choralography" is a tongue-in-cheek combination[9] of the words "choral" with "choreography" to describe the physical movements some choirs incorporate into their performances. While some will look down on this practice and describe it as "kitschy" or "juvenile," we must acknowledge that tasteful choreography that the singers can execute well can create a moving and effective performance that wouldn't have been possible without that choreography.

The majority of choralography incorporated into performances is added by the ensembles themselves, but there are instances when choralography is dictated into the composition by the composer or arranger. Sometimes these directions are marked as "optional" or "suggested," allowing for the ensemble to do what they believe will be the most effective performance.

The majority of choralography in any given performance would have been created or overseen by the music director or by an outside choreographer.

Clapping

While technically a subset of body percussion, clapping should be distinguished on its own as it is far and away the most popular practice of body percussion and because it is so hilariously polarizing in choral music.[10]

This sharp striking of skin against skin can provide a new, interesting color with relatively little effort. Limited amounts of clapping can be especially effective. Extensive clapping can easily become annoying or tedious after a period, and that sharp, fresh new color can suddenly give listeners a headache.

The striking of one's open palms together seems very straightforward; however, there is more variety and nuance than one might initially imagine. The variety of clapping motions can range anywhere from the small movement of one hand gently tapping the other using only the wrist mechanism to a large, full-arm motion of the hands together, using the shoulders, elbows, and wrists in equal measure. Clapping can also involve the fingers of one hand striking the palm versus palm striking palm, as well as whether the hands should be open and flat or hollow and cupped. Most of this nit-picking can feel like straining at a gnat, but multiplying these little changes by the dozens of musicians that

---

9 I would like to stress that this is now the accepted term for this practice.

10 While doing some preliminary research for this text, I asked a variety of my singer and conductor colleagues about what extended choral techniques they felt were important to their craft and difficult for choral ensembles, and well over half mentioned "clapping."

may be executing the practice can make a huge difference. If the composer or arranger hasn't specified anything in particular about the clapping, the style is handled by the choral musicians.

The execution of clapping is surprisingly difficult for some singers. While there are many talented individuals who can sing and dance and are very in tune with their bodies regarding rhythm, not all choral musicians were so blessed (hence many of them are singing in choirs). If you happen to be working with a choral ensemble that often uses dancing or extensive body movements from their singers, you as a composer can ask for difficult clapping rhythms; otherwise, it's best practice to keep a composition accessible for the lowest common denominator. I have seen at least one published score that calls for clapping with instructions indicating "bad clappers are banned" (paraphrasing).

Additionally, clapping can easily get carried away, especially with younger ages, but more mature ensembles are not immune to this chaos. The sound of the clapping can also easily over balance the actual singing from the ensemble.

Whether clapping should be included in a composition or arrangement depends on the desired effect. While clapping is used in a variety of choral literature, it is most often used in, or associated with, folk music settings or arrangements—and not just folk music from North America. I've seen clapping in folk music from every corner of the globe. It is a somewhat surprisingly universal musical gesture.

Snapping

As with clapping, snapping is a subset of body percussion, but one that is common enough to merit its own section. Finger snaps are created when a finger (usually the middle finger) strikes against the palm of the hand at a fast velocity. We can get our finger up to sufficient speed by holding our finger against our thumb and releasing it by pulling away our thumb.

In Western music, finger snaps are most often associated with jazz and other related styles, particularly swing, with snaps on the offbeats. Finger snaps in aleatoric constructs have also famously been used by Eric Whitacre to imitate the sounds of raindrops in "Cloudburst."

Stomping

Stomping one's foot on the ground is found in dances from several cultures and can be employed effectively within choral performances. The sound of the stomp will depend on several variables, including the materials found on the performance flooring, whether the floor beneath is hollow or solid, the number of musicians performing, and the materials that make up their shoes. Stomping can be incredibly effective with a hollow, hardwood stage and hard-soled shoes, and underwhelming with a solid, carpeted stage and thick rubber-soled shoes.

The number of musicians will have the most obvious effect on the sound. The more musicians present, the greater the opportunity for a louder stomp. This effect may not go over as well or be as convincing with a very small or one-on-a-part group. Of course, be very careful with large groups on temporary or collapsable risers, as one can find numerous videos on the internet of choir risers collapsing mid-performance.

Finally, the materials of the performers' shoes will also be an important factor. Whether the soles of the shoes are thick or thin—or made of rubber, leather, or another material—will factor into how loud an individual stomp will be, as well as whether it's accompanied by the higher frequencies of harder materials. These factors may or may not be under your control but mentioning them in the score to remind the musicians may not hurt.

Example 14.27: Ko Matsushita, *Three Insular Songs of Yaeyama and Miyako Islands*, "Karimatanu Kuicha."

Copyright © 1997 edition KAWAI. Used by permission.

Requiring multiple singers

Aleatory

The word "aleatoric" comes from the Greek word for "chance." This word describes a rather broad category of any music that is left to the discretion of the individual musician to create. Aleatoric music has been incredibly popular in the choral community in the last fifty or sixty years and for good reason. This technique is not unique to, nor did it originate in, choral music. However, it can be used very successfully in several ways that are specific to our art form.

Composing with aleatoric elements is not difficult, but two things must be kept in mind: how the musicians enter the aleatoric passage, and how they exit the aleatoric passage. In some ways, these elements are the most challenging part of composing aleatoric music. It's very important whenever composing aleatoric music that you include clear and concise instructions to perform the passages.

There are three common aleatoric methods found in choral music today. The first example involves directing one or more sections to sing a written melody or phrase at their own tempo and expressive discretion. Specific to this technique, the melody or phrase is sung through as written. This technique will create an effect where the general contour on the melody will be perceived but it will be "blurred" by voices moving at their own pace. There are numerous examples, one of which can be found in "Deus, qui illumianas" by Julio Dominguez.

Example 14.28: Julio Dominguez, "Deus, qui illuminas."

(1) *Opcional. Cada cantor libremente con su propio tempo.* [Optional. Each singer freely with their own tempo]
(2) *Repeticiones ad libitum.* [Repetitions ad lib.]

© 2003 CM Ediciones Musicales

Another example of aleatoric music in the choral context includes shorter, repeating constructs, where the singers are directed to sing a melody or phrase at their own discretion and directed to repeat it at will for a period. Depending on the melody or phrase being repeated, as well as the section or sections performing, this device will provide a similar blurring effect, but adds to it the feature of repeating or "looping."

This effect is quite common and highly effective in choral music—especially with medium to large choirs. It creates a texture like particles in a snow globe. One of the drawbacks produced by this effect is that depending on the ensemble performing the work, the music you compose, and the way it's performed, these aleatoric constructs can sometimes come off as dense, thick, and opaque in texture. This viscous effect is mostly caused by louder dynamics and somewhat heavier vocal production. To help mitigate this issue, you can give directions that indicate that the singers should vary their dynamic levels slightly, as well as varying a bright and dark placement of their voice from repetition to repetition. But understand that that direction is more suited to choirs that have some level of vocal training, even if it's only rudimentary.

You may see these constructs presented between repeat bar lines or you may see them in a box. Either way, both are usually followed by a thick line either on the staff or with no staff. Again, there are numerous examples of this effect in the choral canon. A great example can be found in the "Sanctus" movement of *Chichester Mass* by William Albright, where the second sopranos and divided alto parts are given separate constructs with staggered entrances. Not only do these constructs have their own unique melodic gesture, but also they have their own dynamic levels and expression markings.

Example 14.29: William Albright, *Chichester Mass*, "Sanctus."

© 1980 Henmar Press Inc., New York Reproduced by permission of Faber Music Ltd. All Rights Reserved.

Like repeated constructs, another example includes directing the singers to stay on a given pitch and repeat the recitation of a set of words for a period. This variant creates an effect where the harmony is static but the repeating words give a sense of activity. This effect can be useful when trying to present a frenzied or chattering effect. Be warned though that this technique can put an emphasis on any sibilances and "t" consonants present. While not necessarily detrimental, it's something to keep in mind if one is composing a passage that is softer, darker, and generally very hushed in nature. Having numerous sibilances and "t" consonants can be an unwelcome feature in such a passage. On the other hand, this effect will fit right in with a spooky or creepy aesthetic if desired.

Example 14.30: Gabriel Jackson, "In Nomine Domini."

* Repeat *ad lib.* independently of the conductor, in a rapid *parlando*

Music © Oxford University Press 2010. All rights reserved.
Text © The John Bradburne Memorial Society (www.johnbradburne.com). Reproduced by kind permission. All rights reserved.

Other aspects of a performance can be executed in aleatory. These aspects can include, but are not exclusive to, choralography, body percussion, and vocal affect, as well as any other pitched, unpitched, or non-vocal technique mentioned in this chapter. Less common aleatoric techniques include instructing the singers to sing or speak something specific to themselves such as their names. The possibilities are endless, and the limit is your imagination and the ability of the vocal ensemble.

Extended Techniques and Special Effects

Pointillism

This effect is produced when a melody or line is shared between different voices singing one note from the line or, in other words, different voices or parts singing an individual note of a melody in alteration. Again, this technique isn't unique to choral music, nor did it originate with it. However, one might argue that this technique is most effective in choral music, especially when involving solo singers. This effectiveness can be seen in at least one example: "Psalm 150 in Kent Treble Bob Minor" by Jaakko Mäntyjärvi, in which seven singers are directed to sing just one pitch and syllable of a melody. In this case the syllables are determined by their rhythmic order rather than their pitch order. When sung at tempo, it creates the idea and contour of a melody but with a different vocal color on each pitch.

Example 14.31: Jaakko Mäntyjärvi, "Psalm 150 in Kent Treble Bob Minor."

© 1999 SULASOL, Helsinki. Printed by permission.

Mixed affect

Simply stated, this effect calls for half or a portion of the choir to sing with normal phonation and the other half or the remaining portion sings with some sort of affected sound or tone. Very often the effect called for is whispering against normal phonation, as it creates a sentimental or poignant effect that blends well. Other effects, like those listed in this chapter, may also work well. In theory, one could have three or more effects simultaneously, although intelligibility and intonation may suffer.

One popular example is half of the choir singing and the other half whispering, as can be seen in Whitacre's "hope, faith, life, love."

Example 14.32: Eric Whitacre, "hope, faith, life, love."

© 2003 Walton Music Corp. All rights reserved.

Shepard tone

A Shepard tone is an aural illusion of a forever rising pitch. Historically, this effect was first made by having a tone produced electronically with octave doublings. As the pitch slides higher, the lower pitches become louder and the higher pitches became softer, which would be replaced by the lower pitches. On a loop, we perceive it as a pitch that is always ascending. The same can be done in reverse or from higher pitches to lower pitches.

Replicating this sound acoustically by live musicians is possible to an extent. Hans Zimmer famously incorporated Shepard tones into his soundtrack for the film *Dunkirk*, and most recently in choral music, Abbie Betinis incorporates Shepard tones in her composition, "Bar Xizam." While electronically the rising pitch can be doubled in octaves and lined up perfectly with precise fades, a live performance by live singers will require an execution that's a bit more organic. Betinis writes for the sopranos and altos to glissando upward in pitch with *messa di voce* markings in an aleatoric construct. The effect, while it doesn't perfectly replicate the electronic Shepard tone, still gives an illusion of continuously rising pitches.

Other techniques

Pre-recorded audio

This effect involves a hybrid performance of live musicians performing along with a pre-recorded audio track. At one point in the mid and late 1970s, giving a hybrid performance with pre-recorded material was very popular, as can be seen throughout the colossal work *Mass* by Leonard Bernstein. One of the more recent examples of performing with pre-recorded audio is *Triple Quartet* by Steve Reich in 1999, in which a live string quartet plays with a recording of two string quartet performances.

Today, most choral performances with pre-recorded music are found in K-12 school choirs performing show tunes or arrangements of pop music. The popularity of this technique with choral ensembles in art music, however, declined quickly through the 1980s and hasn't seen widespread use since then. That isn't to say that such performances shouldn't be undertaken or that composition shouldn't use this effect if it's what you desire. Weirder things have returned from the 80s.

Singing into instruments

This is a technique—used occasionally in wind band music—where musicians are asked to sing into their respective instruments. Doing so uses the instrument as a resonator and extends the vocal tract. In most of these cases, phonating into an instrument will mean that articulating certain words may not be possible.

The most ubiquitous example of singing into an instrument is the kazoo. Phonating into a kazoo is how it actually makes sound. Another standout instrument for a musician to sing into is the piano. This technique is best accomplished by pressing the sustain pedal, leaving the dampers up, and allowing the strings of the piano to resonate sympathetically to the sound of the voice. This can create a very delicate, gossamer, reverberating effect. This effect would require very soft sounds or for other parts to be tacet as the reverberations could be easily covered.

Singing into your hand or a mitten

Very much what it sounds like, a singer uses their bare or mittened hand to cover their mouth while maintaining their normal vocal production. This technique creates a similar effect to a muted brass instrument. It can be especially helpful when trying to have a choir diminuendo to nothing in a more convincing way—for example, the chorus in "Neptune" from *The Planets* by Gustav Holst. This is best used with an off-stage choir as it can be a bit strange to see a whole choir with mittens onstage. Or perhaps you don't mind mismatched mittens onstage and you'd rather lean into that mittened aesthetic.

Singing with amplification

While singing with amplification is a standard practice of popular music, it can be a touchy subject in the classical world, at least among vocalists. Except in the case of performances in extremely large or outdoor venues, traditional classical musicians have resisted using amplification in most circumstances. However, with the improvement of technology and the imagination of some composers, classical musicians have been cautiously dipping their toes into using amplification for various reasons.

Sound reinforcement can help make narrators and less-trained soloists project over a very large choir. Additionally, amplification can provide a whole avenue for electronic effects to use on the voices. These possibilities can include (but are not limited to) looping, harmonizers, reverb, phasing, compression, and auto-tuners. These effects have been used very successfully for solo singers as well as small groups. An example of this technique can be found in a live performance of *Hymnodic Delays* by Ingram Marshall, in which a quartet sings into four microphones with their voices being manipulated electronically.

An entire genre of contemporary music composition has revolved around amplified sound. While this genre is not my specialty, my understanding of the prevailing theoretical principle is that if one instrument or voice is being amplified, everything needs to be amplified and mixed together to create the most cohesive aural experience.

Because of the limitation of the number of microphones available, as well as the physical limitations of gain-before-feedback, limiting the number of amplified singers would be prudent unless the funding, equipment, and engineers can be obtained. Generally, this technique works best with one-on-a-part ensembles or very small chamber groups.

Time will tell whether this new trend becomes a more widely accepted practice among classical musicians or whether it becomes passé in the same way that pre-recorded music seems to have become.

Singing with helium

The act of inhaling helium from balloons and speaking in at a higher pitch has been a popular pastime whenever helium balloons are present. The result is that we perceive the pitch of a singer to be much higher than normal and the vocal tone somewhat pinched and squeaky. Its use in concert performances is somewhat rare, but still a possibility. However, proceed with caution, as inhaling helium can cause asphyxiation due to lack of oxygen, which may lead to light-headedness, nausea, or passing out. While it's not likely to be fatal in low doses, the risk increases among children. For these reasons, the practice isn't necessarily recommend by the author.

While there are some instances where musicians are asked to sing after inhaling other gases, they will not be covered here as they can be quite dangerous to the health and safety of the musician—even more so than helium. The payoff doesn't seem worth the risk.

Continuing Study

Suggested Exercises

Short
> » Discuss why it's important to respect the vocal health needs of singers.
> » Identify the major categories of extended techniques and special effects. Name three different techniques in each major category.

Long
> » Use one of these techniques (or a combination) as the basis for a motif to build an entire composition around.

Suggested Listening

Chichester Mass - William Albright
"Sequenza III" - Luciano Berio
"Bar Xixam" - Abbie Betines
"Newsreel/Narration" from *Airplane Cantata* - Gabriel Jackson
"Past Life Melodies" - Sarah Hopkin
Great Southern Spirits - Stephen Leek
"O bone Jesu" - James MacMillan
"Psalm 150 in Kent Treble Bob Minor" - Jaakko Mäntyjärvi
"Pseudo Yoik" - Jaakko Mäntyjärvi
Hymnodic Delays - Ingram Marshall
"Karamatanu Kuicha" from *Three Insular Songs of Yaeyama and Miyako Islands* - Ko Matsushita
"Sound Patterns" - Pauline Oliveros
"Nicolette" from *Trois Chansons* - Maurice Ravel
Praktisch Deutsch - Einojuhani Rautavaara
"Epitaph for Moonlight" - R. Murray Schafer
"Miniwanka" - R. Murray Schafer
Partita for 8 Voices - Caroline Shaw
Ipsa Dixit - Kate Soper
"Roncesvalles" from *Path of Miracles* - Joby Talbot
"Cloudburst" - Eric Whitacre
"Leonardo Dreams of His Flying Machine" - Eric Whitacre

Chapter 15

Engraving Choral Parts

There are only twelve notes. You must treat them carefully.
— Paul Hindemith

When speaking with colleagues in the choral world about writing this book, nearly all of them—many without solicitation—mentioned something along the lines of, "Tell them to make their scores legible!" Whether it's handwritten or digitally engraved, legibility and clarity of intention are paramount to a successful performance and marketability of a score. It's shocking to see in the age of Finale, Sibelius, Dorico, and the like, how often choral musicians will get sent a substandard or even an indecipherable score from a composer or arranger.

The principles of engraving are important for any composer or arranger to understand, even if you have no desire to be a professional engraver. Even without getting into the weeds too deeply,[1] there are some things that you must keep in mind before sending your score to an ensemble. Choral music contains a few minor details related specifically to our genre that are different to other instruments or group of instruments and that should be noted.

Many notation issues are preemptively taken care of with the advent and proliferation of digital notation software such as Finale, Sibelius, and Dorico, many issues are preemptively taken care of. However, even with these programs, I have still seen errors in manuscripts from students and professionals.

---

1 If you do want to get into the weeds, I highly recommend *Behind Bars* by Elaine Gould.

Layout and Front Matter

Choral scores should be organized with the high voices placed highest and each subsequent lower voice placed beneath.[2] Choral parts should be grouped together with a bracket. The individual clefs used by each part are discussed in Chapters 4 through 8.

It's common practice to label each staff with the full name for the first system, with the subsequent systems using abbreviation. It is also possible to use abbreviation for the first system, so long as there aren't any other unconventional voices or instruments and there's no ambiguity regarding which part is which. As choral music can be flexible, and staffs can be divided, combined or omitted for space, I strongly recommend having names (abbreviated or otherwise) on every system and avoiding unlabeled staffs for any reason.

Solo voices can be grouped together above the choral voices and do not require a bracket. I have also seen solo voices placed above the part the solo comes from (like an orchestral score).

---

2   Elaine Gould, *Behind Bars: The Definitive Guide to Music Notation* (London: Faber Music, 2011), 462.

Divisions

Divisions in choral music can be written in several acceptable ways. The only overriding principle should be the goal of clarity and ease of reading. Divisions can be written with stems together or stems separated.[3] If the two parts are rhythmically the same, stems together is strongly preferred. If the note values are different between the parts, or if there is voice crossing in the parts, stems separated should be used to provide the most clarity and ease of reading.

If only one divided part is desired (for example, just the second sopranos with the firsts tacet) the part can be written with the indication for just second sopranos. However, probably more familiar to the choral musician is to write the part with stems down and rests written above. Either is acceptable. Writing "2" or "II" into the part is far less common with the choral musician than with instrumentalists and may lead to some confusion.

---

3   Gould, *Behind Bars*, 466.

Parts written with different note values can share a single staff, but if the rhythms are extensively different, or there is voice crossing, the part should probably be written on multiple staffs for clarity and ease of reading.

Any time that a part is divided into multiple staffs, those staffs should have a sub-bracket.

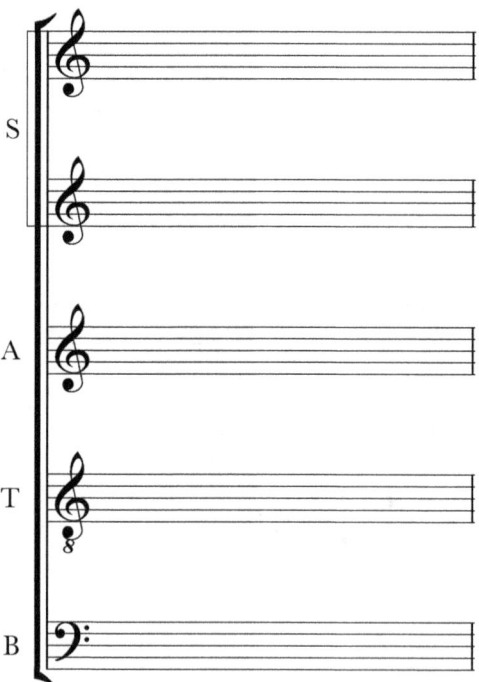

SATB Divisi

There's an unspoken standard certain publishing houses use consistently throughout their catalogs when labeling a choral work. These labels indicate the kind of forces the composition calls for: specifically, how many staffs the composition has and whether the parts divide in any way.

SATB indicates up to four staffs of music: one for the sopranos, another for the altos, etc. It is possible for SATB music to be written on two or three staffs and for "SATB" to indicate that. SSAA and TTBB also indicate the same scenario.

In the case where any extra staff is given to any part that letter would be duplicated in the label. For example, if you had two staffs for two soprano parts with the altos, tenors, and basses remaining united throughout, the label would change to SSATB. The same would happen if you had two alto staffs: SAATB. If one has two staffs for each part—eight staffs total—the label should be written SSAATTBB. Beyond 16 voices can sometimes be cumbersome, and it might be easier to just say "For 17 voices," and indicate what those voices are later in the notes or description.

Double choir is indicated with the parts for each choir divided by a forward slash. For example, if you have two choirs of SATB in a double choir composition, the indication should be SATB/SATB.

The word "divisi" indicates whether there's divisions within those staffs (regardless of how many divisions are on each staff). Even if you only have one part divided in a single measure, the work is labeled "divisi." Unfortunately, this label isn't the most helpful indication because it doesn't help the conductor determine how extensive the divisions are nor how challenging those divisions may be.

The Full Score

Unlike orchestral scores, where each musician is given only a part for their own instrument, in choral music each musician is basically given the full score to read from. Historically, this was not the case, and singers would read their own individual part from a corner of a part book that was shared between all the singers.

When distributing a choral score to the musicians, you should give them a performance edition that includes the full score. This practice is done for a few reasons, first being because most singers can't sing pitches out of nothing and need to refer to other parts. It's important that they see the context of the other parts to have a chance at finding pitches. This ability is especially important with works written outside of a single modal or tonal center. Second, seeing how the other parts are written and how their part fits into the whole allows choral musicians to more quickly refine their performance into a larger context. Third, it's much more practical with choral ensembles of all sizes and voicing configurations—which may vary from season to season—to purchase a single octavo that can work for any musician of any part in various ensembles. Rather than having to purchase a particular number of soprano, alto, tenor, or bass parts, it's much easier to purchase scores for the number of musicians in the ensemble.

Remember in your writing to try to keep multiple staffs to a minimum, if possible. The more staffs on the page, the more likely it is that your music will involve one system per page. This isn't out of the ordinary and singers are used to it; however, if your music is a quicker tempo, or for some reason there are only a few measures per page, singers would have to read from scores that can add up to several dozen pages and would need to flip through their octavos rather rapidly at times. There are many times when this is simply unavoidable, but if you can, keep staffs to as few as possible or practical.

There are a few exceptions to giving singing musicians the full score. These may include when a choir is singing with an orchestra or a significant number of instrumental players and a full score may be less helpful to the singers or would be cumbersome. In this case, a better option would be to give the singers a choral score that includes all the vocal parts (including any solos present) with a keyboard reduction of the instrumental parts.

Another exception may be in cases of extensive divisions and parts for large works such as Tallis' "Spem in alium." Printing all 40 parts onto a page may be unhelpful for choral musicians in this case. One option may be having some of the choral parts available and other choral parts in reductions to avoid a crowded, overly busy score for the musicians to read from.

Text

Placing text properly is crucial to a clear and legible score. As we've previously established (including in Chapter 2) half of choral music is the text so it's important to get it correct in the engraving. The examples used in this section will be in Latin, Greek, and English, but the principles will apply to other languages as well.

Words are placed beneath the staff with the syllable of each word placed beneath the corresponding note that the syllable should be sung on. This placement of words and syllables underneath their respective pitches is called underlay. Hyphens are placed between each syllable and in the case of a single syllable or the final syllable of a word an extender is used to indicate how many notes share that syllable. Maintaining clear underlay, which is reinforced by slurs, is important for ease of reading and clarity for the musician. More on slurs in the following section.

If the underlay from one division is different from the other, the text for the upper part is placed above the staff. The staff may also be divided into two different staffs if space allows, but may not be necessary.

Take care that the size of the words is not too small. It's a fine line between the words being too small to read and too large so it takes up too much room and looks a little cheap. However, I would strongly recommend you err on the side of the text being too large than too small.

Syllabification

As mentioned previously, dividing multisyllabic words into different syllables requires splitting the word with hyphens. Dividing the word is a bit complicated and at times goes against what is intuitive. To make matters worse, there isn't a consensus in the publishing or engraving community about how to divide every single word.[4]

The overriding principle should be intelligibility to the singer. There are several rules of thumb including separating compound words (day-light), separating double consonants (writ-ten), dividing between prefixes, roots and suffixes (un-faith-ful), and treating diphthongs and triphthongs as single-

---

4   Gould, *Behind Bars*, 441.

syllables (dire, wire).[5] Some of these principles also apply to other languages, including Latin. Elaine Gould's book goes into much more detail and is a great reference.

However, there are numerous exceptions to each case and sometimes specific exceptions to each language. When in doubt, consult how a dictionary divides the syllables: for example, *Merriam-Webster* for American English, *Oxford English* for British English, or *Collins* for French and German. Most dictionaries offer a word syllabification between the part of speech and the definition in each entry.

Polyglot Editions

In an effort to save money, publishers will sometimes publish polyglot versions with mixed languages. They will try to underlay both texts into one version for general use. In general, these can be terribly confusing (even after first glance); it looks messy and confusing on the page and can result in a score that is difficult to read and sing from. I recommend creating specific editions made for that specific language rather than a shared version containing both. Having said that, I know that editors and publishing houses have their reasons why polyglot editions for specific cases are preferable.

Other Considerations

If you have a syllable or word held out over multiple pitches and over multiple systems and pages, it can be helpful to provide the word again in parenthesis. In the following edition of the "Sanctus" moment from *Missa Gloria tibi Trinitas* by John Taverner, a reminder of the syllable is given in a parenthesis after each rest.

Example 15.1: John Taverner, *Missa Gloria tibi Trinias*, "Sanctus."

---

5   Gould, *Behind Bars*, 442.

Engraving Choral Parts

Syllabic Slurs and Phrasing

In modern choral music, slurs confirm the underlay and indicate how many notes share the same syllable. This confirmation is especially helpful if it's not entirely clear how the underlay is meant to be divided. If the music is syllabic and there's only one syllable on a note, no slur is necessary.

It should be noted that scholarly editions choose to not employ this device, but virtually all modern performance editions do. I suspect that this is the case because a large amount of the music set in scholarly editions is melismatic and the worry is that it would overwhelm the score and distract the reader.

Slurs should not be used to indicate the musician perform in a legato manner. Instead, this should be indicated as an expression marking in italic text.

Beaming

In the past, choral scores would use beams to confirm the underlay of text and indicate how many notes shared the same syllable. If the word setting was syllabic, the old practice was to flag each individual eighth and sixteenth note. This practice is antiquated and no longer acceptable; it should be avoided at all costs as it creates a busy score that is much more cumbersome to read.

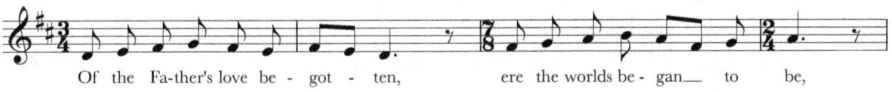

Now, the expected practice is to beam according to rhythmic groupings of the meter, which show where the beats are in each measure.[6] Eighth and sixteenth notes are only flagged when there is no other corresponding note to beam it with.

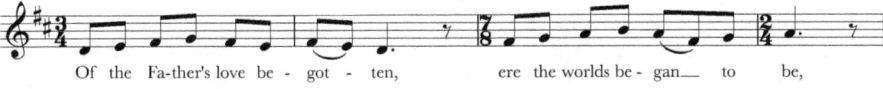

---

6 Gould, *Behind Bars*, 435.

Breathing directions

As stated previously in Chapter 3, you are not required to dictate every breath to the musicians. However, there may be instances when you will want to state explicitly where you would like the singers to breathe or not to breathe. Using rests will be the clearest way to indicate where you want the singer to breathe. If you'd rather use a comma or checkmark[1] to indicate a breath, that is also acceptable, but often not as precise or as clear as a rest. If you don't need that much control and would rather yield to the singer's needs for breathing, a comma will do that.

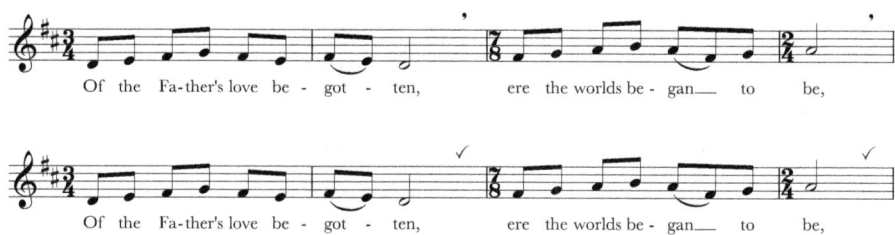

To my eye—as a singer and as a conductor—I would rather see a rest in the score instead of a comma or a checkmark. It's clearer, cleaner, and leaves no question about the composer's or arranger's desire or intention. It also indicates to me that the composer is sympathetic to my needs as a musician and thinking very intentionally about where and when breaths should be taken, and final consonants should be placed. Maybe this isn't the case at all, but that's how it reads to me at least. Whatever you choose, be consistent and refrain from using rests part of the time and breath marks the other part of the time. Stick with one approach.[2]

Use a dashed slur to indicate where the ensemble should not breathe. Indicating "no breath" or "N.B." is not necessary but doesn't hurt.

---

1   In the choral training of my bachelor's and my master's, commas and checkmarks indicated two different kinds of breaths and were not interchangeable. A comma indicated a breath on the beat while a checkmark indicated a breath on a subdivision between the beats. I haven't seen any other institution follow this practice.

2   Harold Rosenbaum, *Choralstration: A Practical Guide for Composers of Choral Music* (Self-published, 2022), 25.

Expression, Dynamic, and Technique Markings

Because the words are already placed below the staff, vocal parts require that expression, dynamic, and technique directions are placed above the staff. This practice is the opposite of what one would do with instrumental parts where the expression, dynamic, and technique markings would be placed below the staff. This will feel counterintuitive for composers and arrangers who work mostly with instruments, and it may take some time to adjust the habit.

The exception to this rule is if you have divided parts on a single staff and you need to provide separate expression or dynamic markings for the separate parts. This is better in limited instances; if you find yourself using this exception frequently, it might be better to use separate staffs for each part.

Keyboard Reductions

In a cappella music, a keyboard reduction is very often included for the ease of a rehearsal accompanist. These reductions are simply a smaller grand staff under the normal choral parts and are meant to help a rehearsal accompanist (or the conductor) play the parts if reading open score is not feasible. While adding a keyboard reduction is not required for an a cappella work, it is highly advisable for the marketability of your work to most of the North American market. Some conductors will not even bother looking at new music if it doesn't include a keyboard reduction. And while there are many fine rehearsal accompanists who can read open score fluently, in my experience most pianists—even ones who majored in piano performance—cannot. Keyboard reductions are not required, but strongly encouraged for accompanied choral works.

There are two schools of thought regarding keyboard reductions. The first is that it is a reduction and representation of everything that is written on the individual singers' staffs. The second school of thought is that it is actually supposed to be playable by a single keyboardist with ten fingers. I have seen both approaches—or at times, a combination of both—and there appears to be no consensus one way or another. As the reduction is meant solely as an aid for rehearsal and is not pivotal to the performance, do what you feel works best to aid the musicians and don't stress too much.

When creating your keyboard reduction, words, slurs, dynamics, and other articulations are not necessary to include. Only the pitches, durations, meters, and key signatures are necessary.

Some editors and engravers will label their reductions with the fussy "Piano (for rehearsal only)." This isn't necessary, especially if you've already said that the work is a cappella in the front matter. We all know what a reduction is at this point and that for an a cappella work it's for rehearsal only. Also, while many rehearsals take place with a piano in the room, there are times when rehearsals are done with an organ, portative, or electronic keyboard and the word keyboard is inclusive of all those instruments.

If you are creating a choral part for a choral-orchestral work, an orchestra reduction is going to be crucial for the success of the choral musicians. Cue notes are not nearly as helpful as a reduction. If the choir plays a large role in the work, a reduction of the entire orchestra score will be necessary. There are many instances when the choir will be tacet. In those cases, truncating down to rest bars is completely acceptable instead of creating a reduction for hundreds of bars when the choir doesn't sing. If the choir plays a more limited role in the work, omitting sections is acceptable so long as an orchestral reduction is there for several measures before the choral musicians enter—or in some tempos, perhaps more than a dozen measures. If using rehearsal numbers or letters, I would recommend creating a reduction for one or perhaps two rehearsal markings before the choir comes in.

There are few things as frustrating for a choral musician as getting a choral score for a large choral-orchestral work and seeing few or sometimes no pitches for reference or only one instrument's part. I've encountered this in a choral score for Ravel's *Daphnis and Chloe*, which almost feels like it was designed to set up the choral ensembles for failure. There are moments when all I've seen is one line (from some obscure instrument that really was no help) and other times when there's a key change that the choir isn't made privy to. Set up your musicians for success.

Printing and Other Considerations

Fortunately (or unfortunately) there is no standard paper size for choral scores. Typically, commercial octavos from major publishing houses will range between 6" x 9" (15.24 cm x 22.86 cm) and 8.5" x 11" (21.59 cm x 27.94 cm), but they can also range all the way to 9 x 12 inches (although this is very rare). If you're working with a choir and emailing manuscripts for them to print, they will almost certainly print them on whatever printer paper is most easily available to them.

Each publishing house will have its own paper sizes to match its engraving standards. Should you publish through one of these houses, their engravers and editors will do this work for you. Should you choose to publish on your own, choosing a paper size that allows for the score to be easily read is the most ideal. For more details about music formatting and engraving, please refer to *Behind Bars* by Elaine Gould.

Publishing for Digital Distribution

This is still a relatively new field for choral music, but one that is gaining speed rapidly. There are two outcomes with digital distribution: sending digital files that are then printed and sending digital files for use on a tablet device.

When distributing for the former, it is recommended to format for US Letter or 8.5" x 11" (21.59 cm x 27.94 cm) as that is most likely what it will be printed on. Formatting for A4 paper is also acceptable, but it will be slightly taller than US Letter.

Regarding the latter, there are very few guidelines at the time of printing, but formatting for US Letter or A4 are both acceptable. Consider that the most popular tablet in use today, the Apple iPad, has a screen ratio of approximately 4:3 and the most common app for singing from scores is forScore. Now, to avoid having to format multiple editions for a variety of devices or final formats, distributing for print should be the focus; however, there may come a time in the not-too-distant future when digital distribution for devices will become the priority.

Continuing Study

Suggested Exercises

Short
- » Discuss the different engraving practices between choral and instrument music regarding parts, divisions, slurs, and expression, dynamic, and technique markings.
- » Discuss the general accepted practices of beaming in modern choral.

» Discuss the general principles that make an effective keyboard reduction.

Long
» When engraving a score, double check the following throughout your work:
- Is the score layout correct?
- Is the divisi labeled correctly?
- Are stems pointing in a way that is helpful?
- Is the syllabification correct? Have the syllables been divided correctly?
- Have hyphens and extenders been used correctly?
- Are there slurs to reinforce the underlay correctly?
- Is the beaming correct?
- Have breathes been indicated clearly?
- Are expression and technique markings in the correct locations?
- Is there a helpful keyboard reduction?
- Is the formatting suitable for printing or digital distribution?

Chapter 16

Closing Thoughts

Since singing is so good a thing
I wish all men would learne to sing.
— attributed to William Byrd

    The conclusion of this book does not by any means indicate having amassed all the knowledge possible to create flawless choral music. I hope this book provides some real value but remember that there's no substitute for learning by doing. So much more is learned in the process of creating, failing, revising, and revising again. You will learn best by engaging in the creative process as much as possible.

    Listen to what your performers tell you about the piece, even if the criticism feels harsh. Remember, the performers are your first audience. If they don't like your music, they won't buy it, they probably won't perform it, and they certainly won't commission you. It's best to find feedback in a workshop situation or with smaller groups and where you can have exchanges and revisions well before a commission is due.

    Understand that it takes time. There will be many points of frustration in this pilgrimage to proficiency. Writing and arranging for choir can't be mastered overnight, but competency—even mastery—is attainable through time and diligent effort.

In this chapter, I would like to provide for you a few ideas to help you continue to learn and grow in your ability to write proficiently for the choral idiom. These are all activies that I have practiced on a regular basis that have all contributed to my knowledge on the subject.

Habits for Continual Practice

Join an Ensemble

This isn't entirely foolproof, but joining an ensemble will give you ample opportunity to learn and sing through large amounts of repertoire. You'll learn firsthand what works and what doesn't. You'll be able to hear how other sections do with learning and singing various works. Even if you feel you can't sing very well there are ensembles that fit your skill set, as mentioned previously in Chapter 9. Most importantly, you will gain more empathy for the musicians you're writing for because you are one of them.

Attended As Many Performances As You Are Able

Going to performances will inform you about a wide variety of different compositions, especially at a variety of skill levels. You'll find other compositions you like and can see whether they're successful in performance. You'll see firsthand how different compositions land with their audiences. You'll also find what literature choral ensembles value and what they feel defines their mission.

Visit Rehearsals

Attending rehearsals is easily the most undervalued activity for a composer, especially because they are free to attend. Nearly all choral conductors I know or have met will welcome you into their rehearsals if you ask them politely. And if they have extra copies of their music, they may lend you some to follow along. During breaks, you may even have a chance to speak to the singers about what they like (or don't like) singing and why. Again, be polite about it. Never assume that you are entitled to be in a rehearsal (even if they are performing one of your compositions or arrangements). This is their space and their time; you are their guest.

Listen to Recordings

While not as informative sometimes as live performances or rehearsals, recordings are a treasure trove of different compositions from all different epochs. Recordings are especially helpful if you don't have that many different choral organizations of different abilities that you can attend in person. And as I hope every reader is aware, nearly every recording of every composition can be found online. Always check your local library, including any university libraries you may have access to, as these can be much more cost effective. Many of them also let you have access to their paid subscriptions, should they have any to offer.

Study Scores

While wonderful on its own, studying scores really should go hand in hand with actual listening so that you can hear what it's like to execute it. I say this as a warning because if you learned how to study choral writing from studying the scores alone, you may have a warped idea about what successful choral writing looks like. Beethoven's *Symphony No 9* or *Missa solemnis* are great examples of scores that need to be studied with a performance.

In addition to playing through or following along while listening, try singing through some of the parts yourself, especially if you don't feel like you have a great voice yourself and don't want to join an ensemble. Most literature can be found at university libraries. Additionally, anything composed roughly 100 years ago is in the public domain in the United States[3] and may be available at the International Music Score Library Project (also known as Petrucci Music Library, imslp.org) as well as at the Choral Public Domain Library (cpdl.org).

Copy Music by Hand

Copying music by hand was a somewhat common practice used by several composers from the seventeenth and eighteenth centuries, including Handel. This was an exercise that one of my counterpoint teachers felt strongly about and had us do for class assignments. It forces you to take time to understand more closely how voices work and what voices are doing. Think of it as another way to study the score. This practice is especially good for tactile learners.

Join a Professional Choral Organization

There are a few professional choral organizations in the United States, including the American Choral Director's Association (ACDA), the National Collegiate Choral Organization (NCCO), Chorus America, and globally, the International Federation for Choral Music (IFCM). Each organization has a

---

3   Copyright and public domain in the twentieth century will vary from country to country and from composer to composer.

slightly different mission, goal, and demographic. These organizations will assemble conferences with performances, interest sessions, exhibits, and meet-and-greets between composers and conductors. Some of these conferences may even have special schedules or tracks curated for composers. Professional organizations are a great way to keep up to date with what is happening in the choral realm, both in North America and beyond, as well as to network with choral musicians around the globe.

Conclusion

Never forget what the amateur, first-time singer needs. Remembering their needs is not just important for the majority of choral musicians, but will also serve you well when composing music for more advanced musicians. As a professional musician who has been incredibly fortunate to perform alongside some truly outstanding musicians, I can forget that I breathe rarified air with these ensembles. I will sometimes get caught up thinking about what these groups can do and forget that these groups—while laudable—do not represent most choral groups in the world.

I have put a strong emphasis throughout this text on writing what is idiomatic and respecting the capabilities of the musicians found in vocal ensembles at every level. One of my fears for an unintended consequence of this book is that you will cease to push the envelope or think outside of the box. I fear that I may discourage you from exercising creativity in expanding what choral music can and should grow into. My consolation is that doing it from a more stable, idiomatic starting point will help you get there faster as you avoid the pitfalls of many of your predecessors.

I am constantly being taught what choirs can do well and how to play to their strengths. Even while writing this book, I have been learning principles of vocal writing that I had never considered previously and relearning some principles I had forgotten. Choral ensembles are capable of some truly outstanding, breathtaking singing. It continues to amaze me what the human voice can accomplish.

How sweet the moonlight sleeps upon this bank!
Here will we sit and let the sounds of music
Creep in our ears: soft stillness and the night
Become the touches of sweet harmony.

- The Merchant of Venice 5.1.62-65

Despite my best efforts to create the highest quality document I can muster this text is not perfect. If you feel I have made a serious error—and not just a difference of opinion—I welcome any well-meaning, kindly-spoken feedback.

Appendix A

Choirs Based on Size

	Level of training	Vocal Ranges	Division of Parts
One-on-a-part vocal ensembles	Usually quite high	Depends on the ensemble, but usually trained extensively.	Not possible
Chamber Ensembles	Usually high	Depends on the ensemble, but very often trained.	Possible, but could be limited
Large Choirs	Varies	Depends on the ensemble	Possible
Extra-Large/ Festival Choirs	Varies	Possible but not guaranteed.	Possible, but with good level of training.

Choirs Based on Ability

	Level of training	Vocal Ranges	Division of Parts
Amateur	Low	Conservative	Usually no divisions.
Semi-pro	Medium to high	Trained ranges.	Standard divisions, sometimes further.
Professional	Usually very high	Trained and sometimes extensive.	Standard divisions, sometimes further.

(continued)

Vibrato use	Preferred Repertoire	Example Ensembles
Usually straight but some vibrancy	Specialized to their specific ensemble make up. Usually very old or very new.	The King's Singers, New York Polyphony, The Real Group, Variant 6, and Voces8.
Varies, but mostly straight with some vibrancy	Variety.	RIAS Kammerkor, Roomful of Teeth, Seraphic Fire, The Sixteen, Skylark, The Tallis Scholars, and Tenebrae.
Variable	Variety.	Atlanta Master Chorale Harvard Glee, Michigan Glee, the Los Angeles Master Chorale St. Olaf, and Westminster Choir..
Varies, but mostly vibrate and less straight.	Usually choral-orchestral repertoire; Romantic and 20th Century.	BYU Men's Chorus, Estonia Song and Dance Celebration Choir, London Bach Choir, and the Tabernacle Choir at Temple Square

(continued)

Vibrato use	Preferred Repertoire	Example Ensembles
Depends on the age of the singers.	Whatever is most accessible from whatever epoch has it.	—
Varies from group to group.	Lots of variety.	Atlanta Master Chorale, Dallas Symphony Chorus, The Holst Singers, London Bach Choir, Minnesota Choral Artists, National Youth Choir of Great Britain, Salt Lake Vocal Artists, and Phoenix Chorale.
Varies from group to group.	Usually broad, but sometimes in a niche.	Ansan City Chorale, Conspirare, the King's Singers, the Los Angeles Master Chorale, New York Polyphony, Oregon Bach Festival, Santa Fe Desert Chorale, Seraphic Fire, Skylark, the Tallis Scholars, Tenebrae, and Voces8.

Choirs Based on Purpose or Function

	Level of training	Vocal Ranges	Division of Parts
Children's Choirs	Varies depending on the group.	Depends, but in treble ranges.	Depends on the group, but generally few divisions.
Primary Education Choirs	Varies, but usually amateur.	Depends, but in treble ranges.	Generally, little to few divisions.
Secondary Education Choirs	Varies, but most often amateur.	Varies. Possibly incorporating cambiatas.	Depends, but usually some standard divisions.
Higher Education Choirs	Varies.	Varies.	Standard divisions, sometimes further.
Religious Choirs	Varies depend on the group.	Varies depend on the group.	Varies depend on the group.
Community Choirs	Varies depend on the group.	Varies depend on the group.	Varies depend on the group.

Vibrato use	Preferred Repertoire	Example Ensembles
Almost never.	Varies, but usually newer rather than older.	American Boys Choir, Cantabile Youth Singers of Silicon Valley, Hong Kong Children's Choir, New Zealand Youth Choir, Singapore Symphony Children's Choir, and Texas Boys Choir.
Almost never.	Varies, but usually newer rather than older.	—
Depends, but usually straight.	Varies, but usually newer rather than older.	—
Varies depend on the group.	Depends, but often very broad and adventurous.	BYU Singers; CSU Long Beach Chamber Singers; King's College, Cambridge; New College, Oxford; St. Olaf Choir; Trinity College, Cambridge; USC Chamber Singers; Westminster Choir; and Yale Schola Cantorum.
Varies depend on the group.	Almost exclusively religious and usually specific to the denomination, although there's some ecumenical sharing.	Cathedral of the Madeleine Choir (Salt Lake City), Choir of Westminster Abbey, Christchurch College Choir (Oxford), Emmanuel Episcopal Church of Boston, Grace Cathedral Choir (San Francisco), Kings College Cambridge Choir, Marsh Chapel (Boston), New College Choir (Oxford), St. James in-the-City (Los Angeles), St. Thomas of 6th Street (New York City), Trinity College Choir (Cambridge) and Trinity Wall Street (New York City).
Varies depend on the group.	Anything goes.	Ansan City Choir, Kansas City Chorale, London Bach Choir, Los Angeles Master Chorale, Minnesota Choral Artists, Phoenix Chorale, Salt Lake Choral Artists, and Toronto Mendelssohn Choir.

(continued)

	Level of training	Vocal Ranges	Division of Parts
Fly-in Choirs	Professional.	Usually extensive ranges.	Standard divisions, sometimes further.
Early Music Ensembles	Usually professional.	Usually extensive ranges, but depends on the repertoire.	Standard divisions, but depends on the group.
Radio/Scoring Choirs	Usually quite high.	Usually extensive ranges.	Standard divisions, sometimes further.
Touring Ensembles	Professional.	Depends on the group, but usually extensive ranges.	Possible, but less likely.
Opera Choruses	Depends on the house, but generally decent.	Depends on the house, but generally decent.	Depends on the house, but generally decent.
Symphonic Choruses	Can vary	Depends on ability.	Depends on ability, but capable of dividing into eight parts and sometimes more

Vibrato use	Preferred Repertoire	Example Ensembles
Depends, but usually straight.	Quite broad, but sometimes depends on ensemble's mission.	Bach Collegium San Diego, Conspirare, Kinnara Ensemble, Oregon Bach Festival, Santa Fe Desert Chorale, Seraphic Fire, and Skylark.
Depends, but usually straight.	Usually from Mozart and earlier, but sometimes new commissions.	Alamire, Anonymous 4, Bach Collegium Japan, Bach Collegium San Diego, Blue Heron, Collegium Vocale Gent, The Hilliard Ensemble, The Monteverdi Choir, The Sixteen, and the Tallis Scholars.
Usually vibrant.	Quite broad, but sometimes depends on ensemble's mission.	BBC Singers, Danish National Radio Choir, RIAS Kammerchor, Swedish Radio Choir, the Tabernacle Choir at Temple Square.
Depends, but usually straight.	Usually ensemble specific; usually very old or very new.	Cantus, Chanticleer, The King's Singers, New York Polyphony, Seraphic Fire, The Sixteen, The Tallis Scholars, Tenebrae, and Voces8.
Generous	Ensemble specific. Classical and Romanic opera.	Metropolitan Opera Chorus (New York), Royal Opera Chorus (London), Teatro alla Scalla Chorus (Milan).
Generous	Ensemble specific. 19th and 20th Century choral-orchestral repertoire	Atlanta Symphony Chorus, Chicago Symphony Chorus, Dallas Symphony Chorus, London Symphony Chorus, and the Los Angeles Master Chorale.

Appendix B

List of Examples

Example 2.1: John Dykes, "Ten Thousand Times Ten Thousand." 15
Example 2.2: Francis Poulenc, *Messe en Sol Majeur*, "Gloria.". 16
Example 2.3: Dominick Argento, *Walden Pond*, "The Pond." 18
Example 2.4: Gerald Finzi, *Seven Poems of Robert Bridges*, "My spirit sang all day." . . . 18
Example 2.5: Claudio Monteverdi, *Il quarto libro de madrigali a cinque voci*, "Si, ch'io vorrei morire." 19
Example 2.6: Claudio Monteverdi, *Il quarto libro de madrigali a cinque voci*, "Si, ch'io vorrei morire." 19
Example 2.7: Felix Mendelssohn, *Sechs Lieder*, op. 59, "O Täler weit.". 20
Example 2.8: Johannes Brahms, *Liebeslieder Waltzer*, op. 52, "Nein es ist nicht auszukommen." 20
Example 2.9: Robert White, *Lamentations of Jeremiah*. *21*
Example 2.10: George Frederic Handel, *Messiah*, "And He shall Purify." 21
Example 2.11: Gabriel Jackson, "In the beginning was the Word." 22
Example 2.12: Maurice Ravel, *Daphnis et Chloé*. *23*
Example 2.13: Ralph Vaughan Williams, *Flos Campi*. *23*
Example 2.14: Jaakko Mäntyjärvi, "El Hambo." 24
Example 2.15: Wolfram Buchenberg, "Klangfelder Raumschwingungen Oszillationen."
24
Example 2.16: Dominick Argento, "Everyone Sang." 25
Example 2.17: Giovanni Pierluigi da Palestrina, *Missa Papae Marcelli*, "Gloria." 27
Example 2.18: Giovanni Pierluigi da Palestrina, *Missa Papae Marcelli*, "Agnus Dei II.". 27
Example 2.19: Johann Sebastian Bach, *Mass in B minor*, BVW 232, "Sanctus." 28
Example 2.20: Maurice Ravel, *Trois Chansons*, "Trois beaux oiseaux du paradis." . . . 29
Example 2.21: Josef Haydn, *Kleine Orgelmesse*, "Gloria." 29
Example 2.22: Joby Talbot, *Path of Miracles*, "Reconcevalles." 30
Example 2.23: Clément Janequin, "Le Chant des Oiseaux." 31
Example 2.24: Pierre Passereau, "Il est bel et bon." 32
Example 2.25: John Weelkes, "As Vesta was from Latmos Hill descending." 32
Example 2.26: Maurice Ravel, *Trois Chansons*, "Nicolette." 33
Example 2.27: Maurice Ravel, *Trois Chansons*, "Nicolette." 33
Example 2.28: Ildebrando Pizzetti, *Due Composizioni Corali*, "Il giardino di Afrodite." 34
Example 2.29: Benjamin Britten, *Hymn to St. Cecilia*, op. 23. . . . . *35*
Example 2.30: Benjamin Britten, *Hymn to St. Cecilia*, op. 23. . . . . *35*
Example 2.31: Michael Tippett, "Dance Clarion Air." 36
Example 3.1: Wolfgang Amadeus Mozart, "Ave verum corpus" K618. 42

Appendix B   335

Example 3.2: Wolfgang Amadeus Mozart, "Ave verum corpus" K618 in two bar phrases.. 43
Example 3.3: Wolfgang Amadeus Mozart, "Ave verum corpus" K618 in four bar phrases.. 43
Example 3.4: Wolfgang Amadeus Mozart, "Ave verum corpus" K618 with breathing at commas. 44
Example 3.5: Samuel Barber, *Reincarnations*, "Anthony O'Daly." 49
Example 3.6: Eric Whitacre, "Go, Lovely Rose.". 61
Example 3.7: Ludwig van Beethoven, *Missa solemnis*, op. 123 "Gloria in excelsis.". . . 64
Example 4.1: Carl Orff, *Carmina Burana*, "Floret silva." 71
Example 4.2: Johannes Brahms, *Zwei Motteten*, Op. 29, No 1 "Warum ist das Licht gegeben.". 72
Example 4.3: Gabriel Fauré, *Requiem*, "Introit and Kyrie." 72
Example 4.4: James MacMillan, "O bone Jesu." 72
Example 4.5: Ralph Vaughan Williams, "Silence and Music." 72
Example 5.1: Anton Bruckner, "Os justi." 77
Example 5.2: Cyrillus Kreek, *Taaveti laulud (Psalms of David)*, "Taaveti laul Nr. 121 (Psalm 121).". 77
Example 5.3: Frank Martin, *Mass for Double Choir*, "Kyrie." 77
Example 5.4: Francis Poulenc, *Un Soir de Neige*, "La bonne neige." 77
Example: 6.1 John Dowland harmonization of "Old Hundredth." 81
Example 6.2: Johannes Brahms, *Ein deutsches Requiem*, op. 45, "Wie lieblich sind deine Wohnungen.". 82
Example 6.3: Gabriel Fauré, *Requiem*, "Agnus Dei." 82
Example 6.4: Vaclav Nelhybel, "Estampie Natalis." 83
Example 6.5: Francis Poulenc, *Quatre petites prières de Saint François d'Assise*, "Salut, Dame Sainte.". 83
Example 7.1: Anton Bruckner, "Os justi." 88
Example 7.2: Frank Martin, *Mass for Double Choir*, "Gloria." 89
Example 7.3: Frank Martin, *Mass for Double Choir*, "Credo." 89
Example 7.4: Francis Poulenc, *Figure Humaine*, "Bientôt." 89
Example 8.1: Bob Chilcott, "High Flight." 93
Example 8.2: Gabriel Jackson, "In all his works." 94
Example 8.3: Benjamin Britten, *Friday Afternoons*, op. 7 "Fishing Song.". 97
Example 8.4: Benjamin Britten, *War Requiem*, op. 66 "Offertorium." 97
Example 9.1: Johannes Brahms, *Drei Quartette*, op. 64, no. 3 "Fragen." 106
Example 10.1: John Sheppard, *Missa Cantate*, "Sanctus." 135
Example 10.2: Felix Mendelssohn, *Sechs Sprüche* op. 79, "Weinachten." 135
Example 10.3: Sergei Rachmaninoff, *All-Night Vigil*, "Bogoroditse Devo." 137
Example 10.4: Felix Mendelssohn, "Jauchzet dem Herrn, alle Welt." 137
Example 10.5: Herbert Howells, *Collegium Regale*, "Magnificat." 138

Example 10.6: Healey Willan, "The Three Kings.". 139
Example 10.7: Johann Sebastian Bach, "Singet dem Herrn," BWV 225. 140
Example 10.8: Gustav Holst, "Ave Maria.". 141
Example 10.9: Trond Kverno, "Ave Maris Stella." 142
Example 10.10: Frank Ferko, *Hildegard Triptych*, "O vis aeternitatis.". 143
Example 10.11: Eric Whitacre, "Water Night.". 144
Example 10.12: Ēriks Ešenvalds, "Vineta.". 144
Example 10.13: Györgi Ligeti, "Lux Aeterna.". 146
Example 10.14: David MacIntyre, "Ave Maria." 147
Example 10.15: Judith Bingham, "Gleams of a Remoter World.". 148
Example 10.16: James MacMillan, "O bone Jesu.". 149
Example 10.17: Herbert Howells, *Requiem*, "Psalm 23." 150
Example 11.1: Hyo-Won Woo, "O Magnum Mysterium.". 155
Example 11.2: Gabriel Fauré, *Requiem*, "In Paradisum." 165
Example 11.3: Benjamin Britten, "I lov'd a lass.". 166
Example 11.4: Morten Lauridsen, *Mid-Winter Songs*, "Lament for Pasiphaë." 168
Example 11.5: Morten Lauridsen, *Madrigali*, "Ov'è, Lass', Il Bel Viso?". 169
Example 11.6: Howard Hanson, "Prayer of the Middle Ages." 169
Example 11.7: Francis Poulenc, *Un soir de neige*, "La bonne neige." 170
Example 11.8: René Clausen, "Ubi Caritas." 171
Example 11.9: Maurice Duruflé, *Requiem*, "Introit." 172
Example 11.10: Francis Poulenc, *Gloria*, "Qui sedes ad dexteram Patris." 173
Example 11.11: Dominick Argento, *I Hate and I Love*, "1. I Hate and I Love." . . . 174
Example 11.12: Jean Langlais, *Messe Solennelle*, "Benedictus.". 175
Example 11.13: Sergei Rachmaninoff, *All-Night Vigil*, "Bogoroditse Devo." 175
Example 11.14: Joby Talbot, *Path of Miracles*, "Burgos." 176
Example 11.15: Abbie Betinis, "Cedit, Hyems." 177
Example 11.16: Tarik O'Regan, "O vera digna hostia." 177
Example 11.17: Francis Poulenc, *Gloria*, "Qui sedes ad dexteram patris." 178
Example 11.18: Sergei Rachmaninoff, *All-Night Vigil*, "Voskreseniye Khristovo videvshe." 179
Example 11.19: Mack Wilberg, "Arise, O God, and Shine"/"Rejoice the Lord is King." 179
Example 11.20: Gabriel Jackson, "O Sacrum Convivium." 180
Example 11.21: Francis Poulenc, *Un Soir de Neige*, "Bois meurtri, bois perdu." . . . 181
Example 11.22: Allen Koepke, "Wade in de Water." 181
Example 12.1: Josquin des Prez, "Ave Maria Virgo Serena.". 186
Example 12.2: William Byrd, *Mass for Three Voices*, "Agnus Dei." 186
Example 12.3: William Byrd, *Mass for Four Voices*, "Agnus Dei." 187
Example 12.4: William Byrd, *Mass for Four Voices*, "Agnus Dei." 187
Example 12.5: William Byrd, *Mass for Four Voices*, "Agnus Dei." 188

Appendix B   337

Example 12.6: William Byrd, *Mass for Four Voices*, "Agnus Dei." 188
Example 12.7: Sergei Rachmaninoff, *All-Night Vigil*, "Voskreseniye Khristovo videvshe." 191
Example 12.8: Joby Talbot, *Path of Miracles*, "Roncesvalles.". 191
Example 12.9: Giovanni Pierluigi da Palestrina, *Missa Papae Marcelli*, "Agnus Dei II." 192
Example 12.10: Johann Sebastian Bach, "Komm, Jesu, Komm," BWV 229. 193
Example 12.11: Josef Rheinberger, *3 Geistliche Gesänge*, Op. 69, No 3 "Abendlied.". 193
Example 12.12: Wolfgang Amadeus Mozart, *Requiem*, K626, "Kyrie." 194
Example 12.13: Giuseppe Verdi, *Requiem*, "Sanctus." 195
Example 12.14: Ildebrando Pizzetti, *Due Composizioni Corali*, "Il giardino di Afrodite." . 195
Example 12.15: Benjamin Britten, "Jubilate Deo.". 196
Example 12.16: Jocelyn Hagen, *The Notebooks of Leonardo da Vinci*, "Perception." . 197
Example 12.17: Caroline Shaw, "and the swallow.". 198
Example 12.18: Johann Sebastian Bach, *St. Matthew Passion*, BWV 244 "Befiehl du deine Wege.". 199
Example 12.19: Carol Barnett, *An American Thanksgiving*, "McKay.". 200
Example 12.20: Tarik O'Regan, "O vera digna hostia." 200
Example 12.21: Judith Bingham, "Water Lilies." 201
Example 12.22: Eric Whitacre, "Leonardo Dreams of His Flying Machine." 202
Example 12.23: Stephen Leek, *Great Southern Spirits*, "Kondalilla." 203
Example 12.24: Gabriel Jackson, "Hymn to the Trinity (Honor, Virtus, et Potestas)." . 204
Example 12.25: Maurice Ravel, *Trois Chansons*, "Trois beaux oiseaux du paradis.". . 205
Example 12.26: Mack Wilberg, "Arise, O God, and Shine"/"Rejoice the Lord is King."205
Example 12.27: Gabriel Jackson, "Orbis patrator optime." 206
Example 12.28: Gabriel Jackson, "Orbis patrator optime." 206
Example 12.29: Johann Sebastian Bach, "Singet dem Herrn ein neues Lied," BWV 225. 207
Example 12.30: Johann Sebastian Bach, "Singet den Herrn ein neues Lied," BWV 225.208
Example 12.31: Frank Martin, *Mass for Double Choir*, "Sanctus." 209
Example 12.32: Frank Martin, *Mass for Double Choir*, "Sanctus." 210
Example 13.1: Josef Haydn, *Vierstimmige Gesänge*, "Die Warnung." 215
Example 13.2: Johannes Brahms, *Zigeunerlieder*, "He, Zigeuner, greife in die Saiten." 215
Example 13.3: Gabriel Fauré, "Madrigal." 216
Example 13.4: Lili Boulanger, "Soir Sur La Plaine." 216
Example 13.5: Edgar Cosma, *Les Amours des Poètes*, "Quand vous voudrez." 217
Example 13.6: Edgar Cosma, *Les Amours des Poètes*, "Rondeau." 217
Example 13.7: Edgar Cosma, *Les Amours des Poètes*, "Les Roses de Saadi." 218
Example 13.8: Edgar Cosma, *Les Amours des Poètes*, "Es-tu brune ou blonde?" . . . 218
Example 13.9: Thomas Tomkins, "My Beloved Spake." 222
Example 13.10: Josef Haydn, *Kleine Orgelmesse*, "Credo." 222

Example 13.11: Johannes Brahms, "Geistliches Lied," op. 30.. 223
Example 13.12: Herbert Howells, *Collegium Regale*, "Magnificat." 223
Example 13.13: Herbert Howells, *Collegium Regale*, "Magnificat." 224
Example 13.14: Maurice Duruflé, *Requiem in D minor*, op. 9, "Sanctus." 225
Example 13.15: Stephen Paulus, "A Savior From on High." 226
Example 13.16: Benjamin Britten, *Ceremony of Carols*, "Wolcum Yole." 227
Example 13.17: Benjamin Britten, *Ceremony of Carols*, "Deo Gratias." 227
Example 13.18: Jocelyn Hagen, "See Amid the Winter Snow." 228
Example 13.19: Abbie Betinis, "Cedit, Hyems." 229
Example 13.20: Howard Helvey, "O Quam Gloriosum." 229
Example 13.21: David Hamilton, "The Moon is Silently Singing." 230
Example 13.22: Gabriel Jackson, "Ave Regina Coelorum." 231
Example 13.23: Eric Whitacre, *Five Hebrew Love Songs*, "Éyze shéleg!". 233
Example 13.24: Tarik O'Regan, *Triptych*, "Threnody." 233
Example 13.25: Gabriel Jackson, "The Spacious Firmament.". 234
Example 13.26: Eve Duncan, "Stars." 235
Example 13.27: Dominick Argento, *I Hate and I Love*, "Let us live, my Clodia, and let us love." 237
Example 13.28: Dominick Argento, *I Hate and I Love*, "You promise me, my dearest life." 237
Example 13.29: Dominick Argento, *I Hate and I Love*, "Was it a lioness from the mountains of Libya." 238
Example 13.30: Ēriks Ešenvalds, "Vineta.". 239
Example 13.31: Ēriks Ešenvalds, "Vineta.". 239
Example 13.32: Ēriks Ešenvalds, "Vineta.". 240
Example 13.33: Bob Chilcott, "The Singing Heart." 241
Example 13.34: Ēriks Ešenvalds, "Stars.". 242
Example 13.35: Igor Stravinsky, *Symphony of Psalms*, Movement I.. 246
Example 13.36: Giuseppe Verdi, *Requiem*, "Sanctus." 247
Example 13.37: Ralph Vaughan Williams, *Sea Symphony*, "I. A Song for All Seas, All Ships." 248
Example 13.38: Ralph Vaughan Williams, *Sea Symphony*, "I. A Song for All Seas, All Ships." 249
Example 13.39: Richard Wagner, *Tristan und Isolde*, Act One, Scene Two. 251
Example 13.40: Richard Wagner, *Tristan und Isolde*, Act One, Scene Five. 252
Example 13.41: Ralph Vaughan Williams, "Serenade to Music.". 254
Example 13.42: Ralph Vaughan Williams, "Serenade to Music." 255
Example 13.43: Richard Wagner, *Tannhäuser*, Act Three, Scene One. 256
Example 13.44: Richard Wagner, *Tannhäuser*, Act Three, Scene One. 256
Example 13.45: Richard Wagner, *Tannhäuser*, Act Three, Scene One. 257
Example 13.46: Franz Schubert, *Deutche Messe*, "Zum Sanctus." 259

Appendix B 339

Example 13.47: Johannes Brahms, "Begräbnisgesang." 260
Example 13.48: Igor Stravinsky, *Mass*, "Kyrie." 261
Example 13.49: Igor Stravinsky, *Mass*, "Sanctus." 261
Example 14.1: Aaron Copland (arr. Irving Fine), "I bought me a cat." 270
Example 14.2: Stephen Leek, *Great Southern Spirits*, "Kondalilla." 270
Example 14.3: Claudio Monteverdi, *Vespro della Beata Vergine*, "Dixit Dominus." . . 271
Example 14.4: Claudio Monteverdi, *Il quarto libro de madrigali a cinque voci*, "Sfogava con le stelle." 271
Example 14.5: Maurice Ravel, *Trois Chansons*, "Nicolette." 272
Example 14.6: Jaakko Mäntyjärvi, "Pseudo-Yoik." 273
Example 14.7: James MacMillan, "O bone Jesu." 274
Example 14.8: Francis Poulenc, *Quatre Motets pour le temps de Noël*, "O Magnum Mysterium." 275
Example 14.9: Andrew Maxfield, "For the Future." 276
Example 14.10: Todd Kitchen, "Refraction Sacrée." 278
Example 14.11: Sarah Hopkin, "Past Life Melodies." 279
Example 14.12: Judith Bingham, "The Drowned Lovers." 280
Example 14.13: Eric Whitacre, "Leonardo Dreams of His Flying Machine." 281
Example 14.14: Frank Martin, *Five Ariel Songs*, "Act V, Sc. 1." 282
Example 14.15: Carol Barnett, "Cindy." 283
Example 14.16: Jeffrey Van, *A Procession Winding Around Me*, "Look Down Fair Moon." 283
Example 14.17: Eric William Barnum, "The Sounding Sea." 285
Example 14.18: Carol Barnett, "Cindy." 286
Example 14.19: Jaakko Mäntyjärvi, "Pseudo Yoik." 288
Example 14.20: William Walton, *Belshazzar's Feast*. *289*
Example 14.21: Gabriel Jackson, "Rigwreck." 290
Example 14.22: Gabriel Jackson, *Airplane Cantata*, "Newsreel/Narration." 290
Example 14.23: Arnold Schoenberg, *Pierrot Lunaire*, "Nacht." 291
Example 14.24: Peter Gritton, "Dry Bones." 292
Example 14.25: Andrew Maxfield, "The Door." 292
Example 14.26: David Hamilton, "The Moon is Silently Singing." 294
Example 14.27: Ko Matsushita, *Three Insular Songs of Yaeyama and Miyako Islands*, "Karimatanu Kuicha." 297
Example 14.28: Julio Dominguez, "Deus, qui illuminas." 298
Example 14.29: William Albright, *Chichester Mass*, "Sanctus." 299
Example 14.30: Gabriel Jackson, "In Nomine Domini." 300
Example 14.31: Jaakko Mäntyjärvi, "Psalm 150 in Kent Treble Bob Minor." 301
Example 14.32: Eric Whitacre, "hope, faith, life, love." 302
Example 15.1: John Taverner, *Missa Gloria tibi Trinias*, "Sanctus." 314

Bibliography

Ades, Hawley. *Choral Arranging*. Delaware Water Cap, PA: Shawnee Press, 1966.

Adler, Samuel. *The Study of Orchestration*. New York: W. W. Norton & Company, 2001.

Akst, Lee and Kristine M. Pietsch. "Is Vocal Fry Ruining My Voice." Accessed 26 June 2024. https://www.hopkinsmedicine.org/health/conditions-and-diseases/is-vocal-fry-ruining-myvoice#:~:text=Vocal%20fry%20is%20the%20lowest,produce%20sound%20(your%20voice).

Atlas, Alan. *Renaissance Music: Music in Western Europe, 1400-1600*. New York: W. W. Norton & Company, 1998.

Berlioz, Hector and Richard Strauss. *Treatise on Instrumentation*. New York: Dover Publications, 1991.

Burkholder, J. Peter, Donald Jay Grout, and Claude V. Palisca. *A History of Western Music*. New York: W. W. Norton & Company, 2006.

Collins, Don L. *Teaching Choral Music*. Upper Saddle River, NJ: Prentice Hall, 1999.

Corgliano, John. "Fern Hill." Accessed April 29, 2024. https://www.johncorigliano.com/works/fern-hill-full-orchestra

Davids, Julia, and Stephen LaTour. *Vocal Technique: A Guide to Classical and Contemporary Styles for Conductors, Teachers, and Singers*. Long Grove, IL: Waveland Press, 2021.

Davison, Archibald T. *The Technique of Choral Composition*. Cambridge, MA: Harvard University Press: 1946.

Garrett, Matthew L. and Joshua Palkki. *Honoring Trans and Gender-Expansive Students in Music Education*. New York: Oxford University Press, 2021.

Giles, Peter. *The History and Technique of the Counter-Tenor: A Study of the Male High Voice Family*. Adlershot, UK: Scolar Press, 1994.

Gould, Elaine. *Behind Bars: The Definitive Guide to Music Notation*. London: Faber Music, 2011.

Haynes, Bruce. *History of Performing Pitch: The Story of "A"*. MD: Scarecrow Press, 2002.

Kennan, Kent and Donald Grantham. *The Technique of Orchestration*. Upper Saddle River, NJ: Prentice Hall, 2002.

MacGorman, Venita. "About Those Chimes." Accessed April 29, 2024. https://area9.handbellmusicians.org/about-those-chimes/

McCoy, Scott. *Your Voice: An Inside View*. Princeton: Inside View Press, 2004.

McKay, George Frederick. *Creative Orchestration: A Project Method for Classes in Orchestration and Instrumentation*. Allyn and Bacon, 1969.

McKenzie, Duncan. *Training the Boy's Changing Voice*. New Brunswick: Rutgers University Press, 1956.

Norfolk and Norwich University Hospitals. "The Normal Swallow." Accessed April 29, 2024. https://www.nnuh.nhs.uk/departments/speech-and-language-therapy/swallowing/the-normal-swallow/

Ostrander, Arthur E., and Dana Wilson. *Contemporary Choral Arranging*. Englewood Cliffs, NJ: Prentice-Hall, 1986.

Plantenga, Bart. *Yodel-Ay-Ee-Oooo: The Secret History of Yodeling Around the World*. New York: Routledge, 2004.

Potter, John. *Tenor: History of a Voice*. New Haven: Yale University Press, 2009.

Ravens, Simon. *The Supernatural Voice: A History of High Male Singing*. Woodbrdige: The Boydell Press, 2014.

Rimsky-Korsakov, Nicolai. *Principles of Orchestration*. New York: Dover Publications, 1964.

Rosenbaum, Harold. *Choralstration: A Practical Guide for Composers of Choral Music*. Self-published, 2022.

Saint-Exupery, Antoine de. *Airman's Odyssey*. Orlando: Harcourt Brace & Company, 1942.

Sataloff, Robert T. and Karen M. Kost. "The Effects of Age on the Voice, Part 1." Journal of Singing 77, no. 1 (Sept/Oct 2020): 63-70.

Schrock, Dennis. *Choral Repertoire*. New York: Oxford University Press, 2009.

Sevsay, Ertuğrul. *The Cambridge Guide to Orchestration*. Cambrdige: Cambridge University, 2013.

Sharon, Deke and Dylan Bell. *A Cappella Arranging*. Lanham, MD: Rowman & Littlefield, 2012.

Shepard, Philip. *What the Fach?!* Self-publihsed, 2010.

Strimple, Nick. *Choral Music in the Nineteenth Century*. New York: Amadeus Press, 2009.

Strimple, Nick. *Choral Music in the Twentieth Century*. New York: Amadeus Press, 2005.

Titze, Ingo R. *Principles of Voice Production*. Upper Saddle River, NJ: Prentice Hall, 1994.

Thomas, Andrew. "The Organ in Some Striking Orchestral, Operatic and Choral Contexts." The Musical Times 151, no. 1912 (2010): 59–68.

The Walt Whitman Archive. "Song of the Exposition No. 8." "U.S. Editions of Leaves of Grass." Accessed April 29, 2024. https://whitmanarchive.org/published-writings/leaves-of-grass/1881

Watson, Derek. *Dictionary of Musical Quotations*. Hertfordshire: Wordsworth Editions, 1994.

Index

A

Agility   69, 76, 80, 86
Alamire   127, 333
Albright, William   299, 306
Aleatoric music   298
Aleatory. **See** Aleatoric Music
Alto   9, 68, 74, 75, 76, 80, 81, 87, 91, 92, 93, 94, 96, 99, 105, 112, 117, 119, 122, 134, 139, 160, 167, 171, 172, 177, 179, 187, 188, 228, 230, 246, 299, 311, 312
Amateur Choirs   111, 124, 196, 328
American Boys Choir   117, 331
American Choral Director's Association   323
Amplification   213, 304
Animal noises   269
Anonymous 4   127, 129, 133, 333
Ansan City Chorale   115
Anthems
    Full   221
    Verse   221, 263
Argento, Dominick   17, 18, 25, 173, 174, 236, 237, 238, 242, 262, 263
    I Hate and I Love   173, 174, 236, 237, 238, 263
    Walden Pond   17, 18, 242, 263
Arranging   3, 4, 5, 6, 39, 46, 210, 213, 321
Ars Nova Copenhagen   132
Athematic
Atlanta Master Chorale   108, 114, 329
Atlanta Symphony Chorus   131, 132

B

Bach Collegium Japan   127, 132, 333
Bach Collegium San Diego   126, 127, 333
Bach, Johann Sebastian   6, 28, 38, 69, 76, 80, 110, 114, 115, 124, 125, 126, 127, 132, 140, 151, 185, 192, 193, 198, 199, 207, 208, 211, 329, 331, 333
Badings, Henk   262
Barber, Samuel
    Reincarnations   49, 66, 132

Barnett, Carol   200, 283, 286
Barnum, Eric William   285
Baroque   2, 10, 21, 37, 85, 92, 105, 115, 126, 129, 130, 134, 192, 193, 279, 280, 281
Bass   85, 88, 138
    Baritone   85, 138
The BBC Singers   127, 128, 133, 148, 333
Beaming   315
Beatboxing   285
Beethoven, Ludwig van   63, 64, 66, 287, 323
Bells   240
Berio, Luciano   266, 306
Bernstein, Leonard   263, 264, 303
Betinis, Abbie   174, 176, 177, 229, 262, 303
Bichordal. **See** Polychordal
Biebl, Franz   141
Bingham, Judith   148, 151, 201, 202, 207, 211, 280
Blue Heron   127, 333
Body percussion   294
Boulanger, Lili   216, 262
Brahms, Johannes
    Liebeslieder Waltzer   20
Breathing   41, 44, 316
    Stagger   44
Britten, Benjamin   6, 34, 35, 38, 95, 97, 165, 166, 196, 226, 227, 263
Bruckner, Anton   66, 77, 88, 151
Buccal speech   270
Buchenberg, Wolfram   24
Byrd, William   186, 187, 188, 211, 263, 321
BYU Men's Chorus   110, 329

C

Cambiata   90, 98, 99, 100, 116, 119
Cantabile Youth Singers of Silicon Valley   117, 331
Cantus   129, 333
Cathedral of the Madeleine Choir   123, 331
Chamber Ensembles   106, 231, 263, 328

Chansons   29, 31, 32, 33, 38, 205, 262, 272
Chanticleer   129, 333
Chanting   271
Chasons   216, 263
Chicago Symphony Chorus   131
Chilcott, Bob   93, 241
Children   4, 9, 68, 90, 94, 95, 96, 97, 98, 111, 112, 115, 116, 117, 118, 119, 122, 194, 225, 226, 227, 305
Children's Choirs   116, 330
Choir of Westminster Abbey   123, 331
Chorale   108, 114, 115, 124, 125, 126, 131, 132, 198, 207, 208, 329, 331, 333
Choralography   295
Choral organizations   323
Chordal   197
Chord Spacing   164
Chorus America   323
Christchurch College Choir   123, 331
Clapping   295
Classical   105, 126, 130, 134, 333, 340
Clausen, René   171
Clef   68, 74, 75, 79, 85
Collegium Vocale Gent   127, 132, 333
Coloratura   80, 87, 93, 99, 113, 114, 119, 125, 126
Community Choirs   123, 330
Consonants   51, 54
Conspirare   115, 126, 133, 333
Cooper, Irvin   95, 98, 99
Copland, Aaron   151, 182, 270
Corgliano, John   264, 340
Cosma, Edgar   217, 218, 263
Coughing   286
Countertenor   59, 74, 91, 92, 93
Cricothyroid-Dominant Production   48, 76, 79, 91, 92, 272, 282, 284
CSU Long Beach Chamber Singers   122, 331
Cymbals   213, 214, 236, 238

D

Dallas Symphony Chorus   114, 131
Danish National Radio Choir   128, 333
Debussy, Claude   38, 184, 211
Digital Distribution   319
Divisions
  Double Choir   140
  Extensive   143
  Standard   136
  Three-Part   138
Dominguez, Julio   298
Donizetti, Gaetano   80
Dorico   307
Doublings
  Octave
  Unison   171
Dowland, John   81
DuFay, Guillaume   210
Duncan, Eve   98, 235, 341
Dun, Tan   242, 263
Duruflé, Maurice   172, 221, 224, 225, 263, 264
Dykes, John   15

E

Early Music Ensembles   126, 332
Emmanuel Episcopal Church of Boston   123, 331
Ešenvalds, Ēriks   38, 66, 143, 144, 151, 238, 239, 240, 241, 242, 263
Estonian Philharmonic Chamber Choir   133
Extensive Parts   145

F

Faburden. See Fauxbourdon
Falsetto   272
Fauré, Gabriel   47, 72, 82, 132, 164, 165, 216, 221, 263
  Requiem   47
Fauxbourdon   81
Ferko, Frank   143
Festival Choirs   109, 328
Finale   307
Fine, Irving   151
Finzi, Gerald   18, 38
Flutter tongue   272
Fly-in Choirs   124, 332
forScore   319
Fricatives   281, 282, 292
  Unvoiced   292
  Voiced   281
Front Matter   308
Full Score   311

G

Gackle, Lynne   95
Gargling
Gasping   286
Gibbons, Orlando   263
Glasses   240
Glissando   274
Glossolalia   287
Glottal stop   287
Gould, Elaine   307, 309, 314, 319, 341
Grace Cathedral Choir   123, 331
Grantham, Donald   3, 341
Gritton, Peter   292
Grunting   287

H

Hagen, Jocelyn   197, 228, 263
Hamilton, David   229, 230, 294
Handel, George Frederich
   Messiah   21, 109
Hand wah
Hanson, Howard   169
Harp   225, 263
Haute-contre   91, 92
Haydn, Josef   29, 30, 214, 215, 222
Helium   305
Helvey, Howard   229, 263
Heterophonic   196
Hiccup   288
Higher Education Choirs   120, 330
The Hilliard Ensemble   127, 129, 333
Holst, Gustav   114, 141, 304
The Holst Singers   114
Hong Kong Children's Choir   117, 331
Hopkin, Sarah   279, 306
Howells, Herbert   133, 138, 150, 151, 221, 223, 224, 263
Humming   275

I

Intelligibility   247
The International Federation for Choral Music   323
International Phonetic Alphabet   8, 12, 37, 52

J

Jackson, Gabriel   22, 94, 145, 180, 182, 204, 205, 206, 211, 230, 231, 234, 263, 290, 300, 306
Janequin, Clément   31
Josquin des Prez   186, 204, 210, 211

K

Kansas City Chorale   124, 331
Kennan, Kent
Keyboard Reductions   317
Key Signatures   50
King's College, Cambridge   122, 133, 223, 331
The King's Singers   105, 106, 114, 115, 129, 329, 333
Kinnara Ensemble   126, 333
Kitchen, Todd   277, 278
Koepke, Allen   181
Kreek, Cyrillus   77
Kverno, Trond   142

L

Langlais, Jean   175, 221
Large Choirs   108
Larsen, Libby   263
Lasso, Orlando di. See Lassus, Orlande de
Lassus, Orlande de   38, 211
Latin   12, 16, 30, 74, 85, 312, 314
Lauridsen, Morten   4, 167, 168, 169, 183, 263
Layout   308
Leek, Stephen   202, 203, 270, 306
Ligeti, György   143, 145, 146, 151
Lip quaver   276
Lip vibration   277
London Symphony Chorus   131
Los Angeles Master Chorale   108, 115, 124, 131, 132, 329, 331
Łukaszewski, Paweł   66, 151, 211

M

MacIntyre, David   147
MacMillan, James   66, 72, 145, 149, 151, 183, 264, 274, 306
Madrigals

American 168
English 31, 32
Italian 19, 31, 271
Mäntyjärvi, Jaakko 24, 273, 288, 301, 306
Markings 317
Marshall, Ingram 305, 306
Marsh Chapel 123, 331
Martin, Frank 77, 89, 140, 208, 209, 210, 211, 282
Mass
  Agnus Dei 26, 27, 37, 186, 187, 192
  Benedictus 26, 134, 175, 209
  Credo 26, 27, 29, 37, 89, 134, 222
  Gloria 16, 26, 27, 29, 37, 38, 64, 66, 89, 173, 178
  Kyrie 26, 27, 72, 77, 194, 261
  Sanctus 26, 27, 28, 37, 134, 135, 194, 195, 208, 209, 210, 225, 247, 258, 259, 261, 299, 314
Matsushita, Ko 297, 306
Maxfield, Andrew 276, 292
McKenzie, Duncan 98, 341
Melismatic 17, 22, 26, 28, 315
Melody and Accompaniment 204
Memorization 61, 62
Mendelssohn, Felix 20, 134, 135, 137
Meter 14, 15, 16, 17, 18, 315
  Mixed 18
Metropolitan Opera Chorus 130, 333
Microtones 277
Minnesota Choral Artists 114, 124, 331
Mixed affect
Moaning 288
Monophonic 190
Monteverdi, Claudio
  Madrigals 19, 271
  Vespers 271
Mormon Tabernacle Choir. See The Tabernacle Choir at Temple Square
Mozart, Wolfgang Amadeus 29, 30, 42, 43, 44, 65, 66, 87, 126, 194, 219, 333
Mumbling 287

N

National Collegiate Choral Organization 323
National Youth Choir of Great Britain 114
Nelhybel, Vaclav 83
New College, Oxford 122, 331

New York Polyphony 106, 115, 129, 133, 329, 333
New Zealand Youth Choir 114, 117, 331
Norwegian Soloists' Choir 132
Notre Dame Polyphony

O

Obbligato Instruments 228
Ockeghem, Johannes 210
Oliveros, Pauline 306
One-on-a-part vocal ensemble 104, 328
Onomatopoeic 202
Opera 58, 129, 130, 332, 333
Opera Choruses 129, 332
Orchestra 243, 264
O'Regan, Tarik 177, 200, 211, 233
Oregon Bach Festival 115, 126, 333
Orff, Carl 70, 71, 264
Organ 219, 263, 342
  Registration 220
Oropharynx 52, 167, 273, 275, 293
Oscillation 275
Ostinatos 199
Overtone singing 278

P

Palatal clicking. See Tongue clicking
Palestrina, Giovanni Pierluigi da
  Missa Papae Marcelli 26, 27, 38, 54, 192, 211
Parry, Charles Horatio Hubert 221, 263
Pärt, Arvo 6, 38, 66, 151, 183, 211, 263, 264
Passereau, Pierre 31, 32
Paulus, Stephen 226, 263
Percussion 236
Phoenix Chorale 114, 124, 331
Phrasing 315
Piano 214, 262, 318
Pizzetti, Ildebrando 33, 34, 38, 195
Placements, forward and back 273
Pointillism 301
Polychoral 208
Polyglot Editions 314
Polyphonic 191, 250
Polyrhythmic 201
Polythematic 194, 195
Poulenc, Francis 11, 16, 38, 77, 83, 89, 170, 173, 178, 180, 181, 183, 211,

275
Pre-recorded audio   303
Primary Education Choirs   117, 330
Professional Choirs   114, 158, 323, 328, 332
Prosody. See Stress

R

Rachmaninoff, Sergei   6, 133, 137, 175, 179, 191, 211
Radio Choirs   127, 332
Ramírez, Ariel   264
Ranges   7, 90, 94, 98, 99, 104, 114, 127, 128, 328, 330, 332
Rautavaara, Einojuhani   291, 306
Ravel, Maurice   23, 25, 29, 32, 33, 38, 205, 211, 272, 306, 318
The Real Group   106, 329
Religious Choirs   122, 330
Renaissance   2, 6, 10, 21, 31, 32, 36, 37, 74, 81, 85, 92, 105, 115, 126, 127, 128, 129, 134, 191, 192, 193, 221, 340
Rheinberger, Josef   140, 183, 193, 211, 221
RIAS Kammerkor   107, 329
Rilling, Helmut   242
Rimsky-Korsakov, Nikolai   8
Roomful of Teeth   107, 329
Rossini, Gioachino   69, 76, 80
Royal Opera Chorus   130, 333

S

Salt Lake Vocal Artists   114
Santa Fe Desert Chorale   115, 125, 126, 333
Schafer, R. Murray   306
Schoenberg, Arnold   6, 291
Schubert, Franz   66, 215, 258, 259, 264
Schumann, Robert   215, 263
Scoring Choirs   127, 332
Screaming   289
Secondary Education Choirs   118, 330
Semi-pro choirs   113, 328
Seraphic Fire   107, 115, 126, 129, 132, 329, 333
Setting. See Composing
Shaw, Caroline   132, 198, 306
Shepard tone   303
Sheppard, John   134, 135
Shouting   289
Sibelius   307
Sighing   288
Singapore Symphony Children's Choir   117, 331
Singer's Formant   213
Singing into instruments   304
The Sixteen   107, 127, 129, 132, 220, 329, 333
Skylark   107, 115, 126, 329, 333
Slurs   315
Snapping   296
Solos   147, 148
Soprano   8, 9, 32, 40, 47, 58, 59, 68, 69, 70, 74, 75, 76, 80, 87, 95, 96, 104, 105, 109, 112, 113, 117, 119, 122, 134, 139, 157, 162, 163, 170, 171, 176, 177, 179, 180, 187, 188, 205, 230, 232, 246, 311, 312
Sounds from nature   269
Speaking   289
Sprechstimme   291
Staheli, Ronald   4, 211
Stamina
    Performance Related   55
    Rehearsal Related   55
Stanford, Charles Villiers   221, 263
St. James in-the-City   123, 331
St. Olaf Choir   122, 331
Stomping   296
Strauss, Richard   78, 340
Stravinsky, Igor   45, 66, 246, 261, 264
Stress
    Melodic   14
    Metric   14
St. Thomas Church Fifth Avenue   123
Stucky, Steven   151
Stuttgart Vocal Ensemble   132
Swanson, Frederick   98, 99
Swedish Radio Choir   128, 333
Syllabic   13, 17, 20, 26, 28, 315
Syllabification   17, 313
Symphonic Choruses   130, 131, 332

T

The Tabernacle Choir at Temple Square   110, 128, 329, 333
Talbot, Joby   30, 145, 151, 176, 183, 191, 211, 306
The Tallis Scholars   107, 115, 126, 127,

129, 329, 333
Tallis, Thomas   107, 115, 126, 127, 129, 134, 145, 151, 312, 329, 333
Tavener, John   127
Taverner, John   66, 314
Teatro alla Scala Chorus   130, 333
Telescoping   29
Tenebrae   107, 115, 129, 132, 329, 333
Tenor   79, 138, 340, 341
Tessitura   40, 46, 47, 65, 105
Texas Boys Choir   117, 331
Text painting   31
The Monteverdi Choir   127, 333
The Philippine Madrigal Singers   133
The Sixteen   107, 127, 129, 132, 329, 333
Thyroarytenoid-Dominant Production   48, 76, 79, 284
Tippett, Michael   35, 36
Tomkins, Thomas   221, 222, 263
Tongue clicking   291
Toronto Mendelssohn Choir   124, 331
Touring Ensembles   128, 332
Trill   279
Trillo   280
Trinity College, Cambridge   122, 133, 331
Trinity Wall Street   123, 331
Tutti   189

U

Ululation   281
Underlay   36
USC Chamber Singers   122, 331

V

Van, Jeffery   263, 283
Variant 6   106, 329
Vaughan Williams, Ralph   2, 6, 23, 38, 72, 183, 211, 248, 249, 254, 255, 263, 264
Verdi, Giuseppe   194, 195, 247
Vibrato   60, 102, 108, 109, 112, 113, 115, 119, 121, 124, 125, 127, 128, 130, 166, 329, 331, 333
Victoria, Tomas Luis de   211
Vivaldi, Antoni   66
Vocal fry
Vocal Hygiene   268
Vocalise   23, 52, 205, 232, 244
Voces8   106, 115, 129, 329, 333

Voice crossing   136, 156, 157, 169, 170, 309, 310
Voice Leading   57
Voicing   154, 156, 157, 159, 161, 163, 167, 232
  Closed   157
  Eight Parts   161
  Open   159
Vowel Modification   53

W

Wagner, Richard   250, 251, 252, 255, 256, 257
Walton, William   24, 142, 144, 155, 202, 230, 233, 263, 264, 273, 276, 281, 283, 285, 288, 289, 294, 302
Weelkes, John   32
Westminster Choir   108, 122, 329, 331
Whispering   293
Whistle tone   282
Whistling   283
Whitacre, Eric   61, 143, 144, 151, 202, 207, 232, 233, 281, 296, 302, 306
White, Robert   21
Wilberg, Mack   179, 205, 226
Willan, Healey   139, 151, 221
Woo, Hyo-Won   155, 183

Y

Yale Schola Cantorum   122, 331
Yodeling   284, 341

www.ingramcontent.com/pod-product-compliance
Lightning Source LLC
Chambersburg PA
CBHW070324010526
44107CB00004B/406